Remembrance and Song

Nancy Hemenway Barton

Cover art
Front cover: Detail from *Flow of Inner Seeing—Part II,* 94" × 306"
    Embroidered wall sculpture of lambswool, linen, mohair,
    alpaca, and karakul; backed in wool; 1981;
    collection of the Art Institute of Chicago
Back cover: *Night Presence,* 12'2" × 6'4"
    Two-piece wall sculpture; 1984

THE *H*EMENWAY FOUNDATION
145 BRISTOL PLACE
PONTE VEDRA BEACH, FL 32082

Contents

Acknowledgments

Special thanks to all those who have contributed their time and energy to making this edition possible. Several friends and family members were involved in typing or retyping chapters so that we would have an electronic version of the work that could be edited. Robert Barton spent countless hours collating the chapters and ensuring that the text was faithful to Nancy's original handwritten pages and vision. Our thanks also to those who have made financial contributions to the Hemenway Foundation. We welcome and appreciate your involvement.

Foreword

A few years after I retired, Nancy and I found ourselves spending the winter in California. There I began typing up the myriad notebooks Nancy had accumulated over the past decade while she busied herself with even more tapestries. Nancy's handwriting was easy for me to read but often she entered her thoughts in the stenographic spiral notebooks while riding on a train or airplane or while ensconced in temporary lodgings. Since she was next door, I could ask her about passages I could not decipher. When we returned to Maine for the summer we sat down together to correct, edit and revise the three or four hundred typed pages we had accumulated.

In one of the forthcoming chapters she writes how she continued this process three or four times. I have gone over it about the same number. We have shown it to a few friends and family members to ask their opinion of its worth. All have maintained it should be made public; the writing is poetic and the message uplifting.

As I reviewed this text for typos and format I could not help but reflect on my initial reaction as I typed those original postings. I was struck by the lyricism of Nancy's prose. Her words sang to me and it was a pleasure to bring them out into the open. They also revealed aspects of her life that I had not recognized earlier. We were married in 1942 so one would think that after more than sixty-five years of love, parenthood and travel together we must know each other inside and out. That proved not to be exactly so. I had not recognized her various nooks and crannies of privacy and introspection. Like most of us, she had secret opinions of people and events, of accidents and humiliations which she had kept to herself. *Abundance,* her book of poetry, reflects her appreciation of nature and art, of imagination and creativity, of her ardor for her children and friends, and most espe-cially of her joy of living. For the most part, however, the poems do not reveal the important events of her life, nor her reaction to them.

The chapters of her journal do so, at least to a certain extent. She is still cautiously discreet. She almost never complains or derides. Her anecdotes begin with her early childhood, her education, her life abroad and the early development of *bayetage*. She does not include much about her private, domestic life. These chapters are confined to a single decade of her long life, a decade in which she is no longer mothering her brood or worrying about her husband's career. In this buccaneering ten-year period she revels eventually in the world's rec-ognition of her newly invented art form and of the many advantages she received as a consequence. In her first chapter she notes that the limitations she experienced in Bolivia induced creativity. She became inner directed. She discovered that solitude promoted her imagina-tion. She wrote a poem to that effect; it also appeared in *Abundance*.

In chapter 2 she muses about her poetry and includes one in Spanish (in which language she was fluent) and her own translation of it. Paramount in these pages is the death of her mother, and she speaks forcibly about her heritage and what love and faith mean to her. Her mother, Mother Nature, mother of vinegar; the sweetness and bitterness of life itself.

For those curious about the manufacture of a wall hanging, the next chapter is revealing. She notes that she interprets nature, but selectively. "Textures of Our Earth," she reminds us, is a song with many voices and a theme of discovery. Each new tapestry boasts a new simplicity. Still, new shapes, designs, colors, and techniques flow. She comments on the restrictions of the rectangle and how sew-ing and molding wool have helped her overcome them. She tells of how two of her commissions are accepted with tears of joy by their new "owners." And she says she wants a sense of wonder to be in her works. Then she ends by acknowledging with excitement that there is so "much more that I have not discovered."

During the first years of the decade she is describing, she worked in a twelve-foot by twelve-foot cabin used previously by the Reverend Henry Emerson Fosdick on Mouse Island. In 1979, she was able to purchase a summer house near her own on Juniper Point. She reflects on what it does and will mean to her in future years. As the chapter progresses, she tells of still another studio she acquires. This is in the Washington area, on the Potomac River. Early, in the first chapter, she tells how she was fearless in the water and how she would dash in at the age of four, although she did not know how to swim. On the Potomac, as on Mouse Island and her promontory Loft, she had sparkling, blue water to inspire her. So, as she says farewell to Mouse, she moves on—and on, always looking for new paths of discovery.

Where the last chapter spoke of how to make a wall-hanging, the next tells how they were exhibited in various museums: Bowdoin College in Brunswick, Maine; the Virginia Museum of Art in Richmond; at the Neiman Marcus department store in Dallas. It terminates with exultation as museums come to her to ask for a showing rather than vice versa.

In chapter 7 she discusses imagination, inspiration, creativity and beauty. Her goal, she writes, is to express beauty as she sees it. She asks, why is there a right side and a wrong side to everything? She says she wants to be a wrong-sided person. She wants to be different.

In the penultimate chapter, Nancy does just that. She goes off for two weeks to an artists' colony called Cummington, a derelict camp for a bunch of motley aspirants. She had previously applied to the prestigious MacDowell Colony, which she describes in an earlier chapter, but that never came through. At Cummington, her initial prospects appeared dismal but she endured. Nancy found something positive in any situation.

The final episode narrates her five-week tour to Africa. The National Endowment for the Arts sent her to five different countries, under the auspices of the U.S. Information Service, to demonstrate her techniques, to lecture and to show off a small collection of her tapestries. Again, conditions were not perfect. The tour turned out to be arduous and backbreaking, but the results were rewarding. I accompanied her on that trip and came back reminded of the expression. "Behind every successful woman stands an amazed man."

Not so surprised. Ever since high school, when I recognized she was the one and only for me, I had admired her intelligence, imagination, ability and energy. My astonishment and delight were from the adulation she received equally from others. Readers of this recollection of a single decade of her life will find them delightful and thought-provoking pages. Moreover, they will enjoy a fluent, gushing style of writing that is both direct and poetic. Her use of prose equals that of her lyrics. She avoids clichés. Every sentence is as original as her art. Both synonyms and metaphors gallop across the page in an astounding array of novelty and imagination. A sly sense of humor pokes up, but beyond that is the sensitivity and awareness of all things great and good. It is a pity that she did not continue with her journals, but at least she was able to continue with her art for a bit more than another ten years, and she left the world richer thereby.

—Robert D. Barton
Washington, D.C., 2008

Graduation photo of Nancy Hemenway Whitten,
Wheaton College, 1941

Introduction

Creative impulse has shaped my life. At two I jumped into the sea, to swim. That is my first memory; there was no fear. As I have moved throughout the years of awareness there has always been color to savor and deep caring; always designs and quick pencil lines of living.

I have found room within myself to sing two songs at once, a rondelet of harmony because each line has its beginning in a moment of consonance.

Brought up to believe that a woman's role is one for service to others, most of my graduation class moved on to become mothers or teachers or nurses. Few other major professions were open to us. How often I heard, "If your husband is happy you will all be happy." No maxim is that easy, no situation so flowing. But in caring for three small boys and the homes we shared in Uruguay, Argentina, Spain and Bolivia I still found time to draw and paint and save a part of each day for creative thought. I drew the ladies at the meetings I attended, sketching their hands clasped around handbags, or their crossed feet or a slumped weary head. If pad and pencil were frowned on I looked beyond out into a garden or at the corner of a sunset and planned flights of imagination when I should be alone.

When Bill was ten days old I stood at the American Embassy in Montevideo with Ambassador and Mrs. Briggs to welcome Aaron Copland who had been at Harvard when I was there. Still swollen with fresh milk flowing beneath my gown, I smiled and enjoyed the excitement, asking no favors.

Bob carried the passports and strode each day out of the door of our hotel or home to his orderly office. His very steadiness was a pillar. Mine has been a life of holding the threads of a complex international life without snarling. I have learned the language of living of each country in order to hold the complicated reins, with tender eyes trusting me. I have held a full measure of loving, caring and sheltering close to me and still had the energy to reach beyond and nurture an inner spirit of creativity.

Margaret Mead in *Blackberry Winter* refers to the creative drive which transforms itself in many women from the consuming years of child bearing and rearing to fields of art, music and many other careers. She lived ahead of her time in many patterns. I have moved somewhere between these two paths, balancing my life, always working quietly with relentless dedication, but holding at the same times the gentle reins of my heritage.

Because of the solitary nature of creative art, whether writing or painting or embroidery, there must be counterpoints. It is perhaps for this reason that I choose to elaborate each step, to remind myself of the labyrinth of art I have traveled alone, quite separate from my other life. The need to touch other lives is now as strong and compelling as was my need for many years to circle my arms around my children.

I paint my thoughts onto these pages with compulsion and often with emotion. It is impossible to record all that my eyes and heart remember. My life has no simple continuous thread that can be followed to show the direction, but there are themes of creativity, of inspiration, and of travel that have all contributed to my artistic growth.

Along with these themes flows a sense of love and optimism—one being the other, and always awareness. These leitmotifs and other smaller melodies form a pattern of living that is full of color and intricacy. I am compelled to write down much of my experience and its relationship to my art to share with you.

Blackberry Winter—the frost on the full fruit—perhaps describes in a special way my own life. The fruit has ripened and the frost, important to the harvest and the sweet taste of the berry, is in fact for me the tempering frost of age and adventure. I have so much I must say. The full clean taste of the ripe fruit is my creative spirit. It could not have been so had I climbed to my studio at twenty. The formative years of growth in Uruguay, Argentina, Spain and my own country have made the vines sturdy. The parched summer days of life in the Dominican Republic and Mexico have forced a fruiting that is bright and sweet.

Nancy Hemenway

~ 1 ~

Inner Directed

*B*orn in the month of spring on the threshold of summer in a time for laughter and song is a time for rich beginnings and flowering. My life was planted in warm ground, eager to bear fruit from the moment of birth.

The open country, the tall pines and the rugged shore of New England were my childhood haunts. Much of the wonder and love of nature that inspires my tapestries comes from memories that go back to the age of four. I still think of forest trees as the most inspiring of the world's sculpture, and the changing sea as it coils and rockets against the ledges of granite as the finest drama.

I have learned through the years that beauty is everywhere, not just in the forest or along the rugged shore but in simple plants poking up through city pavement. A sense of wonder that I learned as a child has traveled with me to many exotic lands, and down crowded streets in towering cities.

All my life I have been storing the treasure of nature, first on the family farm in Foxboro and the warm months in Maine, and then in the years of foreign travel. I have seen a lonely dandelion bloom in pavement cracks in a ravaged city and returned to my studio to glorify my discovery in a tapestry nine feet tall.

The delicate shadings on a tulip petal, the lace of orb webs on morning grass and a single feather each has grace and beauty. Because I work in embroidery and textiles, I find myself saying, "How can I explore so much rhythm and flow with my medium? How will I hold the curve of the stem and the floating mien of the dandelion?"

Now that I have grandchildren I want to share with them the sensitive world of blossom, seed and sea, for that is what our lives are. They are learning to step lightly in the grass, to compare the colors of moss and to see the configuration of lichen. My own heritage, passed on from my parents is the treasure I have to share. As children discover each new plant as we test the spiny sea urchin or watch the fritillary float above the goldenrod we are designing a language of the living, a language that has brought me to love and buoyancy and belief.

When Mother was eighty-six we visited together her family homestead in Wells, Maine. She turned to me, smiling, and said, "The fun always seemed to start when I arrived." The joy of life was her first message to me, a heritage of exuberance.

No one can remember the moments immediately after birth but I am certain of the enveloping arms of my mother, holding me to her warm breast and flowing into my small body and new life the depth of her caring heart.

That understanding kept me close when occasionally I found myself, long-legged and weedy, sitting in her lap, rocking back and forth in the wounded and bandaged family rocker. She knew our needs and even with five birds in her nest found the right diet for each.

From Mother we learned to love nature, to walk the wood paths behind our parents, flopping along in their bear paw snowshoes, packing the earth for their fledglings. We picked sugar bags full of coral and chanterelle mushrooms, learned to protect the lady slipper and harvested wild watercress. We also came in dripping many cold days to display a Monarch Cocoa can full of tadpoles or spring turtles. All our cargo was welcomed and admired.

With three Old Town canoes we paddled the reaches of the salt marshes and rivers of Maine, Mother and Dad each pulling a strong paddle. They loved sports and the out-of-doors and traveled the waters of our harbor to the last. Mother in her wide hat sat astern to catch the blue that paled before her eyes. To her, skies were colors, clouds had their names, cumulus, cirrus.

The special literary hour was after bedtime when Mother, exhausted from the day of usual surprises, lay down beside me to recite her favorites, Keats and Shelley. She usually fell asleep, reviving suddenly to remind herself that bread was rising on the kitchen radiator.

My mother and father loved to travel, but they left us only for one night until we were grown. Neither of our parents thought of taking a trip or even spending a Saturday night away in all of our childhood.

On Sundays we were allowed no games or noise; walks in the woods instead, a time to be creative. But at Boothbay Harbor we had Saturday night parties with all the birch furniture piled like cordwood into one corner and the Victrola humming. Winter Saturday nights were quiet times with Henry Turner, the occupational therapist at a nearby hospital as our "always" guest. My parents' unfailing patience, their acceptance of daily living still amazes me. None of us would ever sacrifice our lives in such unselfishness. And yet I know it was the alchemy of love and devotion that sent the joy of living up our five sturdy stems allowing us to grow and delight.

At home as a small child I sewed for my dolls. They were always stylish and above all warm. I hustled around each night putting homemade gowns on my thin blond doll with marvelous joints. She was easy to dress. (I still have her wicker cradle.) Barbara was my glamorous child, another jointed doll with jet curls and wide blue eyes that closed lazily at the slightest stir. Around each one I tucked blankets even when my bare feet ached from cold pine floors. Then I jumped into my wide spool bed and tunneled under the covers with Robinson Crusoe, my collie who came as a stray to our doorstep, to warm my feet.

At our house we rarely went shopping. Somehow yardage and buttons materialized, and often I asked for fabric I wanted. Mother made me beautiful hand-sewn clothes, every detail from rolled linen collars to pleated red wool skirts a perfection. She taught me the skill of fine sewing and attention to detail.

I was encouraged to choose textures and designs for my flowered pillows and drapes for my exotic attic room. I made hats, a flat pique saucer and a green wool brimmer with ocelot that I concocted while in college. My roommate at Wheaton wore my purple dress and matching hat the day her future husband proposed to her. I felt like Madame Chanel.

Color and beauty, in a deeply positive sense, have always been important to me and are among my first recollections. At four, totally entranced by the impressionist palette of the tulips in our sunken garden, I disobeyed, clipped them all neatly and trudged, arms bound around their undulating stems, to give them to my mother.

I am still indignant that Grandmama took her chauffeur-driven car to a shop called The Little Ladies and insisted on buying me an orange dress. I knew orange was my worst color, but in that dress my pastel portrait was drawn by Carola Spaeth Hauschka. I begged to wear a blouse and jeans (called overalls then) but lost the encounter as my solemn face reveals. I was just ten.

My father was the sensitive son of a corporate tycoon. Perhaps typhoon would better describe the juxtaposition of these two men, one gregarious, acquisitive and self-assured; the son, a shy inner-directed boy, deeply moved by color, line and beauty. He was blown before his father's late Victorian certitude into the arms of my sturdy and loving mother. To all appearances her straight brown hair and starched middy were average, but she carried an understanding of life and love for it that made her remarkable.

My father, although the son of a distinguished industrialist, loved art. Reading Mrs. Duncan Phillips's life of her husband is like seeing the reflection of my father on every page. That one should have been given money to start a famous art collection while the other was condemned to run a chicken farm is the Alpha and Omega. My father's occasional rages, his severe headaches, were his outbursts against a fate that curved his sensitive nature like an archer's bow to the point of breaking. Only now, too late to bring him comfort, I understand his need. Submerged in the creative world, surrounded by my tapestries, a multitude of ideas circling my brain, I would be incapable of his labor and frustration; shoveling ammoniac manure, plucking scrawny, lifeless birds, the whole process a daily ritual too disgusting to remember. And yet he did it almost without complaint.

We were invited for Thanksgiving to Grandfather's in West Newton to feast only in medieval tales. The center pieces of fruit complete with honey-sweet persimmons, grapes like crystal raindrops and dishes of candies were a world of wonder to us. We ate greedily, each course passed by the frilled cuffed-and-collared maids, the ceremony crowned by pastel fruited ice cream on angelic beds of spun sugar. Although my appetite was surfeited it was my eyes that danced from one dish to another, from paper hats in favors to rosewood turkey and back to the Limoges. It was a world of vast extremes, so terrifying that my brother Charles, at four, could not eat but sat with his gentian eyes full of tears and dared not to move. I loved it all.

The West Newton house that my grandfather had built for my grandmother had wide fanning stairs with large oval windows. I ran up and down them in my black patent leather shoes singing to myself. I always sang, even in college, never aware of it except as I remember Grandfather saying I should have voice lessons.

Virginia Woolf writes in her memoirs of the agony of her mother's death when she was thirteen. At that same age I began to understand through the death of my grandfather the finality of death. The loss of a parent would have been a hideous blow. At thirteen there is little to look back on and no way to philosophize the adventures of a mature life. The gift of birth has been my greatest thankfulness. Although I have imagined that my advent may have been a natural outgrowth of my father's and mother's love and not a planned arrangement, I have been secure in the feeling that my mother treasured the presence within her, determined that I should be a nourished, healthy spirit, bringing joy to a house shaken by my father's poor health and isolation on a country farm.

Along with the Pierce-Arrows and beach wagons that Grandfather and my Great Uncle Charles meted out, there was our beautiful colonial house in Foxboro with its fan doorway and fireplace, square rooms. The fine paintings, family heirlooms and knowledge of travel made our house a private oasis different from our neighbors, but as children we played happily together. Our parents were friendly, considerate and generous but they never dined with any of our neighbors nor did they come to our house. Our life was very much within our own family except for school pageants and church functions.

The single most important influence on me was my father's distaste at finding us reading. He was lonely and sought our company. Motherless, his father, a great reader, had shut him out as a small boy, and the need to surround himself with activity and warmth was as urgent as a snowbound traveler seeking haven. The excesses of one generation cast long shadows.

We were all taught to use our hands to create a world of our own imagination, in drawing, in designing tree houses, in learning about engines. Most of our learning came from trial and error. Almost none from books. We visited the fine museums, were taught about nature and developed a high degree of visual awareness and self confidence. Books were read in the rare moments of solitude that a large family seldom finds. We were an unusual New England family for we threw our arms around each other. My father never went to the mailbox without kissing Mother. We played strenuous games, vented our joys and hatreds like steam escaping a boiling kettle. No one sulked. It was all easy and open. Pranks filled our lives. We played them on each other in shifting patterns as unpredictable as clouds, moving with the same speed from one rollicking parlor drama to another. Our stage manager was always my loving mother whose incredible patience held fast.

I remember that Mother and I spent a fall morning swinging on birches. I had read Robert Frost's poem and tried my luck on a cluster of birches. My first swing was a whirling revelation. Mother, working in the kitchen, dried her hands and came to join me. When I told the story she always added humor "And the tree I swung on never stood straight again."

What an extraordinary heritage! A youth of laughter and love, each day my eyes and mind honed more sharply to the stars, March maple buds, and the footprint of deer in the fields of snow beyond our clapboard castle. Auden wrote, "Thank you fog for a moment of tranquil oblivion with friends." I cannot write in words the years that were so full. No diary or book can hold them. Remembrance overwhelms me.

I learned before I was ten the magic passages through the Museum of Fine Arts in Boston. I reveled in Egyptian tombs with their double-eyed profiles, the careless exuberance of Sargent's brush and ancient gold images from Near Eastern tombs, some of them my father's gifts to that great museum.

I think of my mother and father often. Mother, alert and joyous, was our center. Her warmth, bright mind and cerulean eyes reflected the heaven she held close.

At public school in Foxboro I adorned my compositions in history and English with drawings. I did projects for Bob, too, who joined my grade in his sophomore year, and I embellished my brothers' casual homework. In my senior year I won the Benjamin Franklin history prize for a special unsolicited notebook full of drawings and colored pictures of American history.

But music was the field I had been assigned to largely by my parents. Mother said, "There are too many artists already in this family." My father had a studio full of sharp pencils and sleek rulers that none of us could touch. Occasionally he designed a formal chair or cornice or drew a laborious coat-of-arms, but that was all. Mother painted flowers. Her huge watercolor poppy for my freshman room at college rivaled Georgia O'Keeffe. She had true talent, but also five babies and no time.

I won a music scholarship to Wheaton College in Norton, Massachusetts. Having practiced all summer pieces of my own choosing I drove with Mother to Boston to Mrs. Grover's for a final polish. Her studio in the turreted top of the S. S. Pierce building in Copley Square had been my weekly haunt for eight years. She was then eighty-six but still teaching steadily. Distressed at the pieces I had chosen, she chose a fresh program starting with the Bach *Prelude*. I had one week to work out my new music.

I seem to remember more carefully chosen remarks about my love of Bach than great playing at my interview, but the scholarship was won for four years. Because of this my major was music, a small department with two professors of limited ability. My creative engine revved along creating a four-foot pile of choral works and piano pieces never played or of any great interest to my major professor. My dedication was intense but not meek and I hold no memories of warmth or shared intellect as I do in Art and English. Practical art was taught by a thin, frightened lady whose caricature done by one of my classmates was titled, "Seeing Much Dubiously." I never took a single course in drawing.

At Wheaton College, I was only eleven miles from home, and I craved independence. My parents promised not to come and see me or call. I could pretend I was as far away as Stanford in California. My parents' loving made independence possible. Always to me the homesick child is the one who lacks true security. They knew how to let go.

I arrived at Wheaton the year a new experimental program called "Elements of Composition in the Arts" was offered to ten entering freshmen. We wrote plays, painted sets, composed music and discussed and wrote poetry. I explored particularly music forms for the dance and theater and the three elements came together in a rainbow of creativity. It was a perfect world.

Often I stayed at the piano until the last bell for locking doors, racing in the frosty air back to my dormitory at the far end of campus. I wrote scores for choral works, a toccata and fugue. I loved the challenge of the rigid fugue form, pressing its limits.

I think back to the years at Wheaton. There were outstanding professors because of the Depression and because women professors were not welcomed at the prestigious men's colleges. In Art History Isabella Seaver acquainted me with Berenson, taught me the early audacity of Giotto and the constrained voluptuousness of Titian. Perhaps I loved best van der Weyden whose Madonna in the National Gallery was for many years my favorite.

At Wheaton in English were the Boas, husband and wife, teaching me contemporary literature and Shakespeare. I wrote about Shakespeare's lack of knowledge of sailing, analyzing his references, especially in *The Tempest*. It was a spellbinding course with nearly always a row of auditors as absorbed as those taking it for credit. In journalism there was Louise Mackenzie, herself a Wheaton graduate. She was young and alive with large glasses and a wide smile that seemed to balance. Her comments were direct without being heartless. I wanted very much to do outstanding work for her. I knew she demanded the best, but in her class I never rose to the triangular pinnacle of an A.

I am loyal to Wheaton for allowing me to roam the campus intellectually, for the rapport with fine teachers.

Although the piano won me my scholarship and put me through college, I continued to say quietly, "I will be an artist." Absolutely no one listened. That didn't disturb me either.

Music has brought my art great sense of rhythm and motion and continuity of form. All my successful works have motion. Music also gives me an expansiveness. Each opportunity to express oneself in a new medium adds a measure to skill and a glory to living. Music, poetry, Spanish have all enlarged my creative vocabulary to give strength and variety to my tapestries. Within my art form all these influences come together in a special flowering that is unique. My medium is a discovery and expression that is deeply individual, springing from many rich sources.

Washington, Fall 1981

Coming through the security checkpoint at the airport this morning two young women commented on my portfolio case and drawing pad. "Oh, I would love to draw. I've tried but have no talent; it takes special talent."

Drawing has been my language since I can remember. It is a language that is so seldom adequately taught at grammar and high school levels that those who are encouraged at home move on into the magic art far ahead of their classmates. It is no strange chance that four generations of Wyeths are artists or that in the Renaissance sons and daughters moved into their father's studios often to become more distinguished than their parents. I believe art is a skill more than a smoldering, hidden gift that finds oxygen and flames.

At the Everett School in West Foxboro where I started my education I remember most vividly our tall angular art teacher, her graying head bent awkwardly above our work. She taught us only one thing that I remember; to draw water glasses with the ellipses viewed from various levels, from the narrow slit of a newly opened letter to a deep oval. I drew that water glass so many times I shall never forget it, looking out the window as I dreamed about what I would like to draw. Nothing about art in high school has remained with me. I do not think we had a special art teacher there, all the emphasis was on music, on memorizing arithmetical formulas and good grammar. College was history of art, reinforcing in detail what I had already come to know from my many visits to the fine museums of Boston and Cambridge. "Practical Art" was of no consequence.

After I married I moved often, my possessions carried in a few bags. Art became again a focal point and the steadying force in my life. Perhaps in part it has been my peripatetic life, the constant changes that have made me need a personal expression, saying what is within myself. Art is a fulfillment, a room of my own. It can flourish in any climate. I traveled to Uruguay with my husband and our year-old son, Bradford. It took our plane three days with many stops. The first months were spent arranging a small stucco house on Larranaga Street, a dusty road with a bar in front where men played *bochas*. We cooked on a wheezing kerosene cook stove that I pumped with the caution of a hot air balloon. Our dining table fitted underneath the stairs and I remember that Bradford's blue eyes came just above its rim. I had Prang textile colors with me and designed linens and lampshades and painted a circus on pink cotton for children's birthday parties. I taught art at the U.S. Cultural Center in Montevideo.

We became friends of the artists in every country that adopted us in our diplomatic travels. The dark trees and moonscapes of Cuneo, the village dancers of Figari are still a part of my artistic vocabulary from the early days in Uruguay.

Spain was the country where art finally surfaced to demand time and space in my life. Bill and Rick had come to complete our family and were off to school each morning. With two or three quiet hours I laid out my watercolors and began to record in a direct way the avenues and villages, the Guadarrama mountains and the clear sky.

One day I climbed to the fourth floor of a gray apartment building to visit Bradford's teacher, a serious dedicated woman with a long braid wound around her head like a crown. She opened the door. I stood there transfixed. Every space on the walls of her modest apartment was covered with vibrant watercolors. Watercolors were splashed and stretched with the monumentality of oil paintings, but still held their effervescence. I learned that her son Fernando was a painter. He came after that visit to paint with me on the Spanish hillsides. Fernando Higueras is now a famous architect in Madrid, but it is his watercolors that should have won his life.

In Madrid I studied drawing with Pierre Matieu. I was his only pupil. He taught me the graceful fluency of a pencil that never leaves the paper and that space make drawing whether it be a figure or a chair. In Spain I also explored the difficult techniques of watercolor portraiture. I painted my first portrait on a trip to Marbella, then just a wide space on the coast road between Malaga and Gibraltar. We lived in a house built around an olive grove without destroying a single tree. There Bill sat patiently for hours, his six-year-old legs dangling over the edge of a chair. I painted with the ends of match sticks dipped in paint as I had no brushes with me. Everyone was struck by the likeness that I was encouraged to paint many Embassy children and finally to hold a show at Casa Americana. Those pictures are a rogue's gallery of my ignorance of the art of portraiture, but painting children has always given me great pleasure. I shared with each child the quiet hours of a portrait, the likeness and style germinating as I grew to know my subject.

I remember later in Bronxville being asked to paint a child we all thought was retarded. I put off the sittings, not trusting my own skill, and finally agreed. I came to understand the sensitive need of the little boy. He talked to me about music and how he loved arithmetic. I will always feel now that it is society and not the boy who was wrong. Somehow, even in an educated neighborhood we had not understood and shared his world.

My first sittings for portraits were always light-hearted visits. We played games, nibbled cookies and talked about what interested the child. I often found a chance to talk about color and could pick for them clothes that best expressed their personalities. One little girl came for her first sitting in a bright blue dress her mother had chosen. Remembering my own portrait in orange I asked Cynthia if that was her favorite dress because I saw her pale skin and light hair in white. "Oh no," she blurted out, "I hate this dress." I painted her in her favorite dress, white organdy that had been tucked under the eaves because her mother had preferred blue. Children know colors and need only to be encouraged to develop their rainbow vision. My parents did that for me.

In Bronxville I joined a ladies' painting class above a garage on the crest of the hill near my home. In winter I lashed my canvas and paints to my sled and pulled my cargo to the studio. Donald Pierce taught me the science of painting, the bleeding colors, the staining and scumbling techniques. As I gathered momentum I quickly moved on to the Art Students League in New York. Each morning I arranged the day, placed dinner in the oven, made the lunches and then dashed for the city. Four engrossing hours of life drawing, portrait painting and most of all observing my peers.

I studied with Fogarty and Brackman and Joseph Hirsch. He was the best. None of them came to class often enough to make my work dependent on his style as so often happens in art schools. I consciously shunned those temptations, seeking my own individuality. Aggressive students often pushed to the best spots whenever a model came. I remember choosing a back corner of the studio to challenge myself to do a successful painting from the least desirable spot.

The League suited me because it is open and has hours for those of us who must live two lives at once. Many had talent and I flourished in their presence. I painted a portrait of an elderly lady in a black bonnet, paring it down to essentials to give the composition austerity and backbone. Two of the best students came to tell me I should paint on my own, that I didn't need a teacher. I thought about it and decided to go to Columbia and study art and Spanish simultaneously. I took a course in painting with John Heliker. He is a kindly man with a delicate paintbrush but he seemed without animation or enthusiasm to encourage others. The dead arrangements with curled leaves and sodden stems revolted me. I stayed only one semester under his tutelage, but continued at Columbia until I received my master's degree in Spanish lyric poetry.

At the same time I read and studied art on my own, but most importantly I worked. Our bedroom, originally an artist's studio twenty feet square, had high gambrel eaves and open beams. A clean north light flooded in to fill the space. A heavy stone fireplace loomed in one corner holding the openness and strength of my workshop to the earth. There I had my grand piano, my easel and portrait stand and my bed.

Often I would paint for three or four hours after the children were asleep. One late night I found my brush daubing colors while I came to a terrifying reality. I must make a choice. My impulse to give myself totally to art was so great that I began to shake. Then the patterns of living surfaced and I knew I would never put art first until our children were grown. No one restrained me. I chose to hold the two worlds together. I have lived the dizzying plunge of a rowboat in gigantic waves, each crest showing a patch of islands before dipping into the hollow again.

I shall never regret hanging onto my life raft those years. My children were my early tapestries and the threads of their lives were not woven quickly. Now is my time. It is a period of energy and joy. Each tapestry is whole. Of all the talents the Bible tells us, "The greatest of these is love." It is a phrase read at weddings and again, just this week, at the funeral of a young friend. I have stayed for love.

It is not fashionable to be a fulfilled artist concerned with love and family. I will never know the other paths I might have traversed, but this one seems full of creativity. Art demands the same patience and attention to detail important to family harmony and offers the same excitement and absorption. Sometimes one hangs on because there is no other way.

Before I left New York to travel to the Dominican Republic I flirted briefly with Portraits, Inc., in New York City. They demanded a yearly production of portraits in five figures and often trips to stay with families while their children were being painted. Bob's transfer to the Caribbean changed all that. Then came Bolivia and the beginning of my life as a tapestry maker.

I learned on a Sunday that I was going to live in Bolivia. Still bruised by months in the Dominican Republic where I had walked alone through a museum with not one picture on its walls, I felt great relief to be going to a country, no matter how distant and exotic, where I knew there was a long heritage of art. From our years in Spain and in Argentina and Uruguay I had often thought about the cultures of western South America and the life of the high Andes. I knew, as everyone does, about the balsa boats on the highest lake in the world and that there was much more to be discovered.

Because of the long and difficult journey we could only go by air in the time allotted, not up over the rim from Lima and across the lake in a marvelous old steamboat brought in pieces to the high altiplano in the nineteenth century. I did that later. It also meant I could not take my oil paints or canvasses with me but only the bare necessities of life. A few will understand that my paints were the only thing I needed, pushing off into unknown territory without family or friends or anything to remind me of my heritage. This was to be my second voyage without my children. Nothing of my creative life of the past was to go with me.

At once I began to turn over in my imagination how I would deal with this arid problem. I would have to take something light and unbreakable that could fit in a small space. Sometimes the most drastic limitations can bring good fortune. When restrictions are placed that seem as though the lungs cannot gasp for even a breath, when the bars are secured around our being, the spirit can still find a way to survive. After all, this was an adventure and I went with someone I loved. That was a good beginning. Immediately I thought of embroidery. I had learned to sew at the age of six and had taken complicated lessons in fine embroidery when I lived in Argentina, more for the gaiety of friendship than for a sense of art. Bits of material, assorted packages of needles would not take much room. I brought embroidery floss, choosing the colors as I would the cadmiums and alizarin and the powerful Prussian blue for my painter's palette. These treasures together scarcely weighed two pounds. No one could complain about that. I understood that my paints and easel would come eventually over the hump of the mountain, by ship to Callao and then by train. I intended only to doodle and save myself as best I could until the tools of my creativity joined me.

Flying into La Paz in 1966, we flew up over the rim of the world on a blue day, coasted the length of the brown altiplano laid like a wide table fringed with white capped mountains that rose like waves above the level of our plane. I learned the names of each peak in the years I lived there, Aymara names from the earliest habitation. I shall always carry with me the power of that first vision. Our plane landed at thirteen thousand feet. From there we moved slowly down a narrow road cluttered with small carts and garlanded with men and women in their bright costumes. The women in bowlers, their handwoven *ayauyo* scarves often holding a tiny baby wearing a pointed hat. The men wore knitted hats with long earflaps against the mountain winds, all of them spinning down the mountains as though they were tightly wound tops, twirling and dipping over the rim of the world as they ran down steep paths burdened with sacks of potatoes, handspun alpaca and other cargo. The circular wool skirts made from *bayeta* were my first introduction to the vivid flower-dyed yardage I used in my earliest tapestries. From this narrow nubby wool I coined the word *bayetage*. It combines the word *bayeta,* meaning handwoven wool, and collage.

In Bolivia, as in Maine, nature is grandeur. There is an expansiveness. Standing at the window of our stucco house in the bowl of the city of La Paz, we were still at 12,000 feet and looked out to see the sharp peak of Mt. Illimani loom from the valley below. In Maine, from the hilltops one has the same limitless horizon, the black islands carry beyond and beyond.

Bolivia was lonely. It is a place to struggle to survive, where even a tree searches for moisture in the ashes of earth so near the face of the moon. There also I learned the narrow dimension of diplomatic life as I had never known it and was forced to curl in upon myself and seek a secret world of the spirit. Everyone works hard there to catch enough oxygen to keep even a brave heart beating.

Searching for fringe for new curtains I visited Kunturi, a tiny school of embroidery with four handicapped students. I had bought yards and yards of *tocuyo* that the Bolivians use for dust cloths and sewed long flowing drapes. Its uneven rough cotton surface had attracted me. I wished to find fringe to give it elegance. Kunturi by a miracle was just at the end of my street. I rang a bell to be admitted and then climbed down a narrow path dipping straight over the edge of the cliff to a basement area with three diminutive rooms. Here the girls worked making pillows and knitting sweaters of alpaca. They did not make fringe but I saw that they needed new designs and would welcome my help. Their need transported me out of myself like a great hot-air balloon that suddenly warms and lifts to see a beautiful world spread about. It was at Kunturi that I first saw a narrow shelf full the handspun and handwoven wools brought down in large bundles from the altiplano. The country folk called their wool weaving *bayeta* and *jerga*. One a loose straight weave and the other done in patterns they called *ojo de perdiz* (eye of the partridge) and houndstooth and various other intricate designs. This yardage they sold for garments, but at Kunturi some of the bright shades were cut and embroidered into pillows. These handsome fabrics in all the shades of the Andean wildflowers and the subtle colors of the alpaca and sheep became my new palette. While I helped the girls design new motifs and learn fresh embroidery stitches, I kept a sharp eye on the piles of wools that came and went from the workshop, choosing a variety of beautiful lengths to try my hand at tapestry making.

My techniques are original because I lived at great remove from the rest of the world. In Bolivia we had no television and not even roads or telephones to the outside world. There was no air pouch to carry our letters except the whimsy of mountain mail, and an isolation that is very rare for this century. Added to that was the burden of altitude. That made strenuous exercise difficult.

The Bolivian peasants run up and down the mountains, but most of us walked deliberately at a pendulum pace and chose quiet occupations. As more and more limitations surrounded me my creative need grew stronger. Nowhere in Bolivia did any artist use rough wools in her work. I started with collage, pasting the shapes of bright wool onto paper and adding touches of ink and black cardboard. I made twenty-four naïve mountain scenes, the churches, the *campesinos* packed in trucks careening down the mountain roads, the ladies in their wide skirts and bowlers with babies in pointed hats clinging to their backs. I gave the framed drawings with their small banners of wool to a benefit function at the Embassy. They all sold.

When my paints finally came I was already so deep in my new art form that I continued to apply wool to painted canvases and then gave up my oil paints entirely and began to work only with wools. I did butterflies and fish, giving objects fanciful shapes with color and design and moved gradually into my search for the beauty and design of pre-Columbian artifacts. I borrowed books about ancient cultures and studied fragments of ancient weaving going back to the period the before the birth of Christ to see what stitches the craftsmen had used. During my years in Bolivia and then Mexico I continued to research and develop my techniques always with the figures of pre-Columbian art as my source. These early tapestries I call *Ancient Images of Mexico and the Andes*. It led me finally to the Alaskan and southwest Indian art of my own country where I had just begun to delve when we returned finally to the United States.

The isolation, the constant moving, the sense of living within oneself has encouraged my individuality. Nowhere have I had anyone to copy or to influence me. By the time I left the cultures of the South and returned to New England I had progressed along an independent ledge of living so long that I am forever comfortable there. In the adventure I changed from a person stimulated by the company of others and the warm sense of personalities to an inner-directed spirit, complete within myself. I see the splendor of the world without shadow and am content to lift my face to the sun wherever I am. My art is a reflection of that independence and my techniques are the process that I have worked out for myself like a lone sailor crossing the Atlantic. There has been no one to turn to for so long in my tapestry progression that I have come to depend entirely on the solutions that I discover alone, and now I even guard against intrusion.

When children, friends, home and even the wildflowers and birds I loved and knew were all gone, there was nothing left to do but coil the spring of hope tight within my parched frame and search a new opening for my creativity. My need was so great, and the loneliness and thin air so pervasive. We can only save ourselves. Loneliness and solitude have almost nothing to do with each other. But from one I learned the other while I was in Bolivia.

Loneliness by itself is a sense of separation from the world around you. It is even a separation from oneself when there is nothing close that is familiar and pulsating. Nothing seems able to touch you either by its magnitude or its nearness.

Solitude sings a different song. When one is in tune with her own life, able to feel strongly connected to the world about her, then solitude is possible. In Bolivia, as I came to understand the rhythm of the people and move out beyond myself the loneliness evaporated. Then the solitude for creative endeavor flowed in to warm me, and the beginning of my tapestries was created and embellished in that spirit of inner peace. Once I had caught the fragile message of that magnificent mountain country there was no peak I could not scale. The ancient pre-Columbian images, the deep blue scars of shadow on the jagged promontories, the twirling *cholas* in their *bayeta* costumes were mine forever to make solitude a state of trance and imagination, a part of my past and present, almost as much as the sea and rocks and forests of Maine.

What a curious juxtaposition: When friends talk about moving from New Jersey to Virginia as a wrenching adventure I am thinking silently: "How would they fare if it were Bolivia, Uruguay, Spain, Mexico? Do they know what the world contains? Have they looked at the sun in each hemisphere, face up to its blinding strength?" That makes you strong or brittle. I marvel at the intricate voyage I have taken; the human flesh is so fragile, and yet I have made my way up and down many mountains and sit quietly in my studio almost where I began. All the pieces have found their match in the creative momentum I feel.

Bermuda, May, 1980

We have come to Bermuda to revel in the sun and clean air. For me it is a time of discovery, for I learn that I no longer have children of my own. My three sons, sprung from my ribs as surely as Athena, are men in a world that no longer needs me. This has been true for a long time, but because we have lived apart, each in his own separate city and house, I have not seen it clearly. Together in this hilltop house of grand dimensions with the sea on three sides, the curtains float back to the wind and the sky is clear. There are no corners to hide the truth and I know what I am. I see my children on the beach with the sun of

21

Sorolla on their limbs and I glow with their straightness and assurance. Still I lean longingly to warm a nest that is empty.

The two grandones, Brigitte and Robert, are a tender link; Brigitte graceful and golden opens her arms to me with understanding. We are so much alike in our joy of living.

My balm is art. I am grateful for this week because I see my own fragility. The love I pour into my work is complete. Each needleful sweeps stronger and farther because the tapestries are my only children. They vibrate to my touch. Because of my two families, the warm-blooded triumvirate and now the woolen one, I have more to say, some of it with anguish. All of it with strength.

There's no self-pity and a curious sense of triumph. I am as free as eighteen, perhaps more so for now I have the courage of age. There are no weaklings still in the nest. I am deep into my third life.

Whether writer or artist it seems inescapable the fusion between two creative forces, the role of lover and mother and artist have to add more to a statement. The magnificence of gestation and childbearing, the creative cycle is the pattern of every one of my best tapestries. Artists so often say they do not wish to sell their paintings because it is like the loss of children. There is the same origin and growth and an inability to turn back once the seed has been planted. It will see the sunlight. The subtle confluence of the mind and brush will produce compulsively a tapestry, a Noguchi ring of marble, the filigree of a silver chain. Perhaps the seed-spark is a fissure in a rock, bark looping a straight trunk, always untouched nature, never the large scene.

In Bermuda with all its luminosity only Winslow Homer seems to have caught the array of blues without banality. Fishing between the beach and the outer rim of coral ledges I think of his castaway clinging to the broken hull of a sailboat. He tells a story crowding in textures of aquamarine, cobalt and umber. Even Andrew Wyeth, doing his spear fisherman in a Bermuda bay, resorts to burnt umbers, grays, and just a flick of blue in sky and sea. He paints with a sure brush the icy edges of the Bermuda houses against the sea browns, holding it all together with a play of line.

Because of Mouse Island I have become a lover of islands. There is an urge to withdraw into one's own spirit. The watery fringe sets a limit and dimension. My imagination leaps with each wave to find new meaning. Creativity springs from limitation of circumstance. An island sets these boundaries. Here I can say I have only these shores, these rocks, the special birds that have found their way to this atoll. Here are clean limits. Every cove is different.

Once before I visited Bermuda and savored the jasmine air, the sparkle of white diamond cut roofs in exotic foliage. The pink house that belonged to Eugene O'Neill makes me wonder if he could write there. Is this the place for a craft? What is the pattern of living? Does it allow for solitude and the circumstances of imagination? Is there a rhythm of being for two people, one desiring creating consequence, the other easy sociability and leisure?

The hills fall away in a fragrant garment of morning glory. Patches of pale primrose and a brooch of Easter lily catch the folds looping luxuriantly down to sea. Bermuda seems the rare spot where nature has been kindly treated. No speedways, but rather travel at twenty miles per hour. No calliopes or signs, instead the natural serenity shines forth to touch the white rooftops like gulls perched up and down the coast.

Each fall of rocks or the gray arches formed by the sea's passion are mine. I run my hands along the rims and fissures understanding that I am part of evolution. In a place so small and beautiful I could come to know it. Know it with the same intensity as a jeweler who counts the facets beneath his magnifying glass. It is this complete familiarity, this knowing, that triggers creative surge.

Within the last five months I have drunk the heady air of northern California, Maine and now Bermuda. The constant has been sea and rocks, my *aqua lapis*. Through it, migrating whales, harbor seals and blue heron have cavorted, emerged and disappeared.

Right now, as I stretch along the bluff, an airplane is arriving. It clears the casuarinas and slides beyond the horizon. Grandson Robert says, "I flew up into the clouds." He says it over and over. At four he has already had his first vision of heaven.

Anne Morrow Lindbergh has just written the latest of five journals, *War Within and Without*. Every page holds a special message for me. I read, wanting to fill the margins with notes, exclamation points, almost saying aloud, "Yes, yes!" Even more clearly than Margaret Mead or Sylvia Ashton-Warner with whom I empathize, Anne Lindbergh has a special sensitivity for nature. She loves storms as well as sunshine. If one waits for the perfect day she has lost half her life. Lindbergh writes, "There is a lovely storm this afternoon. I go and sit out under a big umbrella to watch the different trees and leaves take it."

So often I have sat indoors watching rain patterns on the glass. Or again, tying my hair tight against my head, rushed forth to cleanse my spirit and feel the balm of rain. Our bodies are largely water and crave that confluence. Here in Bermuda I feel the moisture of salt spray and cloudbursts mingled with the sun. The whimsy of seasons and of rain are equally part of me.

In Anne Lindbergh's pictures with her children she holds a special sensitivity on her fingertips. She seems childlike in her communication with them. My empathy swells. My only great sorrow has been the closing off of my own life-giving force. How deeply and eagerly I sought a fourth child! I remember crying myself to sleep those nights in Madrid for need of a pair of small arms around my neck. We laughingly referred to the wanted child as Carmen Barton. A name exactly fit for a Broadway comedy.

Even the barren years of Santo Domingo, La Paz and Guadalajara would have been sweet with a young hand in mine. Instead the bitter ladies who insisted I join the women's club besieged me. I am cheered to read Anne Lindbergh's comment, "I am bored to death with the women . . . nice upstanding attractive American women." And nice upstanding men can bring the same sense of parched time.

These hours in Bermuda are full of beauty. My eyes turn aquamarine in the reflection from the bay. My first two days here I was frantic to do everything and most of all to be with each member of my family. I have not thought of the tapestries I am composing or have a moment to design a plan. I am totally caught in wanting to hug my tall sons, now men pushing middle age, the youngest already thirty. I yearn to be close to my daughters-in-law. The pink sand stretches beyond my window to pink houses and rick-racked roofs. It is all overwhelming. All birds are exotic and new, and that demands me too.

I want to learn to ride a motorbike by myself and head down narrow roads and lanes. Few of my peers would be found riding behind her daughter-in-law on a moped for the reason that the flesh is knitted with old yarn.

For this reason I revere friends in their seventies and eighties who motor-bike through life, swinging the corners, taking their chances without complaint. I think of Alice Acheson, a bright constellation, replacing a worn-out hip with a new ball bearing as though simply changing a tire. Sitting poised and elegant, passing tea to her friends in pink lusterware cups, serene on the surface. I know the high drama, sense the tenuous smile holds pain and love and admire her. She has lost none of her individuality. That is the blessing of years, to be free of censure or free at least of caring.

～ 2 ～

Confluence of Nature

*E*ach lump of swollen gland or fever in my fourteen-year bones frightened me. Crooning over unborn chicks cramped in their shells, wondering, but never wishing to be unborn—wanting each day of light and wonder, even the chicken pox and the tantrum of poison ivy. "Help me, dear God, to be a good girl so I may go on living."

A world of rare excitement. The rain running down my pale hair and thin legs deep in the summer woods. Foghorns panting to repeat the one-cylinder rigs of lobster boats. Parcheesi, more rain, puzzles, card-table houses, and suddenly, college. My left shoulder sloping away like a reefed sail, loaded with books. Infinite wonder, infinite discovery. "Dear God, help me to be a good girl so I may go on living."

I know about love for I watch the song sparrows weave their nest in the wild rose brambles. I already know about love because the gentian eyes of my mother surround me.

I have yet to learn hatred or wars or guile and, although I am at college, I have not looked in the mirror to know myself. I know all that my eyes see, the soft edge of the white-oak leaf and the sharp curve of the wave. I know where the flounder hides with Egyptian eye and the sky reflected beneath a leaf in the robin's egg. I have never found a four-leaf clover, but love and trusting are my lucky plants. Lying in bed with the rain drum-beating the roof, a spider drops slowly on his own thread of life, unafraid on his single security, curling bright legs on an invisible high wire. I weave my life in his pattern, snaring the sun and raindrops, catching corners of the rooftop or branches as he does. Sometimes I will drop straight from the sky, and the thread of my life will be invisible in the dry wind. But I will trust its strength. When the fog drifts in to silence the harbor, carding woolen patterns across the bay, I will weave the pattern of my day through the mist, trusting dark islands for shelter and raspberry fruit for thirst.

Astern, the silhouettes of marriage and childbearing lift and plunge in the shapes of spruce. Ahead, my oars pull me into the current as the salt veil envelops familiar shapes floating beyond; wings of fog greet me. The cormorant circles with new confidence. I find my tempo, moving out beyond the last reef, slicing with sharp oar, lift and pull, lift and pull, moving into the sea of years.

Seasons

I am not gray
Or willow bended
And yet the changes
Flare before my eye.
The cormorant has come
To dry his black wings
In the sun. The smudge
Of spruce on Burnt
Has faded. A field
Of raspberry, risen
In offering to
Take its place,
Fringed with vetch
And Queen Anne's lace.
Triangularity of tree
And sail, less sharp
Beside the pale
Deciduous forms.

I now may see
The eider with her
Young, and wonder where
The heron with black
Crown has gone.

Mysterious, migratory
        game,
Seed drop and wing
        restrain.

When in my boat
With whittled oars
And watercolor brush,
I hear the muffled laughter
Of the thrush, I know
This cycle of the tree
And bird is mine.

Round arms of fledgling
Curved in love,
Turn hard and strong.
Seasons there are
For nesting and for song.

Along the salted shore
The polished rocks
Have seen more wonder
Than one life. Accept
Their gift and witness well
The magic that is mine
Wherein I dwell.

Washington, Spring 1975

A baby blue jay has fallen from the nest next door and my neighbor comes to see if the nest is in my yard. It belongs twenty feet north, in Edie's garden. Where but in America would three educated busy women devote themselves to returning a tiny jay to its rightful nest?

The life of an artist, as I live it, is not a tranquil day of needlecraft and imaginative séance. On my desk at the moment are letters to an architectural firm in New York about a large contract, a note that Sears needs to send bags for our vacuum cleaner, three poems that need work and a request to the Public Welfare Foundation for money for Kunturi in Bolivia.

Along the way I manage five houses, three of them rented. All this is possible because I marshal my options and use every hour, living each sweep of the second hand.

Each morning my art comes first and each afternoon deskwork. Luncheons are increasingly impossible. They are lingering social vacuums. One of my real needs to succeed is to pursue my art form without explanations.

In every art life there are branches and tendrils of expression of different mediums. I find designing for the school in Mexico relaxation and recreation. The pottery I made for Neiman Marcus while I lived in Mexico is a creative idea I would like to explore further. There is richness in variety, in using hands in a new way, but I hold myself to a steady course with tapestry making for there is so far to go—and so little time.

Mouse Island, Summer 1977

Reflective silence is my rare genie here in my studio. Today I am immersed in folds and rolls of wool. Swimming languidly among the alpacas and the crisp froth of organdy, so many thoughts and ideas flow past that I never know at once which stroke will guide the next design—which is the seventh wave.

But as I leaf through my large sketch pad with ink drawings and summer poems of Mouse Island, its rocks and spray, I am suddenly drawn to the pinnacle of summer pleasure. Sitting on my favorite ledge with my sketch pad I hold a séance with the granite folds, like Christmas candy reaching into the Atlantic. I hear a chirping call and there behind me, rounding the point, comes Bob with Brigitte in the bow of our tiny boat, her head a coin of light and her small body as beautiful as God can make. It was a moment of such completeness; Bob's warm loving presence and my beautiful grandone, their joy at finding me, to carry me back to their world and the pleasure of family. How does one explain these special moments that live with us forever? An alchemy of secret formula has placed that moment of my summer day above the fireplace of my life. I savor its colors and motion and its delight.

Washington, Fall 1977

Today is a winter blanket, a wool sky pulled tight across the bed of leaves. Only the bell in the grandfather clock in the hallway below pulses. Long ago it lost track of arithmetic, striking any hour that wheels into its addled woodwork.

I am working on a rainy day here in my turret with the rumble of planes instead of sea. I know I work often from agony, a surprising confession. I have not fully recovered the loss into adulthood of my children. It is a conscious restraint to stay in my own orbit, leaving them to draw their own circles with new centers. They were my first creative expression, a miracle for me of love and tenderness. In some ways my school in Mexico and the trusting girls filled the deep crevasse. Now again I am pulled away to start a new circle. This time it must be entirely my art even though I am not yet comfortable with its self-centered necessity. I see it philosophically, as completing the ability to be alone, to live alone, which is the way for each of us.

Dylan Thomas is reciting his rollicking Christmas poem on my record player. His words paint snow in Wales and the fire at Mrs. Protherow's that I want to share with my own family at Christmas. The poets are an important part of my studio life. Marianne Moore can make a woodpecker rise before my eyes: "up, up like Mercury." I have friends—all of them—as varied as T. S. Eliot and Cole. I wish there were more Spanish poets on records because they are so mellifluous. Each language has its own resonance.

Más Alla	Beyond
Los peldaños de roble,	The stair of oak
la altura, la fuerza	the height, the strength
me agotan. Levantando	draws me. Lifting
mis ohos, subiendo	my eyes, climbing
sin ver dónde voy	without seeing where I go
o dónde he ido.	or where I have been.
Me marea la vista	I am dizzy
el azul, el blanco,	with blueness, white,
el sol, toda la belleza	sun, all the beauty
tan agotadora, mientras	so overwhelming, while
subo, subo las escaleras	I climb, climb the stair
sin mirar más que	seeing only the sea, the
el mar, las rocas.	rocks.
Sabiendo que allí	Knowing that ahead
adelante está el cielo	are the heavens
tambíen, azul.	also blue.

Washington, Winter 1977

The year is ending, one of growth and new directions, strength and frustration and a deeper understanding of the inner drive that I seldom give full rein. I look back at the year and see myself reflectively with some degree of surprise, as a driving, committed woman, perhaps too often in the role of adversary where treacle would serve better. I feel my innate love channeled into strange ways as the outlets I cherished are ripped from my ribs. I am never without direction, only that the unfolding of life sets new and sometimes cruel limitations.

This has been a year of devotion and even adoration of my mother. Her hard-won serenity and her generosity overwhelm me, although it is not a path I choose to follow even though I see advantages.

I end the year feeling no great satisfaction with my progress in art. I enjoy the creative thrust of my work but the accolade is not important. There seems to be no choice once the momentum is begun and I snatch fleetingly at pen or phone to patch up or arrange a chance sociability with old friends. They are the clothespins holding my life to the line. I need them and yet I scarcely have time.

My greatest satisfaction has been my catalogue: the forty-eight pages with color plates and cogent prose. It tells who I am and why. Each reader learns less or more according to his or her insight. The pleasure of it is that it continues to interest those who know me and those who do not. *Salt Veil* on the cover is the poem of my life, the beauty, restraint and the final satisfaction with finite detail.

The most sorrowful are family members—blessedly few—who are unable to accept even my small success. I know their problem and forgive them. Time is too short to dwell in their houses of cramped spirit. I would prefer to throw my arms about them even as I see that chasm widen.

It is a year of pleasure, of success, of disappointment, of pettiness and in all ways an entirely human unrolling of life. I end it reflectively and will not pause to contemplate again for months. I wish to continue to rejoice and savor my good fortune. I scarcely have time for a noonday yogurt or the poems that follow my art.

I feel a closeness to my faith; an uneducated faith without trappings or details, but a belief that everything will unroll in due time and in the best way. I have written a small collection of poems this summer which I have given to Mother and Bob for Christmas. It is called *Summer Song* and I preface it with a quote from the Psalms:
"The Lord is my strength and my song."

Boothbay Harbor, Fall 1979

For years I have heard travelers and Mainers alike say that September is Maine's most beautiful month. Now I am sharing these thirty days of gold wind and silver water. This year is my revelation. No one has mentioned the fall asters, the flat top aster in palest hue running to middle violet and deep royalty. Goldenrod, scorned as a sign of fall, blooms from late July. But in September the ascetic, spare members of the rambunctious family shoot spikes of cadmium like tiny rockets from every untrammeled spot. Dusty goldenrod abound, and scattered in its midst, each spike an infinite cluster, is the white silver-rod in full bloom. So many flowers seem to have clumsy names for their lace and elegance. There is St. John's wort and fleabane. But silver-rod says it all.

September sun, skirting the horizon, a great searchlight low along the water, catches the lick and polish of each day, a brassy beacon turning the islands black as coal. Sun drifts deep into our living room, tickling the wicker, laying warm hands on the black and white alpaca couches.

Fall is a glorious time to fill my arms with field flowers. The houses are empty. No lawns are freshly pruned along hedgerow and road. The brittle stems snap easily. They are hardy blooms asking scarce water for luxuriance.

September is calm with almost no motorboats, only an occasional patch of sail; loons paddling through the cove. The great blue stands each morning on the riverbed of rocks. His serenity and patience, balanced on one leg, makes a mockery of my morning exercises. Surly, the ancient yogis had herons as their earthly model.

Is there some corner of the world that is September forever?

There are rare interludes in our lives when we stop to see detail, to note the pebbles on our paths of coming and going. I can stop at the window on my journey to the kitchen to catch a migrating chestnut-sided warbler, to see the white returning to the eiders' breasts. At the end of a day these are for me accomplishments. Bright as leaves they tell me the roll of seasons.

Although at the edge of the sea there has been no frost, just two or three miles inland the gardens have been blackened. Trees are lightly tinted but a farmer assures me that frost will not burn the fields along our shore until December.

The foliage has a vagrant brush as we drive inland to river towns, Wiscasset, Bath. Portland is nearly barren, its umbrella of elms destroyed. As we head west into New Hampshire the color is bright banners.

The MacDowell Colony is our destination. Last spring I applied to spend two months there, a workplace for creative artists, poets, musicians, sculptors. Each person has his or her own cottage, off bounds to all others save the quiet hand that delivers a lunch to the door at noon. I crave untouched serenity. I know now that I am comfortable with myself and with silence. It would help me to have the evening conviviality of other creative people. I have always worked alone; I have no knowledge of the interplay of ideas or working artists. There is no vacuum, just unknowingness.

Perhaps the single Indian-file progression of my art form is best because of isolation. I remember at the Art Student League, however, that my greatest teachers were my peers. The professor came fleetingly twice a week noting hurriedly as he moved among the easels a detail, a brush area. But studying works in progress of other pupils told me much more. I saw where they failed, occasionally read with dismay the transition of a gifted student from rare talent to copyist. I have always feared the copyist. I will not exploit or touch ideas of others. I demand of myself that my art come from within. Of course, "within" means only internal interpretations because the "without," the center self, is nature. Leonardo da Vinci wrote, "Nature is the only true source of art." I believe that dictum.

Washington, Fall 1978

Today I am speaking at the Textile Museum to a group of Mexican ladies from the Mexican embassy. Washington is full of celebration of Mexican art with antique *serapes* from Saltillo in the now colors of grape, maroon and beige, the photography of Manuel Bravo and various artifacts at the Renwick.

Speaking in Spanish is easy and pleasant for me. I like the way a language filled with orderly vowels slips off the tongue. Over and over I hear, "You seem so relaxed! How do you find time to do such consuming work?"

But they do not want to hear that each day stretches me to my utmost, that I turn from my arms full of wool and my head tracing a wave to fill the dishwasher or greet the phone. Some of that is necessary too. To measure the amounts is the secret formula. It is a formula that perhaps a woman can handle more easily than most men because it deals with flexibility. It involves bending to the moment while keeping hidden and safe my inner thoughts and patterns. I think of my art as I sit in the narrow Sunday pew or ride the bus or peel fresh carrots. No best ideas or completed designs rise from these dual moments, but art is my lifeline.

Barbara Tuchman, Joan Robinson, Agnes Mongan, all distinguished women who have lived long enough to have their faces framed in silver, are reported to not suffer fools lightly. That phrase concerns me because although I am no smarter than I was twenty years ago and certainly less desirable, I find impatience is the lead horse on my creative chariot. Often I seem to be smiling and extending my hand because it is a ritual. Warmth and friends are a necessity, but the boredom of endless pleasantries saps all energy from the creative pulse. "Not suffering fools lightly" merely means, if truth be said, "I am each day a little older, a little less energetic and I have so many miles I wish to go. Forgive me if I do not respond. My heart is a tree, my eyes are waves. I am watching the motion of the clouds, the prisms of stars and I have no breath."

Last night I met Rufino Tamayo. He came to the Phillips Gallery in Washington to crown his show "Fifty Years of Rufino Tamayo," and he is glorious. White hair has made his Indian face elegant against a silver frame. He is seventy-nine but he seems, best of all, so at peace, so vibrant, and he suffers fools like me with charm and delight. Where along the way has he achieved his great capacity to evolve and produce and keep his calm?

Immediately I ask him, because it is the theme that haunts me, "Do you paint every day?" And right on top of it I heap my next concern, "What do you do about telephones and other interruptions?" His answer, said with the assumption that years of tradition have established: "I paint eight hours a day without interruption. Telephones and all that my wife takes care of!" He then added with delight, "I love parties. We go to a great many parties at night. The nights are for amusement." And sleep? "I am very sturdy. I always feel well." How glorious! I learn later about his wife.

I think again why are we women less relaxed. I know I have no wife to answer my phone, plan my meals and arrange my day. Even with the unprogrammed help of a faithful husband, I still must lead two lives. There is family sorrow; who gives them a small luncheon? Children need a vacation; who tends the grandones? All these ancient delights are dimmed before the lost hours without my art. I need the human contact but I live and breathe my art. Am I ready to give up the thirty years of warmth for the candle of creativity? Or is the question even that easy? Bob says flatly he will not live in Maine all year while, across from him, seated in a tall Chippendale chair ornate in red lacquer and gold, I am already choosing a promontory among the spruce for my studio. My whole adult life seems to have been lived straddling two opposing forces: war and home, foreign living and home, children and foreign homes, and now city life versus a studio on the Maine coast. Perhaps distinguished women of far greater merit have met these same challenges by closing their ears to duets of living. The lone women carry the greatest burden of all for they have no one. Perhaps having no one they are simply rowing in the direction of their choice. I am searching for solutions but I am less and less willing to accept an accommodation. That means dulling the edge of creative drive. I must accept that alternative if I compromise.

And so the fools I cannot suffer lightly are those who remember the Nancy Barton of Foreign Service wifery. They want my art, its happiness and celebration and infinite detail, but they also want all that went before. I love more than before, but much of it will be an embrace felt through my tapestries.

Washington, Fall 1979

Mother has left us, slipping away quietly, wishing not to disturb our lives, leaving each of us with a memory of love and understanding that will keep us close to her as long as we shall live. The grandchildren, many of them already mature men and women, and even the great grandones will remember her ultramarine eyes, a true reflection of the sea she loved and with the same sparkle that one finds on a clear day. Mother's life was that kind of weather, from within the sun shone forth.

Funerals seem always to be moments of rare torment and sorrow. Even here amidst the sudden devastation of my loss, Mother's spirit prevails. Her five children and their wives, seventeen of the grandones and two great grandchildren gather to share this deepest of family moments. Each of us has a talent to offer. Some to order and arrange flowers, to select favorite hymns, others to write for the newspapers about her beautiful life that touched so many. The three sons choose the simple pine coffin and arrange for the service. A tiny great-grandson greets the minister conducting the service with his usual merry, "Hi." This is not the departure of an elderly lady who had outlived living, but the celebration of an extraordinary spirit that has flamed to the last hour. I can feel her strength riding the roller coaster of the last years of age, holding fast to the sides and smiling to us as she dipped suddenly over the last rise. How deeply we all care is the measure of our constraint at parting with her.

From this time of revelation and sorrow a new strength will certainly develop in my art. These are the experiences that temper and cool the steel behind the fragile beauty of my world. Mother never expressed unusual pride in my art work. She accepted it as one of many adventures of her various children. It was never a sense of fulfilling for her an uncompleted passage of her own life.

But the headlong drive each of her five children inherited is from Marion Dix Whitten.

I want two things: to emulate as best I can her generosity and love for the rest of my life; and to glorify her living in my art.

California, Spring 1980

I care so much about everyone, about just being. That is what my art says to every beholder. A hummingbird at this moment sways suspended on the wind, his vibrating throat in electrified copper before my window, bursting light of infinite change, visible in every cloud and corner of nature. All of this seeing and flowing, in and out of the caverns of life, gives a momentum to maturity. Not by some exact image or moment of love but the gentle crescent of each experience. The twelfth year, apple blossom birthday, sea voyages, the birthing, ostriches floating over pampas, the *hornero* bird singing by his clay oven house, the beautiful daughters-in-law, the Chinese tree peony in May. There are new lists each time the mind reflects, and each list finds its way into the soft woolen folds of my tapestries.

There are family sorrows and they are snags in a rushing cascade. The shell of my soul touches and glides on. Sometimes I am bruised but not broken, moving with the stream out to sea. Perhaps rocks for this reason inspire me; not only for their singular beauty of textures and shapes but also the impact of their abrasive forces. They test my strength, ignite endurance. They give variety.

What tree would you like to be? I ask myself this. I like the looseness of willow and weeping cherry, but not their bended obsequiousness. One must be statuesque and elegant to be a spruce, muscular and hardy to be an oak. Perhaps I will choose to be a flowering cherry or a sourwood or best of all a Japanese maple. When the world is green my creative branches will glow copper. The structure will reach delicately out to rain and wind, but the wood is hard and enduring. We have such a maple in our garden in Washington. I watch it through the year, raiment always in contrast to the seasons.

If people come some day to stand before my tapestries with the same absorption and communion I share with our russet maple I will fall to my knees in thankfulness. All the bad vibrations about age are lost in the strength and endurance of a beautiful tree and I shall remember. As I walk into a room of martini glasses or across the flowering fields of spring I walk as a tree. My head rises into the clouds, my hands are strong branches, my thoughts are the leaves turning and changing with the mist and sun.

I have no artifice. The simple blue jeans that sheath my legs and the white blouse or sweater have been part of me since childhood. They are the bark, covering my heartwood. If the vine of a small grandone clings to me I am softened and made beautiful by her curling hands rising as tendrils to my face.

Every beautiful tree has scars along its carapace where weather and the whimsy of fate have swept past. I am the same. My core is fine grained and straight. I am filled with thankfulness. Even the foliage of my blond hair has forgotten the seasons. There is as yet no change, no threaded gray, although I do not dread it. Somehow it is of no real importance. The soft gray turning to snow of my sister Harriet is beautiful. White hair has an aura. It is the carded alpaca of my most sensitive tapestries. White on white canvases are the gathering of subtle essences, whether hair and face or wool against woven wool.

I think of the white nimbus about Rufino Tamayo with his polished pecan skin. The white above the cheekbones on Bob's straight head are wings. It is a coronation of life that I celebrate, accepting the seasons.

Winchester, Massachusetts, Spring 1980

This week as I await my turn in the hospital line like a patient commuter, all the family have come and gone and come again. Bob and I have been alone in the dark shingled home of my brother. It is a discrete house with the slanting soft roof of the saltbox dipping down behind a gigantic fir. Patches of New England stone frilled with azalea and juniper circle its prim presence. Along the north boundary forsythia flames.

I have thrown my arms this week in deep communion around my three brothers. The boys, as my brothers are still called, greet me diffidently at first. I find two of them at the end of a day in their tiny office. They labor as hard as bricklayers, bending their bright minds to inventive building techniques and million-dollar profits. They are totally without artifice. During the coffee breaks of their workers, Bradford can be found manipulating a fork lift, Charles pulling great ribbons of siding into position. We all have the same desire to use our own hands in creative ways.

Winchester, Spring 1980

Hospital, U.S.A. 7 P.M. 1980! After ten days in my brother's serene saltbox this is flashbulb night on the strip. What a fine line divides the sick and the visitor. It is like policemen and bandits. We all carry guns, we all shoot and both sides drop in pools of blood sooner or later. Heavy smokers, flaccid relatives, stand at the elevators at 8 P.M. How can one guess except by the thin plastic wristlet with name and number who are there to be mended? Illness is a great exercise in patience. A futility that contrasts with the patience of creativity. The slow progress of a tapestry is above all a construction, a putting together. It is a glowing building, the birth of a child, a sewing up of seams of caring.

All night my semi-private "sweet"-mate has rattled and burped and groaned like a teakettle on the back burner. It is like the trip across Lake Titicaca, a narrow bed, plenty of noise and the bubble of water. The shiny brass trim of the nineteenth century lumbering along the top of the world with a mismatched cargo seems curiously relevant as I perch on my narrow bed with yellow coverlet.

My surgical H-hour is not until two. Yesterday Bob told me, perusing a genealogical chart of my Dix ancestors, "You are a tenth generation here, Nancy." And it is that New England heritage that propels me out of bed, into my clothes until the medication starts around noontime. On my narrow shelf with its rubber sheet I do all the yoga exercises I can, brush my hair one hundred pulls, and think of the painting Georgia O'Keeffe did, remembering the moment of anesthesia until the white dot of cognizance vanished and went blank.

I want to watch this process outside my emotional self, to be clinical and see the poetry, sense the transmigration of the mind and match it to a tapestry. If a stone is so moving, surely singular events I am caught up in must be expressed in strong forms. My detachment from my own body is one of the advantages of my absorption with art.

If American art is deeply involved in spiritual significance, particularly as it relates to nature, then perhaps I meet moments of creativity and crisis on the same level. There is a fusing of faith and wonder, a trust and at the same time a flowering. Nature is more than an object of beauty. It is also clearly to me an exultation of divinity, coming together in subtle forms and juxtapositions that none of us as artists can match.

Moments of pain are also moments of growth both spiritually and creatively. Tucked under my calm skin and straight gaze there is, of course, concern and apprehension. Like childbirth, the moment must come and I move into the pattern of the outer circle of tide, knowing I will be pulled under eventually. I also know that the controlled, almost lighthearted way I dismiss myself to my peers is as fragile a cover as a porcelain rice dish but the agony beneath surfaces later. It will pour out in my art. I am put to the flame to prove the alchemy is pure and strong. What few can guess is the breadth of imagination that reaches deep into me extracting all sorts of phantasmagoria. This might be the moment in which I would wish to be a better bridge player!—and not an artist.

Washington, Spring 1980

Lunch with Jim and Patsy Webb is a special moment. Jim has the finest mind and is the gentlest of the men I know. We talk about his adventures with presidents and his absorbing years with NASA putting the first man into orbit. His caring and intensity boil up and consume him under the quiet skin of a southern gentleman. I see his hand shake with illness and know his sacrifice. Men often give their health for corporate success. He has given his to his country. And Patsy encouraged him and shared his choices.

We succumb to small treacheries, eating ice cream for dessert. A small grace note in his life of sacrifice. There are special men with whom I always have a lively conversation. Jim, John Gardner of

Common Cause, Senator Hugh Scott. They are smarter than I, and I feel exhilarated. Although we talk as equals, none of them has a wife with a career outside her home. They are dominant men in a social pattern that has changed. How am I so lucky to have chosen a strong man who sees so clearly my new role as a woman? But none of these men has a sense of superiority. They are all humanists. Each of us, man or woman, is an individual with spirit and independence. Other talented men talk down to me, inquire about my art as you might an attack of gout and don't listen to the answer. We have good conversations, but I do not trust them in the same way. And, of course, some of them bore me to distraction. The days when "anything in pants" was preferable are as moldy as Limburger cheese. More and more I make feeble social gestures but seek the hours to pursue my work. Family becomes increasingly important and old friends who understand that time and solitude are the oxygen of my art work more than fill my spare moments. I cannot turn back to days filled with tennis and shelling peas because they never existed.

Mouse Island, Spring 1980

America, the beautiful schooner with wide gaff, topsail and her three jibs set, is slipping past my studio. Going out on the morning wind, she turns like a swan to catch the south breeze, the line of her sails close hauled like folded wings.

With Mother's death, the heritage she left us seems suddenly deeper and more important. I knew the sea lay far back within our family life and skills, but I did not know that on both sides were seafarers. My father's family, the Sawyers, came from Yarmouth. Only my great-great-grandfather, Moses Hemenway, a Harvard classmate and friend of John Quincy Adams, chose books and the Bible. For fifty years he led the congregation in Wells, Maine. The delicate spire of his church still stands, trimmed and shuttered. Even his church was close to the sea. He had only daughters and the line of theology and seafaring was broken. But the communication remains.

Mother loved the sea from the earliest moment when she made a small boat from a box. And Mother was drawn to the psalms and deep faith. Surely, a good sailor held the same sense of wonder and belief as land disappeared over the edge of the world and only the line of the horizon lay before him. That line is a quest both in faith and passage. As I hold my mother's worn Bible with brown leather cover I hold my heritage. I comprehend the forces that are mine: love and faith and a sense of the rare beauty at the sea's edge. I wish to express it over and over again as an offering of gratitude. My throat aches. It is almost more than I can contain. I see the line of my ancestors, the parasols, the foot warmers, the rough shoes turning the sod of a New England spring, arms winding brass winches, testing sails. I too, want to make a contribution in strong sons, in beautiful tapestries, to leave behind an unbroken endeavor, a spinning out of my caring to keep the horizon line sharp. A line where level eyes and belief can focus and move on to new generations.

We call that being a New Englander. Toynbee suggests that the harsh climate and soil of the Northeast have shaped us. But so has the rare beauty, the natural abundance of forest and sea. The "work ethic" is the life ethic really. Its source, beauty and faith and living, is a flow of constant refreshment for me if I stay near its stream.

Today I am sixty. I am still sitting on a rock in blue jeans in Maine as I write. The marvel is not so much that the blue jeans I have loved since a small girl are still my costume, but that I have learned a way to record my thoughts both in tapestries and writing. I have always loved the rocks, sea and forest and the life it holds, but it is only now that the right words seem to come.

This seems a day like any other. We swim in the icy bay. As I leave at 6:30 Bob is scraping a cedar rowboat patiently with a pen knife into the most difficult corners. I am in my studio on Mouse Island, working on a free-shaped tapestry of wool called *Moment of Impact*. Bob offers to take me out for dinner but we choose instead a picnic lunch to Boston Island. June 19th is so early to be in Maine. There is no family to share our celebration. A boat ride in our small motorboat smacking each wave like a great fish's tail and then the quiet walk to a sunny cove, a day as indulgent as heavy cream. Bob has bought me a plum-colored bathing suit that fits into the palm of my hand and a new pair of oars. I have rowed to the island for four years with unmatched oars always pulling harder to keep my skiff flowing straight.

I feel gentle and happy accepting the bounty of my life, savoring each moment. Looking back and ahead I see the sun shining. "My cup runneth over." If I were to change my life or redo it I wouldn't know what to wipe out or multiply. I think of the Queen of England who celebrates her birthday in May to satisfy the lovers of garden parties. She never can walk the streets or the woods alone.

I think of Eliza in her small adobe house in a Mexican village with the window we gave her as a wedding present, her opening to sunshine and fresh air. I have fallen miraculously between these contrasts with love and freedom and independence all mine. I have had parents and a husband who encourage me to explore art to the fullest, even if a little late. I have done all the traditional samplers first: "Home Sweet Home," "The Hearth Is Where the Heart Is." I gather myself together to put art first. Each day it is easier as the path is worn into the fragrant landscape. Now and again I will tread on a lily in my path, but must not stop to grieve. That is my choice.

Boothbay Harbor, Summer 1980

Bob and I share the housekeeping. We are balancing now the presence of three grandones, a high school mother's helper and a new college graduate working as an apprentice in my studio. We eat, sleep, swim, sail, send out and receive messages from friends, museums, corporations, carpenters, bricklayers, relatives. An hour today will provide time to shine the face of our cottage. Best of all in four decades we have rarely been angry at the same moment. This has saved us enough energy to accomplish what Sisyphus failed to achieve. The single rock I push up and over the rim of my art tables is my burden and ecstasy. Each time I achieve the lip of the mountain I am encouraged to reach down into the valley of the unknown and start up again. Much of this is possible because we are domestic jugglers egging each other along.

I leave small reminder lists on the floor at the entrance to our bathroom. "Sasha and Lisa's beds need to be changed." "Brigitte is missing a sock that is in the motorboat." "Call the plumber." "Thank you for seeing about the insulation in the Loft." "Water the lettuces in the garden that I transplanted last night." "I love you."

On the row to Mouse Island I make a new list for myself in my head. The head of the board of trustees of the Portland Museum of Art is trying to reach me by phone, two wicker chairs haven't been returned from recaning. I need to talk to the local travel agent about flights to Africa. Where will I get the exotic shots for our African adventure?

Our life could be a large snarl of yarns, sure to knot and break. Neither of us pulls too hard. As we unwind the day, kisses come easy and often and our fingers in the complex web of living have a hidden patience that must be hereditary. It is a very good idea to always have outsiders in a home, everyone is a bit more civil. At least those of us with staunch New England ancestors will think twice before we speak rudely. We both have an actor's love of audience and want to keep the chorus happy.

Everything that was Mother's now has the aura of the moon's nimbus. I have flowers by her picture, cherish the scarf that matched her cobalt Liberty silk dress, row in her cedar boat to my studio, each gesture full of remembrance. I look about me as children and grandchildren walk the field with Bill and hear him say, "Every blade of grass has family meaning. We are a strong, close family like few others in this world." He suggests we overpower others, but only as love and loyalty are overpowering.

I see that I am in many ways mother; Mother and myself. I want to be her image in making our family strong and I stretch out to be her other side: the deeply creative half that lay dormant most of her life. On the mantle of our upstairs fireplace I have a watercolor still life that she painted. My brothers and sister have chosen her flower paintings. I have one large red poppy she painted at my request for my freshman room at Wheaton College. But the picture on my mantle is of a translucent plate, and china pitcher. Their texture and the milky consistency of glass, the varied colors of white against crimson curtain are as exact as a steel rule. As sharp and right as frost.

Saturday and Sunday, picking greens in the garden, cosseting a family, a babysitter, Amy Gray, my apprentice. Bill's girlfriend and former girlfriend, all here, floating like gay painted lobster buoys on our front porch—I am one side of Mother.

But the hidden side of her is not my lopsided self. The tapestries bulge from my brain. My new studio is blossoming like a flower among the spruce on the other side of the ridge. I feel that once I can give up my blueberry recipe I will shed the housewife's skin and be only a plant reaching up into the light, leaves of creativity reaching out along a sturdy stem. That is what I want. The loving and caring will not wash away. As I shed half myself I leave room for new growth.

Boothbay Harbor, Summer 1980

I am confronted by my Puritan ancestors and cannot escape their steady disapproving gaze. I am also pulled by the sapphire blue of my mother's eyes to the place where I know she will be on Sunday morning. And so instead of sneakers and a racquet, I put on freshly creased pants, scoop up my life jacket and head for church. Today I cross the long bay of Boothbay Harbor, a bright north breeze at my back, to the Wilson Chapel on Ocean Point. By car, a long sinuous drive through the town and down the peninsula; by boat it is an arrow's flight without restraint.

I am there in fifteen minutes, rounding the north edge of a dark spruce island and into the dock where boats hang as tight as suckling kittens. Beyond them the cottages sprout along the inner ledges, the ocean and the elegance of Fisherman's Island, the two Whites lift from the polished sea. Their strength makes me walk lightly, swept with happiness, past the dime store architecture and the slack curtains. All of Ocean Point is a hurriedly made bed, but the islands, they are my New England forebears. They will prevail.

The Wilson chapel is a rock upon a rock. The nave holds the altar and two stone cells right and left. The organist, in cerulean blue, is sitting before her musical altar in one cell like a nun in prayer. From the stone walls, long beams are praying hands interlocked, lifting up into the peak of the roof. Every bench is full, full of migrating souls seeking a quiet branch among the living. Dr. Lucock speaks of death, death that already whispers to him, his white head and shaking hand suggesting he seeks as well as gives comfort. His fragility tells me he is coming to terms with his own life, eager to share his questioning. He speaks of the anxiety, of the fear of losing a child, or husband, not just of losing oneself, and suggests we accept that possibility or the terror of our own passing can shroud all the beautiful days that are still ours.

I was not thinking of death on this blue day. Perhaps this is a good time to do so. When the sky is clean blue and the wind allows no safe haven. I hear his message and am grateful for it. I do have anxiety for those I love. Perhaps I can remember the flavor of what I have heard here in this stone chapel, as cool as a great well.

Back in my skiff I round a feldspar ledge and follow the curve of a spruce island, skirting the shore, making a ruffle along its edge.

The tide is full. I look deep into the sea, watching for unknown rock and measure the bright lobster pots for low water marks. There are folds of granite pulled up into the forest like molten steel. There is an osprey's nest on the west face in the tip of a dying spruce. I hesitate and then head quickly home, skimming and bouncing from wave to wave, the wind flat against me.

There are washed stones on the south face of Ocean Point, as symmetrical as billiard balls. They will be perfect for the aprons of more tipis. I have found rocks I want to explore and feel on the island and am light with enjoyment and freedom.

A small boat, I think to myself, is like a willing pony. I am in charge in a modest way. It is my beck or whim that leads us both and the choices are mine. That is why girls are so often eager horseback riders. That is why my granddaughters all want to run the boat. It is the release, the freedom, the decisiveness that we have been told belongs to the masculine mind. Sailing has some of the same power but the wind is more recalcitrant. There, too, we must coddle. The wind has treachery and strength. That is a challenge, but the obedience, the unquestioned obligation of my rowboat with the tiny motor leaves me free to see the fish hawk and the taffy rock without distraction.

That is the morning's vibrations. Then the afternoon, sailing with friends on a blue, east wind day, a curious phenomenon, for the wind has blown straight from the east with a smile for three days. All our storms come from the east. I do not remember such a wind in all these years that has brought sun. We lift and pull in our sloop beyond the islands of Mouse, Burnt and Squirrel and point resolutely in a heavy breeze for Damariscove. The naked brown earth where a whole colonial village once existed forms the horizon for several miles. Not a single house remains. Sitting alone on the bow I brace my feet and hold a stanchion against the angle of the deck. As we press out beyond Fisherman's Island the wind rushes through a narrow passage laying our sails close to the water.

In this moment, when the sailboat bends and is tested, I see a clear analogy. The two islands are my life, one my family, the other my duties as a woman. Between them the high tide and the rush of air are what happened to my life. Always I have been there, pushing against the two islands of my heritage. Nourishing, with a soft wind that tried not to gust and gale, the shores of these two certainties. The sudden high tide has been my triumph. I have finally swept over the rocks and the momentum at my back leads me lightly along the crests of waves. Nothing can stop me. I have burst forth without injury to either island. They are still constant as I glance back but I move now looking only ahead, filled with joy and buoyancy. Wherever I am going I am unbound and cannot be caught. I have fulfilled. My journey of wind and sea and rock will hold strength and fragility. Together these have been polished for so many years along the far shore of my two islands before the tide rose and pushed me free.

I know that my freedom would be meaningless without the years of confinement. Restraint has taught me to look at the mysterious configuration of each rock, the sprouting of a single seed. But the bigger concept, the delineation of freedom, is for sculptors and large designs. That happens when the wind blows hard and the sea rises without rancor. I have been washed clean, robed in the white curl of waves and sustained by the gust of slanting sails.

Lisa slips along the deck, clutching the rail and comes to snuggle close to me against the spray. I tell her about the two islands and how my toes are touching the sea lightly. I want her to share my exaltation. With her small hand in mine, curled against the wind, she is still on the far side of the two islands, holding to my flesh, caught in the rock pools that are turning her into a graceful adult. The summer we have shared is for her a strengthening and for me a song of love. Sunday she will go back to her mother in Texas, but neither of us will be the same. I give her my place away from the wind, taking only the feel of her warm hand in mine as a memory.

Washington, Spring 1991

Often the sun flowing into my studio in Maine or Virginia fills me with lassitude and I lay down my needle or my pencil and paper. It reminds me I need rest, that the creative drive, like a strenuous sport, demands relaxation. Stretched on the narrow canvas cot in Maine or the frayed chaise longue in my southern retreat, I close my eyes with a deep sense of pleasure. The luxury of total release nurtures every creative instinct. When I open my eyes again the designs will be fresh and tell me clearly where I am going.

Have you ever lain on the forest floor and watched the sunlight filter through the patterns of oak leaves? As a country child I often stopped in play to lie face skyward, to watch the clouds and birds. I have lain with my arm around my grandones, to watch the seagull slide over us in a counterpoint with rushing cloud.

New One

Newborn eyes
    lie back against
        the hammock
            watching the seagull
      float, his wings
    laced between
oak and alder berry.

Small fists rise
    to catch
        the passing
            image, laughing
                softly as a thrush.

A contrail
    ties a ribbon
        on the sky.
            I lie with the starfish
        hand in mine
    gazing
through each leaf.

Wondering at
    the lacy sheath
        framing the wings
            caught in the waterfall
            of winds.

I am renewed by these peaceful moments, and by the evanescent confluence of nature.

The sun is for me a talisman of joy because I am a child of north country. I do not have the tropical need to hide beneath a solitary tree on arid land or scurry like a mole from one shaded corner to another. I notice each day as I work when the warmth and color dips behind a cloud. I sense its passage as it cuts light patterns along the floor of my studio and slips past my work, fringing the tables with citron and gold.

When I have traveled to Africa and watched the herds stamping and whirling in clouds of dust, I understand the other side of the sun. In western Mexico the parched spring is vagrant as torn paper and whole villages shrink in the heat. I came to know the agony of the sun.

But in my studios, tree guarded, one river and one sea washed, I am thankful, for sun and water meet and neither destroys the other. Both nurture my art. In these two places there is softness and flow, not only of waves or the movement of a great river but also the flow of sun between tulip trees or evergreen. I belong to these small areas of earth. Slowly I am growing to know them, their needs and changes. I have watched the dogwood bud hold winter icicle and balance fresh snow. I am watching now in March beginnings of spring, imperceptibly moving to flower.

The Potomac is roiling and tumbling, its brown shoulders hunched with spring thaw. The song is wind in the great trees. There is crescendo and sudden pianissimo, like a Brahms symphony with chromatic color filling the measures.

Occasionally a jet blunders past, using the river as guide. It is easy after a while to screen out the surge and roar of airplanes as I do the outboard motor in Maine. One learns to see and hear what is beautiful, selecting out the static, for there is almost no place left without intrusions. I too am an intrusion and want to move between the rocks and trees in silence.

The Loft, Summer 1981

On my drawing board are books piled about, some open to strong pictures. There is Eliot Porter's *The Place No One Knew* and *The Eternal Sea* with quotes from Hemingway, Heyerdahl and Walt Whitman. Usually I look at the pictures filling in my own imagined words, but this gray foggy morning I stop to read Melville's words and what Joseph Conrad had to say about tall masts. All of these eloquent men instinctively write of the sea as a woman, quixotic, compelling, sometimes old and gray, dangerous and irresistible. The references to ships are also couched in feminine adjectives and pronouns. Whoever heard anyone say, "What a beautiful ship he is"?

Musing at my desk I see how clearly the lines are drawn not only through our daily ritual of living but through our language. Nearly all the literature is by men. I have found in the many books on my work table only one woman quoted, Marguerite J. Adams. I think of Rachel Carson's *The Sea Around Us* and the poetry of Edna St. Vincent Millay; Marianne Moore with her pithy observations is nowhere to be found. How clearly each has his or her own place. Rocks have no gender for all their strength and beauty, but almost all that is glorious in nature if it has gender is feminine. Those who are quoted are almost exclusively male. It is as though nature is the receptive partner to be admired, even adored, by the most articulate men as they might stop to absorb the vision of a lovely girl entering a room. Nature is certainly feminine because she is equally vulnerable both to the love affair and the abuse of men.

I am a bird-watcher and I have just been on the *Lucy B.* out of Port Clyde to spend a whole day at sea. Our destination, the mighty rocks of Matinicus. The fragile bird life of the Icelandic tern floating across the hard crust of rocks like white streamers and the comical puffins like toby jars somehow continue to survive the ages. What I remember most of that day is the faces of men as they sighted each bird, their gentleness and enthrallment. This is where the masculine and feminine languages we all accept seem to melt together making of us spirits of light without limitations. Bird-watchers are a unisex society. They have grasped the best of our ancient division.

The birds, of course are not so twentieth century. The elder drake has glorious plumage and he will soon withdraw to the mercy of the gulls. But there is a sharing, a unity of life where home is simply a down nest with no dusting or dishes. I hear the elder in conversation below my studio widow. The females seem to do the herding and chattering, just what we expect! Does their language assign to each sex certain indelible rules? I wonder if the sea is masculine or feminine to them.

Who first said "Mother Earth"? Who called the shadowy shape within the vinegar jar "mother"? I grew up reading about Mother Nature and the "merry little west winds" of Thornton Burgess. They were the people I visited as I ran through the woods. They are the people I watch and wonder about from my studio balcony.

At this moment a huge boat with the crusty tin-can name of *Carmac* is gliding past below my cliff-hung Loft. They say a famous actor is aboard. I wonder if he has noticed that the spruce along the dark shore are taller than his floating superstructure. The trees cast shadows across the white hull like artists' fingers. How many men to build such a behemoth? Is it another woman that he has possessed? The bridge of a great yacht sees the inside of the osprey nest, the tops of trees and the outline of islands. It possesses nature like the wood-cutter's saw without savoring the beautiful detail. It is the His world of the ancient whaler, the arrogance of size. It is the big She that is chosen for her girth. Ships and the ocean are variables beyond our comprehension where feminine means small and dainty.

Our verbal patterns are all a mixture as raveled as Spanish moss. If the beautiful in our world bears a feminine nomenclature it is time we share it with men and assume some of the poetic revelations.

~ 3 ~

A New Way of Thinking

Each artist develops his or her style from the environment. Usually it is the place of birth and childhood that burns brightest in the expression of a creative need, sometimes the development comes from circumstances of life. I know of no famous artist who has failed to work with the material about her. There are few "novelists" of fine art, creating fanciful castles and a world of phantasmagoria that has no bearing on their own lives. William Blake perhaps comes closest. When I see his figures and the quality of their chiffon-draped world I know it is from his imagination, and yet I sense that the people were real although the story they tell is not.

What of Dali with his melting watches and wreath-like exaggerations? They are full of the scenery of Port Lligat, his tiny harbor on the coast above Barcelona. The woman he portrays over and over again is Gala, his wife.

To know the artists we must understand their influences, the touches of home, the curve of a cove, the face of a friend. Rembrandt, the greatest of all artists, painted best his reality. All his life he drew scenes of the Bible, adding the fantasy of palaces and halls of splendor of northern Italy, but the flat country, the well of Jesus and the Woman of Samaria are Dutch. His Saskia and the *burgemeesters* are family and friends.

To have had two cultures to bring together, Bolivia and New England; a gift that is offered to very few. I am certainly the only tapestry maker who has lived in Maine and La Paz and chosen to work in wools and with embroidery and appliqué to make my art from. Already this difference, this clear-cut advantage means that the technique I choose and the art I design will be original and different.

When I invented the word *bayetage* in Bolivia to describe my work I did not know that the word *bayeta* also belongs in the vocabulary of the southwest American Indian. *Bayeta* in the Andean countries means handwoven lambs wool. It is a colonial Spanish word long since forgotten outside the altiplano except for our own North American Indians who lived where the Spanish made the first settlements in New Mexico and Arizona. They took the linsey-woolsey linings of red from the coats of the Spanish soldiers and unraveled the wool to spin it again into their own rugs. That is why the natural shades of their rugs were sparked by red in early designs. It gives me a sense of pleasure and unity to learn that the Indians all along the western spine of our hemisphere share a heritage. Their art like mine is a coming together of two cultures.

After the early tapestries of pre-Columbian design has come my return to my native soil. A strong recollection of the mountain years derives from the materials I continue to use. Much of my yardage still comes from weavers who work for me in Bolivia. To that I have added wools from Ireland and Southern Africa and New Zealand, silks from Madagascar and organdy from Switzerland. The travels that have been such an important part of my life in time as well as in cultural fulfillment have also made it easy for me to meet and share with weavers around the globe the pleasure of our interest in fiber and art. My workshop is the center of a large map—the pin with the bright point from which I can reach out by letter or cable or telephone to corners of the earth to choose materials for my tapestries. Part of every day must be dedicated to planning ahead a year or more in advance what I may need for yardage. I am demanding of originality of texture, of freedom of weave, and I pay the prices I must for the fine floating lengths that are on my worktables.

"Textures of Our Earth" has been a song with many voices and a theme of discovery. I have created more than sixty tapestries to the exaltation of nature and in particular to the world of Maine where I was born and which I care for deeply. Many of the tapestries were literal; *Winter Weaver Quahog* and *Spruce Fall* are examples. There has been a steady change and evolvement in my understanding of nature from the earliest work through *Salt Veil,* catching just a breath of the seas' motion and through *Epiphyte,* a monumental perpendicular statement on brown alpaca with organdy and white wool.

While my traveling museum show of 1977 and 1978 was still on view I had already evolved beyond anything displayed to a greater distillation of the natural world. "Textures of Our Earth" has carried me far beyond my former work; in freedom of my medium in subtlety of color and also in monumentality. If pre-Columbian art was a fascination, acquired as an adult by intellectual insight into the beauty of the early artifacts, I was also confined by their lineal limits and the strong declaration of design. With my newer work, delving into nature, there are fewer restraints. The simple objects in nature such as tree trunks and a seedling pine, the shapes of shells are now a part of my inner eye. I see them and yet I move on to interpret nature more from a sense of rhythm, a power of the wind and fog and from a strength I feel in the seasons and the elements of our planet. I choose consciously to see as acutely as I can all that stretches about me and to select and bring together independently what seems significant to me.

More and more I am laying my wools across the long tables with the same freedom of clear line that I would use for an etching or a pencil drawing. The uninterrupted patterns flowing along give motion and a sense of atmosphere. They seem to declare what the eye never sees but the mind understands.

Each day I enlarge upon the scope of my *bayetage* medium. There is a wide area between painting and sculpture that neither of these traditional mediums can fully express. *Rock Lichen* is texture, a contrast of hard rock and a crisp flowering of plant life. In *bayetage,* texture is also realized. Sculpture may achieve texture, although inadequately, but color is forfeited. Only in my wool technique can color and texture meet, enlarging a minuscule fragment of nature into a tapestry that may have heroic proportions and give a true sense of the celebration of nature.

That same expansion finds its way into my organdy tapestries. Nearly all my designs are larger than life. A murex hanging of organdy is seven feet high. Embroidered in wool on organdy, it hangs suspended to catch the light. Other organdy hangings embroidered on both sides of dandelions, nautilus, marsh grass all magnify the exquisite structure of their natural forms. Where windows look out on a barren city scene, I hang my transparent art to form a world of light and delicacy.

Washington, Spring 1978

From my tree series several important new techniques have surfaced. The uninterrupted overlay of yarn is the most important. I lay my wool generously with a definite mental image above and below the layers of wool appliqué. I achieve motion and texture and also a subtle but intentional perspective. With thin yarn I sew it under a fiber or two in a running stitch. Occasionally I use couching but this makes a somewhat jerkier line.

A curious trick of the eye conveys a different image when a design lies flat with the viewer looking down. The same design stretched against a wall shows nuance and contrast. It is important to hang each design as I progress to check the vertical image.

I have learned to give weight to the bottom of the canvas, as in painting, by color, mass, texture. Again, motion on a flat surface is largely lost, and if I can create it in a horizontal frame I know there will be impact and strength when it is hoisted up on rods against the wall. Or in the case of organdy hangings, left to swing free in space.

The organdy hangings edged in wool frames are a special area of creativity quite different from my wool-on-wool tapestries. They are embroidered so that they may be viewed from either side. In the deep bay window of our Georgetown house I have a perfect spot. Suspended on a slender bamboo rod that runs from one window lintel to the opposite side, I have double-faced organdy hangings—changing the designs from time to time and studying their quality.

It is essential for an artist to hang her work so that she may evaluate change and progression. Often unsuspected elements emerge. The early morning impact of a work is very revealing. I even consciously leave a room and detain myself at some small chore in order to return and view a new work with a fresh glance.

Painters use mirrors to catch flaws in design and color, and of course the same is true with tapestries. What may appear as perfect symmetry to the direct eye suddenly becomes lopsided when seen in reverse. And not just symmetry but whole areas of a hanging or painting may focus anew though a mirror image, showing fine precision, a marvelous casual effect, or reversely, a totally unworkable neglect. A mirror is a second pair of eyes.

With my *bayetage* art form I have found a new way to express nature. Eliot Porter has brought the nests of birds and the cadmium patchwork of the Grand Canyon alive with his camera. Mark Tobey, with his million milkweed brush strokes, delicate and incisive, creates a fresh painted image in such rare poetic passages as *Edge of August*. And now with wool and needlecraft I hope to approach these giants. They are as important for their imagination as for their skill. They reach large masses of viewers without condescension or accommodation. I hope to accomplish a sense of wonder in my tapestries. That is my intent.

Washington, Spring 1977

Our attic is being restored from a windstorm. It lifted off a quarter of the mansard roof, pouring rainwater down the tall stairwell, sluicing across the face of an ancient Peruvian painting. By a miracle not a raindrop touched my tapestries.

This small cataclysm has been my good fortune. In redoing the ceiling and walls we have thrown the two large rooms together to make a studio eighteen by thirty feet. Sunlight moves from early salmon pink across the city sky to black clouds, absorbing the silt of the city, shooting like lasers through the patterns of the falling sun.

As I stand before my large tables, my creative altarpiece, I find I move my hands and arms, and do a ritual reliving of the sweep and motion of the sea. It curls over and out of my circled arms, spills and lifts in foamy lightness, breaks above the fragile coils, stretches and pushes out. I am coming to know the guild of the sea as I might the artful patterns of a bird's flight. I intend to catch and structure in wool the strength and pattern. As in so much in life, we look but do not understand or know what lies around us.

My lineal technique, the motion of flowing wool yarn across many unexpected textures, is my great discovery. Especially in nature I feel the complex lines have so much to say. Strong rhythms of nature are all about me. Not just the rhythm of fertility and growth but a great sweeping and lifting surge of forest and sea.

I have watched my small grandson lying in his carriage with his cloud view. I have lain beside him to share his skyward vista and to see the white pine curving down, the lifting up, the blue spruce with arms stretched back, palms upward.

In my studio I lift my arms, twist and hold them to bring my flesh close to the posture of the beauty of each branch. From there the yarn flows through my fingers and onto the wool yardage to make the tracery I see and feel. It is a continuous circumstance, innate and undramatized. As in painting there seems to be a brain message—to my arms and out along the rough woolen tapestry. My touch, light and unmeditated, blinds what I have seen and distilled to the canvas in a continuous rhythm. Rhythm, rhythm, rhythm. If my tapestry does not have this flow it is not truly mine.

Washington, Spring 1978

Epiphtye is such a large hanging that it covers my three tables and drops to the floor. It is fourteen and one-half feet long by seven and one-half feet high in brown and white alpaca. At first it was not satisfying in either color or texture, and after much thought I decided to overlay the alpaca with organdy, cutting long slits and gashes down through the organdy to reveal the rich wool giving the perpendicular momentum of the epiphytic plant pulled down by the earth's magnetism. One third of the canvas will be exposed, and long thrusting columns of white combed alpaca will punctuate it.

One of the most difficult aspects of a large work is the time it takes to complete it, and therefore to see the evolution from original composition to finished work. I have made a careful pattern, life size, of what I originally conceived to be the design. Hung along the entire studio wall, suspended over the wool, it is too intricate, and I begin to simplify, seeking the essence of the heavy trunks and cross-hatched branches. Before, I have used horizontal linear patterns, now they are perpendicular. The intricacy of the layers of design give great depth.

Epiphyte

The seed
of a bird
on a lonely bough
high above the earth
bursts and drops
fresh roots, air spun,
twisting down, down
until an armature
of wood begun so
subtly spreads

to overcome
a gentler host.

Adventitious branch
constructing sculpture
from epiphytic heritage
explodes rock and soil
covering forest, simply
by existing without toil.
Its secret strength, ability
on air to thrive, while
a trusting host needs
nourishment to stay alive.

MORAL: Sometimes just breathing is enough.

Mouse Island, Fall 1978

I lay my cheek along the curvature of granite ornamented with a bracelet of quartz. It is encrusted with mica. My own presence, so ephemeral beside this stoneness, is somehow enhanced. I feel fulfilled in the knowledge that long after I am gone these same rocks will uncurl their rolling patterns to the sea. My flesh to their flesh is a unity I crave. Their magnificence penetrates to the fragile column of my spine. Where I will someday splinter before the sea, rocks are supreme. Even they may change their configurations in a storm as brutal as last winter's.

Interaction of stones and water are my new source. Why does the sea wash each stone on every surface equally? Every object about me suggests forms and thoughts that merge to create patterns in my mind. Stretched on sand I watch water triangulate with the tide, covering ovate shapes. The counterpoint of two elements, one so strong against a fluid force of equal predictability. Here in this contrast of shape and similarity of purpose lies a whole series of tapestries and poems.

Washington, Winter 1979

Everyone is talking about the new East Wing of the National Gallery and the Edvard Munch exhibit. The flame of his talent burns strong on the January sky of Washington. Superficially, the exhibit is an extravagant sociological legend. Munch, neat in bow tie and Edwardian jacket, as seen through his art, is a fire burning out of control. Color and luxuriant paint portray the agony of childbirth, the terror of young death. Like Virginia Woolf, the presence of death in his family before he was twenty scarred him and drove him to an outpouring of visceral aching.

Guides walk us through the galleries talking of his prints, of his life, of his use of imagery. It is all so academic. I rush ahead out of the verbiage to shiver and stare into the heart of this sensitive, beautiful man, painting his agony beneath the studied control of his tall image. Opulence is rare in the Nordic landscape—I understand better now after my trip to Sweden, and see the craving and the torment that is Munch.

Washington, Winter 1979

With the New Year Amy Gray has come again from Wheaton College to work in my studio.

Pink-cheeked with her blond hair cut straight, she flowers like a camellia, smiling and eager, learning the art of tapestry making as she works with me at the tables in my attic. I am composing a tapestry for the Morris Rosenbergs for Palm Beach. They came to my show at the Textile Museum and asked me to do a work for them. I asked them to tell me what they liked best from "Textures of Our Earth." They chose first *Epiphyte*, the abstract alpaca trunks on organdy and brown wool, and secondly *Surge II* on white mohair. Both are new works not shown before in any other museum. For me this is ideal as a commission as it represents a natural progression of my work. I have done two sketches, one of a rock ledge in organdy with a touch of blue velvet and slices of organdy slanting down across the brown wool. The other is a wave pillar, twisting in the wind before the crash. They have chosen the first, *Rock Shelf.*

Washington, Winter 1979

For three months I have sewn and surveyed, folded and sliced though the organdy to create *Rock Shelf.* The Rosenbergs have never seen it or suggested how I proceed. In the end, after the hard and soft edges have been juxtaposed, I have added two columns of alpaca with a dark streak of brown bending like trees rooted into the pale scarce earth of the ledge. Every stitch is done with care and precision. It is bound and finished like a fine French garment. I feel it is a refined and elegant work. Helen Rosenberg chose the design over the wave motif and it is much more cerebral. I knew before I presented the sketches which one she would pick. I am happy with it. I feel as I used to with portraits that a commission is my work and my interpretation but also, because I am intuitive, it must include the person who asks to share my art. By the very act of choosing a Hemenway tapestry it is an act of love of nature, texture and line that declares the interwoven quality of our two lives. So the creative development in my studio of an idea includes my patron.

Morris and Helen came tonight to see "their" tapestry. We sat on the orange velvet couches making polite conversation as nervous as a parent waiting for word from the delivery room. Finally Helen said to me, "Aren't you nervous?" I laughed, "Yes, of course, why don't I go get the tapestry?" And I did.

I felt calm because I had made it as beautiful as I know how, without compromise of a single stitch. Helen hugged me and we both burst into tears. Occasionally that happened to me when I did a portrait. A humbling experience because the guide to my hand, the knowledge that the flow of creativity remains a mystery.

Washington, Fall 1979

As I start the preparatory drawing for the *Flow of Inner Seeing* I am filled with optimism and trust. My eyes and imagination are acutely active as I face into the unknown. For five months, while I have been working on *Tipi–Waterfall*, I have been thinking of the Kidder tapestry. Now nothing interrupts my passage into new ideas.

This new tapestry must have line and texture and create a sense of ambiance in the narrow hall where it will hang. I want the visitor to be propelled through the long corridor with the slightly curving walls. Its six-foot width and twenty-six-foot length and low ceilings give it the dimensions of a grape arbor. For this obvious tunnel I wish to give a sense of space transcending architectural limitations.

I want motion and strength to give flesh and blood to my tapestries. They are not to be artful decorations but pulsing and warm. This separates me from the embroiderers I know. I do not want just design but exaltations, bell ringing of the beauty around me.

In tapestry I see atmosphere totally different than I did as a painter although there is a similar evolutionary process. Where painting was figures and landscapes, my emphasis now is to distill what I see. To capture that essence means constant drawing, observing, even the sensual feel of my fingertips along the ridges of rock and the wet sand of the beach. There is a surge of creative understanding when hand and eye join in a unity.

The development of my tapestry technique came as the result of deprivation of basic conventional art materials. In *Flow*, limitations of space require new solutions and imagination to give power and grace to the long, narrow hallway.

I have thought of including the ceiling to give the sensation of a cave tapestry like cave paintings or an arbor that guests are spirited through by surprise. I think of taking the traditional fall of textile and folding it vertically for sculptural relief, crisscrossed with a meandering rhythmic wool line. I have not yet received the inspiration that is right. Fragments that exist in my imagination will all be part of the final work, but the main concept is not yet clear.

Dottie Kidder, with her keen perception, sees that the texture and depth within the medium of tapestry far exceed that possibility in paint which offers only room for surface design. Tapestry offers the glow of painting and the dimension of sculpture. It is visual and tactile and perfect for a long wall in the same way that tapestries gave warmth and life to medieval castles. The making will be laborious and will require hours and hours of patient work. *Flow* must be a mood.

Mouse Island, Summer 1979

A quarter of my apple of summer art has been eaten. I am just beginning to savor the flavor of it, to reaffirm the patterns of rocks, and turn eagerly to my series *Aqua Lapis*.

Aqua Lapis I is gray and white *bayeta* with an uneven hem and a white organdy band. It will be entirely rock veins, possibly with a cluster of orange lichen at the seam where the two *bayetas* meet.

Aqua Lapis II is white alpaca brushed to fine duck down and again laid on white *bayeta*. Nearly all the yardage for *Aqua Lapis II* is handspun in grays and white of mohair, karakul and alpaca.

Aqua Lapis III begins to burst the bonds of controlled design, dropping with organdy icicle, the gray woolen rock forms, lichen encrusted. Organdy and wool, first used years ago in *Ancient Images* for the layered fins of fish in the Woodmere Art Gallery, Germantown, Pennsylvania, has lain dormant for ten years but has now returned in the form of sea foam for *Salt Veil*. Organdy dominated *Rock Shelf* and I see the two surfaces, one tweedy, irregular, strong; the other pristine, elegant, reserved in natural juxtaposition; literally as sweep of fog against spruce with angularity and strength—as ribbons of quartz within granite—as layers of light against the sky. Unfolding yardage so finely spun, so clean, sets my imagination jumping like water on a hot hearth. The need for beautiful materials is essential.

This summer is a fresh beginning. Ideas spin from me like ribbons on a Maypole, turning in and out, catching some of the past, leaping into the wind, scarcely captured again. Weaving, weaving, the patterns of creativity. Excitement lies ahead.

The new series of tapestries for a museum tour in 1984 has formulated in a general way in my imagination. I will call it *Aqua Lapis*, saying in Latin exactly what I am working with, water and stone. At one time I thought of calling it *Elements* but that has neither the poetry nor the sensitive quality that I hope this group of tapestries will have.

I hope to discover new details of specific rock formations and the life of the sea. These two elements have limitless possibilities. By defining an area for myself and directing my attention totally to it, I simplify the creative process because I screen out much that is obvious and allow myself to deal with specifics.

New yarns spun by a friend have added vitality and a life of their own to the linear detail of these new *Lapis* tapestries.

When I came to my studio this morning a small wave, probably from one of the early lobster boats, was just hitting against the shore. As it hit and doubled back almost like a collar on a lace blouse it formed the most beautiful fringe. I pushed open the screen and stood there captured by the three or four undulating waves that followed. Each time a new lace collar of different design, all of them of equal delicacy, drifted out to sea.

My first desire in the *Aqua Lapis* series is to develop new shapes away from the rectangle. I shall continue to mix materials, wool and organdy or wool and silk. I want to combine both strong and fragile materials. Almost every inch of this handwoven wool is handspun, something that is so rare and so hard to find in a modern world and extraordinarily expensive.

This early June morning I am working on a *Lapis* tapestry that is two pieces of Bolivian wool. One is dark, a smoky gray that looks almost as if it contained bits of mica. It has the look of the woven, spun, pulled mixture that the glaciers have given to granite stretched along the shores.

The other is a much paler piece. It has bands of jet black as if the weaver had one sheep in his flock much darker than the others. The traditional wool, which is always the most expensive, is white. Here the black is woven coquettishly, a few dark warps at a time with a random feeling that makes the yardage unusual. It is the same kind of ingenuousness found in a child's drawing. The Bolivian weaver, no doubt thinking more in economic terms than any other, felt that he should not waste the wool and the results are sparkling.

I have tried to find weavers in the States to weave the same way. Even if I take them a sample and say, "Copy this exactly," showing them the different bands of color and different shades of gray, they are unable to achieve it.

Washington, Winter 1979

Flow of Inner Seeing, twenty-two and a half feet of tapestry eight feet tall is unrolling on the large tables in my studio. After four months of collecting textures from my Maine world I am ready to lay the sculptured wool and weave the abstract design. Each section is carefully catalogued. Because of the size I must know in advance exactly where I am going and which texture I need to integrate into each part. Because there is no wall long enough to hold it, I try to imagine the vertical impact. Appliquéd sections will be analogous to the gray background so as not to protrude and command. I plan to use slivers of wool joined by sinuous handspun wool and overlaid with embroidery. The small thin layers of wool melt into long patches of silver gray stitches.

Washington, Winter 1979

The Blue Ridge Mountains flaunt their name and place in a magnificent sea of cobalt peaks. They flow and ripple west from the Virginia plains, a great ocean with undulant generosity. Standing at the top of the first ridge I, too, want to move west. They seem like a great soft carpet that will cosset my feet. It is still to the eye almost a wilderness with only a fleck of white farmhouses and not even a column of smoke visible.

During the night a seven minute frosting of snow has stretched to cover every horizontal surface. I saw Aldebaran as I closed my door, paling before the moon's splendor, and now the sun is piercing the wound of my curtains to wake me.

Dark hours are for rest and the womb of dreams. I should prefer never to miss a sunrise as long as my eyes have sight. Each day has its own perfections, whether rowing to Mouse Island or sitting chin in hands along an icy window ledge. I celebrate it. Nature continues to give me peace and strength. Life in cities holds less and less meaning. I feel in the transfer a return to the elements of life and the eventuality of my own ashes. The city fails to offer the reconciliation I find in the mountains.

For two days we have walked slowly to the rhythm of our heartbeat along the slopes that slide east and west from the Skyline Drive. My exhaustion vanishes with each new valley. The trees lie about like discarded toys felled in October and still not cleared and we move up and down weaving through branches, almost losing the trial.

At the river of our first hike, icicles and water slip and freeze in iridescent stalactites above moss as green as beryl. I have not brought a camera because I want to behold only with my eyes allowing the impact of the green, frosted with icicle, to be a distillation. For me this is what we continue to call "abstract art" or "minimal art," or even perhaps "the new realism." I follow no blazed trail in my tapestries, only the inner voice choosing the path.

For six months I have been at work on the *Flow of Inner Seeing* tapestry. The original sample of wool was woven last spring. There are delays and reverses in delivered fabrics and even in the finished lengths. After Mother's funeral I flew to Portland for a long, bitter day of redesigning the new grays, the light gray warp with bits of dark mohair and linen in brown. Slowly it has come together, but I need to escape from its demands. I look up unto the hills whence cometh my strength.

Washington, Spring 1980

The *Flow of Inner Seeing* is done! It is part of *Aqua Lapis.* It is up and it is successful! Dottie Kidder is thrilled. The narrow hall of her entry cuts the drama of it, but it is strong and fragile at the same time, full of texture and motion, compelling the viewer from the entrance in irrepressible urgency. Although I know it would be better with a longer view, it still captures the eye at close range. Such a challenge I have never faced. It is by far the largest commission to date and we had thought at one time of doing both walls of the hall. Now I feel that one is sufficient. I cannot imagine the same intensity on both sides, but I plan to continue the design, to complete the total tapestry, to say what I want it to say, shout what I want to shout.

Mouse Island, Summer 1980

Today is for sculpture. A black on black tapestry, twelve yards of folding, descending, handspun wool more than eight feet high have been on my work table waiting for me. I am calling the sheer angular cascade *Basalt.* I think of hard stone with veins of color. Against a white wall I expect it to be dramatic, demanding attention. I have already lined and folded the fabric. I have hand sewn the rough surface. I have cleared the studio for this new work.

Sculptured forms lurk closer and closer to the surface. In the Fogg Museum at Harvard last spring I found two abstract Japanese prints that flashed me a clear signal. I looked at their pristine line, the spare black and white calligraphy of brush and thought, "Oriental forms—simple curve and mass in ORGANDY and WOOD!"

First I choose a long roll of paper and unroll it until I sense its proper length. The first sculpture will be seven feet, seven inches long. Size is the first decision even before the flow of poems that surround my drawings. In my new Loft I can fling my sense of size up to rafters that float sixteen feet above the floor and a hundred or more above the sea. I am already measuring my ideas against the grandeur, spreading my creativity like wings. My ultimate challenge from now to 1984 will be proven or defeated in my Loft. If each work survives on stark walls between the scarves of sky and sea I shall succeed. Dimension comes first. Each idea speaks for its own size. I know the shape before I start, sometimes from drawings or photographs, but just as often from an inner compulsion, knowledge as clear and defined as though the sculpture already stands before me.

Other materials affect me dramatically; why polished wood and organdy cross my brain I do not know. The juxtaposition of ideas is outrageous. But the confluence has lingered and today, a rainy, quiet day when no one will seek me is a magic moment to consider new textures. The calm is deep, reaching to the farthest fathom. One black-backed gull wails overhead like a hungry child. Rain smothers the harbor, punching holes in the sea like spikes driven into tin.

Boothbay Harbor, Fall 1980

My antenna lifts unseen to capture something memorable each day. Today I remembered that a friend from Bolivia, a lady who has devoted her years in the mountains to handicapped children, also has a rare sense for bargains. I learned long ago that she had stuffed and punched into boxes a treasure of alpaca shawls which she hopes to sell at a profit, probably to be used to mend the bones of some third world orphan. Once or twice a year my need for yarns and fabric brings me back to this cache. Today I have telephoned New Mexico to barter again for the thistle-combed shawls. I offer the most I can possibly afford—a lump sum of $1,700 for all that she has. The gentle voice with the steel computer undertone seems to waver. Finally I seal a bargain and know that from the stripes and blotches and gentle flow of gray and browns I will fashion many of my *Aqua Lapis*. The eye caresses these shawls as it sees a peach bloom baby or an Angora kitten. Combining them with other handcrafted fabrics and handspun yarns they will turn strong and compelling. They are a palette of seventy grays and browns and blacks, no two identical. Their originality and strength have come from the ubiquitous alpaca trotting the altiplano, with incongruous coats above delicate legs like dowagers dressed in sable.

When the ponchos come I shall see them mostly as rocks and floating spaces. Their rectilinear form can be folded and shaped in limitless ways. The idea of black and white, the most arresting combination in art, as Franz Kline has proven, is a combination I want to explore. My new tapestries are to be freer, more sculpted than embroidered, more mass than line.

I choose certain materials like these shawls with specific ideas and creative design in mind and often find that in the end they engulf me. What I eventually create is often a total surprise. Some will be simpler, great gashes of white in the black stripes like strong brush strokes.

The tapestries of this summer move inexorably into the realm of wall sculptures. Much of the sewing now needs to be on the wrong side. Every fold, flowing like the salt-honed rock, requires long hours of hand sewing so that the fiber will curl and undulate without apparent restriction. I have learned these techniques fashioning clothes, turning my own hems and pleats and flounces. Now I see the years of training as a new language for my art.

Washington, Winter 1980

From Winterhouse, the twisted path drops in layers of oak leaves and Christmas fern over the rim of rock to the Potomac. Below, reckless and willful, the river gushes and pummels. The spring rains burst the deep veins to fold back and climb the rills again. With fingers of ice and ruffs of frozen lace the rocks hold and rebuff the stream. Patterns of water bend back, collide and flow into each other like clouds on a windy day. There is so much going forth that the sheer power of downward water casts itself back against the stream and hesitates before it sweeps on. Beautiful to behold the ascent and the backward glance or a great river! This is Robert Frost's "West Running Brook" country:

> Black stream flung backward
> On itself, in one white wave
> And the white water rode
> The black stream forever.

Climbing, leaning into the hill again, I pull to my studio among the tulip trees, carrying the motion and intensity of the Potomac with me.

I have made no sketches or photographs, only the imprint of careful watching to guide and suggest the ascent of a descending river. Sitting on a polished rock in the sunshine I close my eyes and begin to savor the feel and dance of the Potomac so different from the sea.

Instinctively I begin to understand river motion. I want to know its patterns and make myself part of its forward pull and churning power. I see in my imagination a correlation to my own life of travel and the press of motion always upon me. The curling, the smiling, the reluctance to leave each haven, each a view of the bend of a long river, but also the compulsion to rush on.

What does this mean in creating a river tapestry? Will it be torment or pleasure?

It will, in the end, be life. The ascent I see is the tentative holding pattern of frail wool and embroidery saying "Here is momentary beauty. Here I have looked back with longing but also with need to create a sensitive moment before I move on."

As the folds of Bolivian *bayeta* and African yarns ripple across the wide, white tables in my studio, I must design the essence of the Potomac, the return upon itself of the passions and the grace notes of living and the memories of many years.

Ascent is not only a return but a building of stairs of pure water in wool. Clouds and celestial figures crowd the painting of Murillo and El Greco. Theirs are pictorial ascensions, each a vivid scene peopled with biblical figures. I have chosen elements of our earth to create the same feeling of lifting, of rising up above water and stone. In the simplicity of the folds, building one upon the other; I strive for the same levitation.

Mouse Island, Spring 1981

Before I left Mouse Island last fall I designed a large tapestry inspired by a stretch of shelving rock above the high-tide line west of the sheltered beach. It had veins of iron that had bled through the quartz and a gray ribbon of granite. I brought samples of yarns in garnet and rust to hold them against the rock. This is something I have never done before but the color seemed so perfect I felt it was a key to the whole design.

At the beginning, in Bolivia and Mexico, I used color lavishly, but then I grew shy of my own bravado and found the subtle harmony of beiges and natural tones more to my liking. They seem to enhance a design rather than dominate it. Color is dominant, willful and I continue to use it sparingly because texture and flow are already two strong elements of tapestry art.

All winter I thought of my rose and gray tapestry but always I yearned to return to the ledge along the beach and study it more. I put it aside waiting for May and Mouse Island.

Today is a morning heavy with sunshine and the lightest of sea breezes. I row to Mouse full of eager expectation.

Tramp and Misty, the island watchdogs, come running down the ramp to meet me. There isn't a bark. The tails wag on the tiny Pomeranian and chunky mongrel as though I had come ashore only yesterday. This is the best of welcomes, animals are so artless. I greet my friends, the family who lives here through the January ice and the April thaws. We hug each other and then I slip away hurrying to the beach and the rose rocks with gray borders. I am a little afraid. Afraid that over the winter I have lost the sense of beauty that this spot inspired. I am writing now as I sit close to the shelving tapestry of granite rock.

I am glad I have waited because the ribbon formation of rock is stronger than I remembered. Nature is always more daring. Beside the protective coloration of mating birds and the shadowy light of the forest there is also the gold of the moon on a dark island and the cardinal bird in the snow.

My rose rocks are part of this drama. They are color but also texture and line. I need this second meeting. Now my tapestry design will melt in my inner eye to form a vigorous strong design. The color and flow come. I see the rust rind of granite, the moist layer below the shadow and pumice smoothness. I will watch these rocks hour after hour without photography or drawing. The tapestry must come from within, simmering gently until it spills over out of my head and hands onto the long work tables.

Progress is a whimsical word. I proceed where an inner sense drives me.

Critical judgment is another solitary journey. Who is there to tell me if there is improvement? There is no one to measure by in a field so untested, a medium so much my own. I say fervently, gripping my bare feet to the pebbled earth of Maine, when someone praises me, "I hope to do better," without knowing what "better" is except in a nebulous way. Inevitably I evolve just by sheer effort and persistent creativity, the long days of work and the weighing and balancing of shapes and textures against the rock shores and the ruffle of sea.

Winterhouse, Fall 1981

Aqua Lapis is not just a title. It is a whole new way of thinking about source material, about the handling of wool yardage and the accomplishment of new techniques. By process of elimination, I have narrowed my inspiration to two sources, water and stone. I can now study more carefully the various facets and reflect on the textures and the quality of these two elements.

Two specific manners of dealing with these two subjects emerge. Particularly for stone I favor a molding of wools, creating deep fissures in the wool by rounded surfaces one against the other, in a random design that has a strong sense of rhythm. *Rock Bloom, Roserock, Strata II* are good examples. I have molded the wool like clay into an undulating pattern. Then with utmost caution, I reverse my design to line the back with layers of natural wool yardage. This is a complicated and tedious process because the sense of flow must not be lost. Sewing by hand in various stitches that hold but do not pull, I catch the surface and lining together. I proceed to add a sense of depth to the tapestry. Finished, the lining makes the outer layer seem more luxuriant, the gentle roll as it hangs on the wall is a miraculous suspension, a defiance of gravity without tension.

My earliest tapestries dealing with sculptural folds were *Mangrove* and *Salt Veil*. For the first of my *Aqua Lapis* series I joined two lengths of alpaca and, working freely, created a rush of fabric in gray and black that could be a cloud or a wave or a glacial rock formation.

The second general category that has evolved in my *Aqua Lapis* is another kind of folding. This is not the undulating subtle curve, but instead a direct acceptance of yardage at its given width and color. Good examples are *Basalt, Ascent,* and *Wave Length II.*

Fabric is my strength in design and also my limitation. In *Basalt* I have folded it back and forth horizontally, creating a strong design and making a clean statement about the yardage I am using. On this black angular tapestry I have embroidered other black yarns with just a grace note of steel blue. The variety of color within black is itself a revelation. The surface design conforms to the warp and weft of my yardage. The embellishment gives a sense of the rich embroidery of nature so clearly a part of rock and sea.

In *Ascent* I choose a gentle curve as guide to the folded tapestry. Using a narrow *bayeta,* the handspun, handwoven wool of the Andes, I folded and lined the entire work. With intricate embroidery in mohair alpaca, karakul and lambs wool it becomes in my imagination the spring eddies and flourishes of the Potomac River, close to my studio. I see, as I embroider deep into the cascading folds, the inverted eddies and the confluence of water as it rushes over the floor of the river.

Some of my new tapestries combine the molded fabric with folded techniques as in *Strata I.* Wide folds begin and end the angular U-shaped composition, but at the curve joining these parts, a twisted and molded area holds the two flat extensions together.

Tapestry making is a miracle of art because it has limitless dimensions. Now after many years as a painter, always handling color at the end of a long brush or a palette knife, working against a flat surface, I know I can never return to these restrictions. There is a sense of communion with my medium in fiber, a chance to touch and mold and create a sweeping movement that is much more my own personality. It says what I want to say. The variety is endless because it holds three dimensions, is open to color and nuance, to shape and mood. It deals also with subject matter that is not valid in paint or in sculpture. How could an artist have a painting show simply about the details of a rock, or a fleeting feel for part of a wave? In non-representational art this is possible, but the artist is limited to expressing it through color alone.

Contemporary artists are struggling to escape the bondage I left so many years ago. The hard metal and wood constructions of Stella, the shimmering layers and contortions of Tom Holland, even the subtle sophistication of Ellsworth Kelly are all in defiance of flat canvas and traditional rectilinear limitations. None of them can have the nuance that textiles achieve. Their surfaces are angular or flat. They have no way to hold the flowing roll of their canvas or their construction as I can in wool and silk.

I have had the good fortune to be a woman in art. Along with the limitations of shape and stretched canvas, men have little knowledge of the art of sewing except to bind our torn flesh or tailor a suit. Society has placed a taboo on their creativity in our western culture and only recently are men considering embroidery as anything but women's work. In Abomey in Africa, where the Amazons guarded the king's palace, the men were and still are the embroiderers. I have worked with eighteen husky energetic men, sitting on mats on the ground, embroidering with them, and I know the excitement they feel in their work. In our western culture I still have a whole art medium to myself.

From the beginning I have sought the adventure of a new art form that "fiber artists" have scarcely considered. Most women have wrapped great hanks of jute and made visceral sculptures, all of them imitative of each other and scarcely moving away from the loom. What excited me most is the absolute knowledge that there is much much more I have not yet discovered.

The changes in my style and understanding of my medium are dramatic. Each new period from the pictorial pre-Columbian to the undulating *Aqua Lapis* is only a span of fifteen years. What is vitally important is the strong thorough base of my artistic training. I haven't simply bought myself a loom or some needles and yarn and started to experiment. Twenty years as an artist, painting and drawing, lie before my adventure in textiles.

~ 4 ~

Textures Are My Medium

*H*unger and fulfillment are shared by those who choose creativity. The creative way, the compulsion to see all faces of the prism of the world, comes without asking. The tinder to the flame is a self need. Even with the two elements coming together, the inner drive and the knowledge, there must be a third element, call it space or solitude. That is what feeds the leaping flame.

Mouse Island and now the Loft are for me the third element. The row to Mouse each morning has been sudden unleashing of ecstasy. The path of my oars and the furrow of the cedar rowboat stretching behind make each day an emotional roller-coaster, the keen anticipation looping away from the mainland of my life and suddenly the calm of Mouse and the view beyond.

I have left that now for a wider working space with the same limitless view. I have given up the daily severing of one world from another that even a small island close to my cove has provided. I shall miss that. In its place I now have room for expansive tapestries. There is no limit to the size; the air is so much grander at the Loft, and I am ready for that. I wonder how I ever managed to unroll tapestries larger than the actual size of the small room I had on Mouse.

Every artist shares this experience of growth in some measure. It brings us close without words or patterns of society.

The creative mind, once nurtured and allowed to run unencumbered, is an amazing friend. It fills every corner of my being. There are still vast unrecognized areas and only physical strength restrains me. It means that while I am raising funds for a political campaign or listening to poetry on my tape recorder, I am observing the earth and the light for new tapestries.

As I work in my studio with an ever increasing number of waste-baskets placed close at hand, I still find it natural in my absorption to push wool ends and scraps onto the floor. I think of Julia Child cooking her television meals with both hands flying. The peas and pots fall where they may. Creativity must be an interrupted act. It must season, nourish, grow and be self-pruned. It is a full house, not a vacuum. For this reason a studio is essential, a place where a half-worked idea can crystallize and develop without repeated folding and dustings.

There is a correlation between tidiness and creativity. It has been explored at Harvard University in studies of preschool children. The well-washed, neat child whose blocks are piled in even rows at supper time is not the questing original. Nature is extraordinarily untidy. Its ocean curls and bites at the edge of land, leaving the earth crust like a half-consumed cookie. Trees, some of them self-pruning, lose their branches into the forest like collapsing chimneys. A swept forest floor will never surprise with a ruffle of trillium, May apple or lady slipper. The exposed seed is made sterile, and so with art.

By chance two fabrics may lie next to each other and suggest a harmony that a carefully manicured hand would not suspect. It is a major concern to me that my wools must reside in plastic cases because of moths instead of being lumped and stretched along the shelves for instant access. It exerts my imagination to remember each texture and shade and to pick from my recollection rather than from the impact of a woolly palette. I find more and more I empty everything out as I start a new design regardless of the effort.

One must create for oneself, without a thought of critics, or costs or intrinsic value. The marketplace will adjust if the work is worthy. Learning from nature first and always; learning our symbiotic heritage is what matters. Creating, absorbing into self that symbiosis between the natural phenomenon and our own expression makes superior art. Each canvas or tapestry is a learning, a new comprehension.

There is an important ingredient to me in creative activity. It is a unison with the beauty of life. None of my work is conceived in anguish or anger. None is inspired by tumult. My momentum is exuberance and the stimulation of the requisite detail of the world around me. It is an inner but also a serene belief.

I painted for years, a grade B portrait artist, an average oil painter, a literal interpreter of nature, a slightly above average water colorist.

When our three sons were young, I was up at five each morning and painted my daily watercolor with the first rays of light. It gave me nothingness and peace that my day was already full by seven in the morning. I could share all the remaining hours with no sense of loss for I had communicated with my inner creativity.

I first discovered my unshakable belief in my art soon after I began to work in wools with collage and needlecraft. Much of my initial satisfaction came from the knowledge that my tapestries inspired an electric reaction in their viewers. It came also from a deep unison with my new medium. The tactile elements, the total originality, were fresh and full of possibilities.

Textures are my medium. Neither paint nor clay can give such a living quality as do textures. Bark, rock, lichen, sea foam, all elude the painter's brush. My own creativity is simplicity itself for I see in an uncomplicated way. I often wonder if I look at the world as a bird does or a small squirrel, seeing the obvious shapes with a different eye.

With a magnifying glass I follow the rain ribbons gusting off the roof, rebounding on the pavement, slipping down the bamboo leaves, forming heavy crystal marbles before they splash. Have you ever sat and watched a rainstorm? It is more beautiful than the son et lumière at Chenonceau, a beaded curtain of light and silver. I may never attempt a tapestry from my rain vigil. The idea may crystallize or it may evade me, too presumptuous to attempt. But the seeing will enrich a corner of my mind in ways I cannot know.

A spider's web holds the same intricate message. "We see them and yet we don't," as someone said. "If there were but one, people would come from all over the world to see it." The seven weights of silk thread extruded from the spider's abdomen to make an orb web is a miracle. No man-made machine can weave so fine.

Creativity

Flat along the rock,
flat as a skipping stone,
my veins, veins
of the shelving earth,
nerve ends of salt.
My skin, the skin
of the rock. My bone
quartz and granite.

Past the cold stone,
past the wet cheek,
my eye watching
the tide, knowing
the water curve;
piercing the sea
waiting the prey
and the clean deep dive.

Seabrook Island, South Carolina, Spring 1976

This is my first southern journey to Carolina shores since the Marine Corps days, when I came to New Bern and Camp Lejeune as a bride. Then I ran the Navy Relief Society in return for a tiny cottage, sat on beach chairs, ate on orange crates and went only once to the beach at Morehead City. It is all changed now.

The wide swamps, the low pine and the beaches are all tamed. Condominiums, neat, electrified living; sports cars on wider and wider macadam have changed the wild careless shore.

The Caspian tern, willet and skimmer are more furtive. Quiet and wilderness are now wantonly cut and combed for pleasure seekers, the dollar boys who know nothing of nature. Only a great tidal wave or the gift of a hurricane can save it. What a prayer to offer up to God!

On Seabrook in the early spring the builders have just begun to parcel and place their wares and the long wide beach lies like a fragile oriental scroll. There is a crust of shell life and the vibrating edge of countless sandpiper, sanderling and plover harvesting treasure. I learn now that the sea foam is bunched bubbles, that they pull back, sometimes in strong angular patterns, sometimes softened and finally the edges round completely as the lace froth recedes and vanishes. I know that the wind blowing off the curving waves forms a thin spray that is as fine as silk. I discover that on shallow beaches the sheet of tidal water covers quickly. It caught me with my camera on its outer rim and only by holding my lens far above my head was I able to ford the inner channel to the high beach just in time.

Lying on a dune alone I feel the hot sand and the sun warm me. I want to remember it all. In my own creative shorthand I write sentences, note birds, do doodles of sea foam, but most of all I look. I see the sea edge in twisted loose folds of alpaca and organdy, the delicate sea pattern never quite the same. I will create a tapestry about fragility.

It is only much later as I near completion of this memory that a poem about my life surfaces to form a unison with the edge of the sea.

Salt Veil

Tide has lifted
fresh spun thread
above the sand
shelf. I tread on
lace, clustered
and stretched
changing itself, womanly
acquiescent to the pull
of salt.
Constant tide
neither able nor willing
to escape the ebb and flow.
Salt lace, beautiful
and bitter, covers my
head, pours from creased
brow along shoulder
and fingers spread to catch
love memories.

Engulfed
in new wedding veil,
I dip the salt
across flat palm,
turning my left hand
to accept the ring
of brine flowing me
to caverns out beyond
the rime of lace.
I know the fathoms,
dipping birds, exotic
fish, savored beyond
the beach. But
watching along the shore
as the sea veil forms
I seek the delicate
change within my reach.

Mouse Island, Summer 1977

Early sun, as vivid and uncontrolled as a forest fire, rages into the morning sky, hitting hard the stretched platinum water. As I rest on the ledge before my studio, fishing boats are caught in molten light with fire and reflection as they move slowly from lobster buoy to lobster buoy.

I feel a great lassitude, a need to replenish my mind, my body, before I return to creativity. A sense of ability to grasp the beginning eludes me. I know that solitude is the key. Coming to deal with my creative drive for expression, with the demands of a willful need, sometimes I drive myself against myself. I wonder why I am here and not playing tennis or sitting on my front porch reading the morning paper, or taking an early morning swim. What compulsion forces me to search for the bare spindle of an idea? What will send the rod of yarns and wool whirling until it is a tapestry? My solitude is a key to my liberation. I know that is the true answer. It is an open door away from the tidy controlled patterns of living, a chance to develop and expand my life that a woman over fifty cannot hope to find in any other way unless she has begun at the beginning long ago. And then nearly always she has been an underling, not free to choose her own route. This greatest freedom also requires great discipline for I must travel alone, keeping the hours of solitude separate and steady so that the other hours may truly be mine also. It is a pattern of industry often without visible result that I have followed since early childhood. It is a need to be an individual like no other individual that I have sought and created.

As a girl of eight I practiced on the piano two and sometimes three hours a day without urging. Later my parents were to say they did not wish me to pursue music professionally because I would not have a "normal" life. As a volunteer I worked with a florist, cutting the brittle stems of carnations by the hundreds and sinking them into the moist sand to germinate. I worked at a dairy to learn how to milk cows. When I was fifteen I worked seven days a week and on Sundays rose at six-thirty to sweep the steps and open the double doors of an amusing emporium called The Smiling Cow. I did this because I needed to reach out and be a part of the world more intense than the life of our cottage with the bent birch furniture.

In college I devoted myself to music composition, working until eleven each night and barely making the dormitory at a hard run before curfew. I composed a shelf full of compositions that I played for myself and choral music that I sang one line at a time to test its worth. And then six months in the Library of Congress, I rode past snow and finally cherry blossoms in pursuit of my master's degree in Spanish lyric poetry; "La Mujer Desnuda" of Juan Ramón Jiménez, the Nobel poet of Spain.

But always art fascinated me, museums were my home in many foreign cities and the search of Jiménez for "La Mujer Desnuda," the perfect poem, was my searching for a perfection in art rather than in poetry. Suddenly I realized that my search had to come first and to be whole and I have never forgotten that since. Ask me if I am happier and I will tell you honestly that I am and that in my creative life I rise to pinnacles of great joy as I work. Perhaps the concentration had made my life seem to spin faster than any other I know but it spins free and open and as varied as the light around us as we turn with the earth.

Sometimes, as today, I feel exhaustion. The exuberance will return when I lay the demands of living behind me, and ideas again begin to flow. It will come. I know that now and I do not panic. I have for a long time, as much as five years, to work without seeking to display my tapestries.

Choosing the material to bring to my island is difficult. I settle eventually for grey and white wools, a length of pristine mohair woven by the Zulu in Lesotho, a length of mohair-lox spun by Anna Viljoen, an African housewife from Pretoria. There are also grays in abandoned ribands of natural lambs wool from Bolivia, my favorite *bayeta*. For a counterpoint, I tuck in brown and orange wool from Helen Kirtland in Ajijic, Mexico. All of these weavers have become special friends in my global adventure and they understand my needs.

Yarns run the geographical gamut too, but except for oranges all are earth tones with very few dark shades. Grays and whites predominate, the many natural whites in more than twenty shades and textures. How can I know what to choose, to bring this to this tiny studio for three months? How to anticipate what my new work will be? I have only brought a sampling.

I feel that there is a Mouse Island cycle in my life. As Richard Diebenkorn has painted his magnificent Ocean Park series, perhaps in some small way the adventure of this summer on a small coastal island, two hundred and twenty oar pulls from my cottage, may bring me to implicit knowledge of this outcropping of earth and its relationship to the sea around it.

As I write I see six trees beyond the screen door. There are young spruce and beyond a tender white pine, and farther out a seventh tree sparkles, a glistening white birch, reflecting hot summer time from its white stem. Something as simple as these seven trees could be a whole summer's work.

I am not a minimalist although the idea is tempting. Who would totally reject the spirit of one's time? I wonder how the hard-skinned thin hands of Agnes Martin, that I held so fleetingly, would see those trees or the brush of Diebenkorn abstract them.

At this moment, two large trawlers loom before my window, pulling a weir between them en route to a third barge. The noise and the energy make my studio a Third Avenue El bedroom, the clatter I remember from the old N.Y. elevated when I lived in New York in 1942. A sudden conflict of thought. Maybe this, too, explains the diversity in some abstract poetry and art, the shooting color on a calm canvas.

Mouse Island, Summer 1977

It is already Friday and I have not threaded a single needle. This is as I expected. After such a hiatus it will take time. I have spent almost six months raising funds and creating my catalogue for my museum tour, "Textures of Our Earth." I need to review for myself what these steps to a museum tour that will travel to four museums entail. It all looks so easy: "Sponsored by Bowdoin College."

The director wrote me in August to say that the exhibit would not tour, there was no further interest. His letter to the National Endowment was bland and filled me with indignation. I called the Textile Museum in Washington where Andrew Oliver, the new director, knew my work. He was optimistic and wrote to Bowdoin and the N.E.A., endorsing my show and asking for it for his museum's first major show of a contemporary textile artist.

In September I was invited to Montana and decided to fly on from Bozeman to Seattle, to make the acquaintance of Willis Wood, the director of the Seattle Art Museum. I called him from a pay phone at the gas station asking for only ten minutes of his time to show him my work. He graciously assented. A man of solid museumship, he was director for sixteen years at the Detroit Institute of the Arts, where he built much of that museum. Our meeting was totally felicitous and my third museum fell into place. Then the director from Bowdoin moved on to Richmond, to the Virginia Museum of Art to make a fourth exhibition.

In the spring after much searching for funds I went to see Thomas Haas at the Wool Bureau of New York. I arrived with my long leather case, no small feat in Manhattan traffic, and disgorged my tapestries. They became immediately involved and promised me support for my catalogue and chose other works (that would not be at the museums) to tour the country at their expense. This meant that forty-eight hangings were on view at once across the country, literally from Maine to San Francisco.

This long digression into the unrolling of a finished first-class tour has been a three-year struggle. I have compromised nothing to achieve it except the exhaustion I feel as the tour starts.

In the privacy of this beautiful island with a north blown day I want urgently to recapture the creative swell. I wonder if I sense its essence? I find fields rather than woods enchant me, rocks rather than water. There are no raging seas here, no unattended spruce falls, no violence of any sort. The raspberries fruit and fall soundlessly as the mice scurry to and away from their field grass hutch, leaving in the grass round holes as clear as bullet wounds. Behind my studio, bees fly trajectories from their nest deep in the thatch. Bayberry, its own candle gray-green, knits a leitmotif across the island, sheltering moss and lichen. It is a soft, touchable, comforting place. Birch trees, like succulent celery, intersperse, to give it shape and contrast. I need to go to the outer harbor rim, to Fisherman's Island and to Cape Newagen, to feel the strength and passion of the sea.

The rocks of Mouse give me the strongest impulse. At the very tip of the island, stretching limbs toward Burnt Island, are shelving granite layers, sculptures perpendicular and bold. Everything else is stale in relation to its neighboring vegetation except the rocks. I have brought with me to my studio on Mouse Island just one book, a catalogue of the retrospective (1943–76) show of Richard Diebenkorn. Although I have read the early pages with interest, the Ocean Park series overwhelms me with strength and subtlety, the two elements I feel direct my own emerging style. I have followed his art since the middle fifties when he first appeared as one of the San Francisco Three with Park and Bischoff. His work has changed as drastically as my own. His has a more literal style with figures where mine had natural shapes. Now I understand his luminescent distillation. As I read the explanations of his concerns and influences I realize each of us follows a different road. The great value of studying the catalogue is that it is a private conversation between me and another artist who I feel is successful in his own creative expression. It doesn't matter how different we are in delineation because basically we are involved in the same uncurling of imagination and creativity.

In my tapestries and in the use of wool, luminosity is not one of the terms that applies. Wool has to be different, more architectural, or sculptural if you will, creating a third dimension.

The painterly brush strokes, the layers and layers of color over a primed canvas become in my medium folds of yardage and sometimes layers of different materials with wool and organdy and even cheesecloth. Juxtaposition of colored yarns approximate what I might do with a paint brush. It is the linear quality of the handspun yarn next to the folded and rippling wool that creates the most subtle and sometimes dramatic effect. I handle yarn as I might an etching tool or a pencil with conscious consideration for hard and soft edges.

Boothbay Harbor, Fall 1977

The summer is almost over. Hastily we plan a picnic to Thrumcap, a solitary island between Pemaquid and Ocean Point. It heads like a ship straight out to sea. Here rocks have been hurled like broken toys in all directions. One feels that this is not glacial but sea anger. On the north shore, away from the wind, a beautiful hollow is filled with marsh goldenrod, some of it growing from the heart of crumbling granite and feldspar.

Our friends have spread out to enjoy the view and I slip away seeking textures. Suddenly I hear, "Nancy, look how the wool is pulling around the rocks—see the lace at the edge!" The gift of friends who see what I see and the knowledge that I have in a small way enriched them delights me. We run together over the rocks stopping at ever bend and curve to marvel.

A poet friend asks me why I call my current show "Textures of Our Earth," rather than just "Textures of the Earth"? I explain that I want what I see to be a shared experience. I do not visualize my art as a detailing of textures, coldly enumerated, as much as eye openers that we can all enjoy. My art is meant to be inclusive, as my titles state with their simple directness. With my more abstract work I feel it is necessary to give the viewer a key. Tapestries have titles because they are animate to me. Calling them I, II, III suggests sterility.

It is my nature to be loving and generous, I hope I can share and enrich others as so many have me.

Washington, Winter 1979

After more than forty years I have come to understand the trance of the musician. Although I played the piano and even the cello for a brief time as a child, it was always the compositions that I devised, the improvisations and the intricate lines of the fugue that most delighted. The musician with his violin held tightly clamped between chin and shoulder, his eyes shut as the bow lifted and pulled like a sighing tree seemed to be an affectation I could never quite dispel.

For four years I have been without a piano, for the first time in my life. I sold my piano in Mexico, knowing the narrow space of our early nineteenth-century Washington house could not hold both my tapestry table and the long curved form of my grand piano. It was a present to me from my parents when I graduated from high school.

The piano traveled to Uruguay and Argentina and on to Spain and even into the high Andes of Bolivia. It was a hard choice but by Mexico I rarely played, my life given entirely to the visual arts and my small school in the Mexican countryside. So I sold it without a sentimental thought.

In the intervening years as my tapestries grew larger and larger and gathered to fill a whole room, I occasionally thought about music but not as often as you might expect. The world of tapestry making has been so absorbing; I gathered myself into its woolen folds and absorbed myself in creativity. When the tapestries outgrew our colonial home I found another larger space with eleven-foot ceilings, a lovely garden and a new way of life.

Then I thought about my piano and grieved to think I had sold it like a child to slavery. Perhaps I could find a fine old Steinway! That too was a dream I had had for years. I shopped all the music stores and secondhand dealers and found rickety, pock-marked pianos at huge prices. I called my piano tuner in Maine and pleaded with him to be on the lookout for a good Steinway grand.

We all gathered for Christmas in Portland, filling our son's house to the rafters with merriment. Mother came and Jesus, our Bolivian treasure. It was cold but not a flake of snow fell. When I returned to Washington I had scarcely unpacked my bag and admired my Christmas booty when the phone rang. It was the piano tuner in Maine. He had a beautiful piano, he said, owned by one family. He asked if I was really interested. I assured him I was, hung up the phone, packed my bag and caught the next plane back to Maine. The snow was beginning to fall. In the gathering snow I felt a sense of discovery and exhilaration.

A fragile lady in a quilted robe and worn slippers came to the door in astonishment to see me standing in what had now become a winter blizzard. With frozen fingers she led me to an unheated parlor, removed the paisley shawl and suggested I play. Each note rang out with the clarity of bird song. I felt moved to hot tears down my cold cheeks. A beautiful piano.

I play it now almost every day, but I shall always remember my first hour with my piano in my Queen Anne castle in Washington, the tall wind-swept tapestry of a wave on the near wall and farther away the rising shape of *Aqua Lapis*. I played without knowing where the rhythm from the keyboard caught the life and strength and transport. I composed, without thinking, arpeggios to my tapestries and to the glory of the sound that came from my piano.

The flow of a simple fugue pours through my hands like fresh water on parched leaves. I know suddenly that my art has helped me discover this new dimension, the trance of the musician, for now it is pure sound and lilt and expansion drifting like fog back and forth between my piano, my tapestries and my inner being.

California, Winter 1980

Sometimes we revel to be captured in our bodies. These are the times when creative ideas are pouring from our brains pungent as fresh coffee. There is nothing but celebration in my heart when a deeply satisfying creative series of days brings exultation. It is a mystic communication—a transfiguration.

Often we are cornered in our bodies when overwork and illness reach out and clamp us in their vise. The mind often runs ahead of the body.

Why did Mozart perish in his young thirties? The enigma is how to live the long life, to express both creative gift and need, and to hold the fragile human shape together. It is a constant challenge like a speed skater changing lanes, sometimes moving effortlessly on the inside circle but again stretching the extra miles on the outside course.

Norman Cousins in *Anatomy of an Illness* writes: "I became convinced that the will to live, hope, faith and love have biochemical significance and contribute strongly to healing and well-being. The positive emotions are life-giving experiences."

I believe each of us has a destiny we can fulfill to whatever degree we choose until our time runs out. As Robert Penn Warren writes, there is "a secret knowledge" that steadies. To each of us that secret is different. The body and the mind are the first two: the third is of our own making.

California, Spring 1980

Each morning I wake to an imagination bursting with thought for the day. Where it used to be the rush of small boys scampering to climb into our ample bed and hide under the covers, now it is the scampering of ideas running free from the curves of my brain. They are just as eager and willful.

Today as the half moon slips past the shutters, I look up at the slats of the redwood ceiling and wonder about the elements that have brought my art together. I think of Faulkner and his speech to the Nobel Prize Committee. He believes mankind will prevail. That is a large message. I share his optimism. More importantly, he spoke to the creative generation that would succeed him. He declared that "the basis of all things is to be afraid and knowing that to forget it forever." I rush through the years of my life fearless of the superficial dangers—purse snatchers, plunging planes, the orange flame of war—and still I have never resolved fully my own mortality. That is perhaps my fear and not sufficiently forgotten.

As I watch the light thicken and color of this morning I think of the old "verities" that Faulkner says are essential to true creativity—the "truths of the heart": love, honor, pity, pride, compassion and sacrifice. There are also the waves of childbearing, of physical passion, of travel to far lands, of membership in a family and a culture. Age has brought me these gifts and burdens and in their presence I am fulfilled. I think of the emaciated boy of fourteen in Madrid whom I could not help because his breath was nearly gone, of the arms around my suckling children, the drama of Manhattan rising from a scarf of fog after three years in foreign lands. The memories can start at any month of any year, pushing and shoving to be recalled running on and on like a deep river. All of this is not my creativity. All of the pity, the love, the compassion are there. Only pride is missing. For me it is thankfulness.

Washington, Winter 1979

Poetry fills my studio the days I have long seams to sew. Records and tapes unwind their familiar word songs, prodding me to see the world with fresh vision. I have favorites. Some days I choose to listen to Dylan Thomas or Edna St. Vincent Millay or Philip Booth. Robert Lowell and Millay are Mainers with their own strong variations of poetic vision carefully staked out. Each touches me differently. Lowell lurches from lobsterman to honed intellectual. I see and hear him but he is a truant neighbor. Booth, a shy, quiet observer, comes closer. I feel his poem to his daughter deep in my being.

> remember when fear
> cramps your heart what I told you:
> lie gently and wide to the light-year
> stars, lie back, and the sea will hold you.

Those words, "lie back, and the sea will hold you," are a key to my whole being.

I like to write poetry but now I feel the need to be twentieth century, to compete with the abstract poets. I have eagerly sought the brand new poems with their lists of anguish. They offer no cheer.

In February, as I work among the chimney tops of Georgetown, poems come to me as I start each tapestry. With the new *Aqua Lapis,* the poetry seems deeper, farther inside me, and less animated. Water and stone together capture my sense of conflict and oneness, the strength and fragility that will always be my inner self.

I wrote "A Truth" after waking up suddenly from a nap on a fall day when I had a rare quiet day alone in my tall Queen Anne's castle. It unwound from inside me in anger and honesty. I am amazed at the presence. It seemed important and now, again and again, I try to recapture the hammer beat of pain, thinking I must search this inner honesty I did not know.

A Truth

How I lived all my life in a house
    with the toilet seat up.

Only brothers, (a sister who hid
    under the bedclothes reading.)

Went to school on a bus the color
    of pumpkin.

With unopened books and a fried egg
    between two slices
    of bread, thick as Irish tweed.

And more men, three songs and a six
    four husband.

Shoveling food, mending socks until
    I threw down my needle
    like a larch in a gale.

And said I'd never sew again.

Lived in fourteen houses, that were
    nailed and sawed to please
    somebody else.

The tall pink house built by a bull
    fighter for his girl friend.

And the fat pink house, high among
    snow peaks that used to be
    a beauty parlor.

A truck yard next to it.

And a low pink house, open to the breezes
    —that was hot country.
    Hot from guns, and no rain,
    and bad tempers.

But the rains came, soaking the hearth
    and the last fire of love
    and kisses in me.

How I hurt enough inside, parched
  and aching from too much
  of everything.

Hurt enough to pick up my needle and sew.
  Sew the lost babies,
  the pink houses, the grinning
  toilet bowl into my sewing.

Finding beauty and peace all over again,
  fresh as snow on cold ground.

Finding new freedom, saying nothing.
  watching the lichen grow,
  the spider weave.

Walking. Laying my head low on rock granite,
  next to the salt—
  troubling no one.

Finding the secret stair to my being.
  Closing the door.
  Always quiet.

Sitting with myself and my needle
  troubling no one.

Sometimes missing the warm arms,
  missing cheeks with stubble
  and salt.

Wishing a kiss were more important
  than proper spelling.

Wishing a thought were an idea
  not a dictionary.

Knowing love and babies and caring
  are wrapped tight inside.
  Invisible treasure.

Wheaton College, Spring 1980

Flying straight from San Francisco to Boston, I have come from the mist and salt of redwood country for a conference of mentors at Wheaton College. Tomorrow I will fly back again, richer for my association with the students preparing for careers, and for my friendship with Louise, my former professor of English, and Amy Gray, my student assistant, who have also come to share this morning with me. We are three generations who have profited by encouraging each other. Louise has read my poem "A Truth" to the students. Hearing her reading I am surprised that I feel so strongly the words that uncurl about me.

If my poetry is occasionally angry and my tapestries stronger and stronger, it is because an inner force is bursting from me. I have lived all my life with brothers, sons and a husband. The only womanly figure has been my mother and although she taught me to be feminine and gentle, she was strong, decisive. I have been a leader trying to be led. I accepted that role at twenty-two but not at sixty before many pairs of bright eyes and seeking spirits. I am glad that Louise has read "A Truth." That is how it is.

Louise Mackenzie and I beg off from the head table to sit with students and young mentors. I ask her about contemporary poetry; where I might find self-teaching. For the first time I understand the modern poems are like bright streamers, simply list impressions that have no special message. They do not relate to anything, not even to the title. They depend on fleeting observation. Titles like those on modern paintings are chosen without relationship to even one line or object.

Louise clarifies her image of modern poetry. "But it must have rhythm, without that it is not poetry."

John Ashbery is a leader in this coded poetry. We both admit we like W. H. Auden best for his choice of words and craftsmanship among the poets. "But, of course, he is not a modern poet," Louise quickly adds.

"Your poetry is so strong, Nancy. I expected the thin blond girl with the sensitive face to be a lyric poet. You are not. Your lines do not float. They walk with determination."

I think aloud, "That is like my tapestries. Many of them are very powerful, especially the most recent. There is a correlation."

I wanted to be a first-rate poet by tomorrow's standards, but now I see that poetry is for me a soliloquy, a knowing myself and an expiation. I need to talk with myself about the beauty I see. I am so often living on two, three and even four levels all at once, and that means that two or three of those conversations must be within myself. I am not full of anger. I have no hate. Sadness dissolves at the edge of the sea, the salt lifts my body, suspends it easily and that is what poetry does. It lifts out of me simple thoughts and brings magnified responses.

Anita spreads the folds
of her printed skirt.
We sit on two white chairs
where Mother often greeted
    guests.
We talked, two in the fog—
filled air, sun moving
undefined as dreams.
I lift my hands to catch
the lace of living, hold
the netted beauty of living,
    hold
life, the continuity sewn
from my mother's womb
to me. Thread spun
on through the tall spare
shoulders of my son
and whirling now across
the meadow blooming
    with his young.

Each moment light
as fresh soufflé.
The air is warm
with love. I see
young eider in the cove,
hear the purple finch
coloring the spruce.
A sail cuts like shark
fin into the shroud
of fog. Geometry of
living piling so many
shapes into a summer
pattern, up and up
until I fear
to topple; balance
the airy burden
in my arms, upon
my head and heart.

Some poems have no direct bearing on my art. They are floating milkweed. Poems surprise me, finding their way onto a discarded envelope when I least expect them. Others turn over and over, pebbles in a quick running brook, finally breaching.

I no longer write for publication or perfection of twentieth-century form. There are no lists of agonies and observations wrenched from aching thought waves. Poems bubble out, curving and bending the letter onto the page. As my pencil does in drawings, I am shaping in another way the ideas and observations that needle and thread will take. Sometimes it is only a small cloud of being that dissipates and is nothingness.

Sometimes poetry is also a conversation with myself, livening the long hours of solitude. I have never discovered how other writers of poetry converse with themselves and the world. Do they sit at their desk each day as Hemingway did, demanding the muse, even when only twenty words came? He told me one evening when we dined with Ernest and Mary, just the four of us, at El Escorial in Spain, that this was his greatest agony. The daily search and the slow unfolding. And much of his writing has the sparse, clear ring of the best of the poets.

Did Edith Sitwell suffer the birth of each new poem? She suggests that in poems such as "Hiroshima" that the idea was in her mind long before it fruited. A newspaper article sparked her final choice of words, describing the bomb as a great totem pole.

All of us, whether vivid names or unknown, share some similarity. First, a sensitivity to sound, to environment, to color. Some extrasensory message is delivered to us and inspires us to scratch a message. Tiny children, Chinese monks, all know the tingling birth of a poem. I suspect that solitude or a rare moment of quiet, freely given or sought, is the universal ingredient.

Mouse Island, Summer 1980

Rowing to the island this morning there is a gray haze, a filament of nothingness. I push off from the pier just at seven, avoiding the carpenters at the Loft and swinging into the rhythm of oars and sea. I feel cold and unnourished. The sun has fooled me into thinking another heavy summer day is beginning. In blue jeans, shorts and a cotton blouse I shrink within my flesh to resist the damp air.

Yesterday, walking the beach, I found the key to two new designs. A gray rock with a loop of white tied like a Christmas package, unbalanced and raffish enough to suggest a huge tapestry in gray with white appliqué. At the end of the island the rocks piled up and pushed to an upright position, long thin lines of rock glued together a million or two million years ago, but still holding their surfaces apart from each other.

I visualize each new idea as part of my *Aqua Lapis* series. The space it will fill, the homogeneity and also the contrast must all be part of the development of my exhibition.

From my earliest tapestries ideas have come so fast that perhaps I have not explored them fully. With four years to work on *Aqua Lapis* I am testing my range of imagination within a definite time frame. By 1982 or '83 I will begin to search beyond for still another area of creativity, almost certainly in sculpture, lifting the free-form wool sculptures off the walls and away from their armatures and into living spaces.

The abstract shapes of my new work have been with me since I first came to Mouse Island four years ago. I walk the same rock and see the same granite and lichen each day but it offers something new. It is like the faces of friends. I recognize them instantly but when I come to draw them from memory I am lost. I need even the faces of Bob and our children before me to delineate them in recognizable form. Without them there is no sense of capturing exactitude. In my tapestries I build distillations, but I still need to feel the fissures and study the layered surfaces.

The peace of this island and the simplicity of my tiny studio make all things possible. I do not have a spiritual quest, instead I feel here a flowing froth of creative wealth as though by seclusion and calm I am transformed into the medium of new ideas in the simplest way. I hope to catch the strength and continuity, that "man will prevail" in the cut of every rock. To share the beauty that I see with others is what I used to say. I think now I have changed; that is to say, "To share the beauty I feel with others." Perhaps that is also why the new series, *Aqua Lapis* is more abstract.

The correlation between what my eyes behold and what my creative medium expresses is a new confluence leaping directly from my creative image to the medium of tapestries.

This week I have discovered the flow of wool as a new adjunct to my art form. For nearly two years I have been folding and molding wool, often lining it. Now I see textiles as a freer form, not expressing any reality in nature, but as an outpouring of rhythm. Motion is the important new dimension. A single rock just south of my studio started me on this new adventure. I have walked across this rock for three years and never noticed it. Now in early morning light when the shadow is heavy, the sun cuts the edge of the rock in a new way. I see the deep fissure as a two part tapestry in gray alpaca and lambs wool, falling and rising again. Lines of white slice through it like cream cheese. I pull heavy mohair that I bought in Africa over the folds to cut the face of my new composition.

After two hours of intense work. I wriggle onto my cot beneath my work table and curl up for a nap. Pulling a new design together is the most exhausting work that I know. I drift into sleep knowing that when I wake I will see it with fresh eyes. The passage of time, the mortal enemy I throw myself against, seems suddenly subdued.

Until this is done, I cannot proceed. The state of pure creativity is totally demanding of me. I must forget myself completely and move into the current with a firm oar. Just now, the waves curl in signing a low urgent tune. I hear the swish along the shore like fingers on a harp. That is the song of creating and the dance too. Suddenly the loop of gray wool in my new tapestry *Declivity* has meaning. I understand what the push and pull of the wool fabric can say. It loops low beyond the narrow gash of cleft rock and falls lightly upon itself like a wave against the shore, joining the two halves.

Mouse Island, Summer 1980

Early rowing, criss-crossing the flight of the blue heron with the sun's hot spears between my shoulder blades. Each day as I row I look back to the pier of the mainland with the sun behind me. By one o'clock when I row back again it will have moved above my head and the tide will have crept over the ledges filling the cup of the bay. I am exhilarated today for I have finished *Declivity*. It represents a step forward, a bolder treatment of wool and a new freedom. When the sewing is complete I slip sheets of paper under each section and draw and cut the pattern for the stiff armature on which to mount it. My home has no wall large enough to hold *Declivity*.

I feel such lassitude. It will be a hot summer day, the wind scarcely touching the bayberry bush beyond my studio window. Tide nearly full, lobster buoys stand straight as picket fences, so thick in the shore waters I could skip from one to another. I watch an early lobsterman in his cockle shell. He has a toy motor and a narrow wooden guard on the starboard side where he pulls his traps. While I perch on the rock he pulls two traps. He does not see me but still he dutifully flings the shorts, the baby lobsters too small to sell, back to sea. I marvel that we still have such order and sense of law. Honesty is the ultimate test of civility. The Incas had it. Now it seems a rare prize.

The rocks have lost their beauty today. Even the lichen in cadmium and its silver gray does not touch me. I will read and rest, trusting shadow and light, floating for a day without a sense of time. The apparent quiet of creativity is sometimes the most exhausting. I cannot escape it even if I would. I seem to yawn, heaving great sighs, when I am working on a new design. I call it a great peacefulness, but it also brings the ultimate exhaustion.

How much easier it is to follow the tempo of daily living; to cook a meal, to answer the phone and to weave a basketry of living into one lopsided shape or another. Delving alone into the unknown for a form, an idea that has never been created before, is taking on tremendous odds.

Washington, Winter 1981

What place do people play in creativity? I write about solitude, about seeking the alone place with no telephone, no interruption. The gray chores of living as barren as winter trees I want to leave to others as I sew and write and revel.

As January twists a narrowing thread of cold and ice I begin to seek old warmth. January is sharp. December—we have caroled and candled and unwrapped in an orgy of joy.

Washington has the excitement of an inauguration. How wise to celebrate a new president when we are shrunken to our core, a deep freeze of the spirit. Not many malcontents are going to picket the White House or parade at the Lincoln Memorial with hands and feet white from chill. And this year, the inaugural committee has cheerfully allotted the northwest corner of Lafayette Park for dissidents. It is all so respectable. Who wants to have a playpen set aside for mauling; where they can roast their own chestnuts of discontent without public heed?

There is a whirl of activity that makes solitude seem unreasonable. I want to pour some of myself into the gaiety of living. Some artists play well. Others are all wrapped in the energy of work. Picasso seems to have thrived on both. Matisse surrounded himself with students painting bright sheets of paper for his cutouts. Rothko retreated into the diffuse absorbent canvasses, turning the glow upon himself and his own destruction.

But suddenly there is too much aloneness in my bones. Driven by perfection, my fingers seem to chill and the songs I hum are dissonant or gone.

Creativity comes to a light heart. Each breath of fresh air kindles a new fire. Doors must open; eyes alert. The lines of my tapestries need to flow to that same rhythm, curving and climbing spontaneously.

Even so, I am hostage to politics that has often been my interlude. The politics of international living. Smiling, face front, feet flat on the floor of some creaky platform in Mexico, Bolivia or Spain. I think of the agonized hours that wives spend as background to speeches, ceremonies and parades.

Often I am asked to speak. On my trip to Africa, fat with talking: this time the patient mate was my husband, standing behind MY chair. Somehow the marital setting adds sincerity. It convinces, if wife or husband stand stiff and silent in support.

Now I am hostage to my family. Republican brothers are here to attend the coronation. We have watched parading bands and horses flow past from the Capitol on their way to 16th Street. We have waved to the new president and his first lady. We have heard folk singers, pressed our ball gowns and thighs against hotel mobs and rushed home to the television to see what we have missed.

I long for my studio, the tulip tree, a hundred feet of strength, just beyond my window. After such an orgy, the suffocating hymn of mink and success and money vibrating in my ears, I lose the tune I sang before Christmas. When, where do I begin again the subtle measure of line and fold?

The sure flow of composing from brain directly to my fingertips has been short circuited. I wait for it in my studio, watching the self-pruning of the forest. This may be a pruning too, like the trees I watch. Interludes do that. They have their place.

When the last footsteps, heavy with bags and boots, have left our door, I fold like a crumpled napkin. For all these days a counterpoint has called me while I grated cheese and curried cream chicken. I forget names because my memory is saying, "Hold a place clean for thought." A narrow passage, thin as a strand of hair is all that joins my two worlds. It will take days to replenish the tenuous corridor of my art, to spread it wide across the tables where my woolens lie. I have no plans but art. The rhythm will pick up again, the flow of ideas will come. It has before.

Creativity is more tender now, more subject to the world because it is no longer art of place. IT IS SELF-REVELATION. The whole landscape is my inner being. Much of that is subconscious. It is the child of quiet and absorption in a city where bells are ringing night and day.

Happiness and solitude form a tempting dilemma and the most delicate balance of all. It is a ballet on tightrope without an audience.

Boothbay Harbor, Spring 1981

When reading the lives of other women who have been creative as writers, teachers or artists, I find marvelous friends who encourage and support my own creative drive. I think of Sylvia Ashton-Warner with her life-long need to be an artist, writing about her frustration at pursuing the role of teacher and how the need to sublimate her blazing imagination to circumstance brought her to the brink of self-destruction.

Georgia O'Keeffe, on the other hand, has given it full rein except for brief periods when marriage intervened in her quest for solitude and a place to paint. I know that my whole life is one of creative energy from as early as I can remember; from my imaginary castles staked out below the sheltering canopy of the elms on our farm in Foxboro to the stacks of music compositions and notebooks filled with drawings.

Marriage has been a long continuation of that creative process, a subtle and sometimes conscious effort to bring two very different temperaments together in the most beautiful flowering possible. The exaltation of childbearing, the moment of first life, which is indeed for a mother also the moment of the knowledge of death, has again enlarged my creative consciousness. It now flows into the years of my celebration of life itself through the elements of our earth.

"Textures of Our Earth" was a beginning, a cataloguing of my growing awareness. *Aqua Lapis* defines the two strongest creative forces with that sphere—water and stone.

Sometimes I feel a sense of becoming shrill in my need for one environment, for quietness without another human soul dependent upon me. It takes a fierce independence to disregard the social patterns of a lifetime and the needs of others. Where I was taught to never look in the mirror and that happiness is thinking of others, how can I dare now to "know myself," and move away from the circle of human warmth out along the granite shore and the fog-clad bay? I dare because the motion and texture of the natural world is my home . . . It fills me. It seems eternal and vivid and inescapable in a way that demands my presence. Nothing else matters. My tapestries are fragments of the glory of our earth, trying to catch the overall strength and depth and also the fragile embellishments. The medium I chose from need in Bolivia, the rich wools and the intricate embroidery by some magic age are the perfect alchemy for what I must say about the coast of Maine. There is a degree of sensuousness in wool.

As I return to my tiny studio on Mouse Island for a fifth year I realize that a harmony has evolved between the grains and fissures of the rocks and my art form that is original and powerful.

The discovery of solitude despite hardships of living is something I crave. It is a little like being deaf; suddenly you cut out the sound of human life about you, other needs, and find an inner strength.

That transport only comes from seeking. It is finding the epicenter of a circumstance as undefined as fog or cumulus clouds. Its nothingness—as I reach out to grasp it—is nevertheless its greatness. Not every day brings a sense of oneness with one's self without the electric currents that slice like lightning through a sky, but once I have known the levitation of purely creative moments I seek them with the passion of a zealot.

The Loft, Spring 1981

The Loft is a miraculous extension of the horizon line I have known. Nowhere have I had such a sense of space and freedom. Suddenly I find myself stretching out the lengths of wool by yards instead of feet and inches. What seemed monumental to me in the tiny studio at Mouse and the confines of my attic space in Washington has dissolved before this new sense of infinity.

Already I know that designs will be simpler, more sweeping; the movement and thrust more cleanly hewn. The unencumbered flow will push the limits of textiles as close to the sweep of clouds as I can fold and fashion.

Today from my balcony, where I can stand and see straight out to sea, patterns of flat water pull like lariats at full speed through the ruffled sea. I think *Wave Length,* a tapestry lifting up to the surface through so many, seeking to be formed. Perhaps this pattern of water far out beyond my Loft is the key. I make a rapid sketch and slip down my spiraled, wooden staircase to try it on the long flat tables below. Alpaca, handspun and handwoven, yards and yards that I buy from just one family in Bolivia, is stretched before me. There are lengths of winding sheets in raw silk, in beige and grape and white from my trip to Madagascar. The touch, the comprehension of the skill and patience of these beautiful weavings are as much a treasure as the silver and gold of the jeweler. Once it is cut it cannot be melted back into a single piece like a precious metal. I must study and fold and test my imagination to see the beginning and the ending of my design before I feel free to slice with shears through the warp and weft. Only when I feel I can create a tapestry that has elegance and grace, that glorifies the surface, can I then feel the exhilaration. That is the absolute apogee. No accolade, no self-satisfaction can touch it.

The Loft, Summer 1981

The traffic of the sea passes below my studio window perched on a cliff. Only the tallest masts reach high enough to touch the sky where my Loft rests partially hidden by a giant oak, fringed with spruce and fir.

Often I walk onto the fragile balcony, the catwalk of my skyship, and wave, but no one sees me. I am a shape so small and so much a part of the landscape in jeans and a worn shirt that I am only a spirit. I think to myself that I have become invisible.

Sometimes I yearn to go join the whirling world about me, but I am pulled harder by the need to be creative and the fascination of transforming inanimate substance into movement and vitality. Sometimes there is desperation in my work. I am breathing life into cool yardage as one returns breath to a drowned victim. I cannot leave my post or the delicate chain of my art may be lost forever.

But like the sailors sweeping past the prow of my studio, there are the moments of breathless excitement. The parachute opens when a new design breaks free or the right words tumble into place. That is why I stay. That is why I cannot leave.

With age, too, there comes a sense of proportion. I know the feel of a pulling sail, the excitement of love beyond my winged windows. I share in both feasts without surfeit. One I remember, the other I seek.

People talk about discipline. That is part of it. But what sparks the motivation to continue an idea, a direction? Women who wash diapers and racks of clothes day after day are the disciplined. Men who return to the assembly line of office routine are the constrained.

I am disciplined only in that I do something different and by myself. But I can write or paint or draw or rest quietly on the pine needle floor of the forest and watch sea gulls career above me. The silent world is alive with wonder and never twice the same. Full of impressions, I choose my own tempo. There is no discipline, only a rhythm that propels me. Along the way momentum gathers as I find solutions and test new techniques.

~ 5 ~

The Magic of Inspiration

Walking the Berkshire hills each day past farms and the maple groves has made me realize that farming is in some ways very like the profession of an artist. Here there are pastures and fields that were cleared, many of them, back when the early settlers came and built their first church.

The dark stone walls of the Goshen schist define and contain every area, a sculpture up and down the sloping hills with a fringe of fiery maple at this time of year.

Every farmer has fields. I remember from childhood that on our farm there was the west pasture and the south pasture and the orchard and a pasture to the east. On a southern promontory stood the house and barn as the focal point of our farm. All of this reminds me of art. There is a central place of living where the impressions one collects are brought to be churned, or skimmed off or sheared, but all of the farm is a place for growing and knowledge and for new seasons.

Yesterday, as I passed the fields, I realized that I have winter wheat seeded in the unfinished tapestries that are already on their way to Washington from Maine. I have started them where I know the ground is fertile and I will finish them this winter. Now that snow is about to come there is a north field that I must give my attention to before the winter sets in. That is museums and travel. Because I farm alone without a gallery or professional publicity to help me I must schedule and plan where I want my work to be in two, four and six years and with whom I must share the odyssey of my art.

It is the north field that is usually most on my brain when the productive exhilarating summer months that now stretch for me into fall are over. I have in my mind many ideas as how best to utilize the north pasture, and it will often depend on others deciding to join with me. Also important is the sort of a harvest I have produced during the bright days in Maine.

The analogies are clear to me and perhaps also say in no small measure why I find the path of art so perfect. If I am a farmer growing art I am up with the first light. I work hard all day with only my own council as to where the time is best spent. My imagination dips to turn over the wonders of our earth and like a farmer I am surrounded by nature and it fills me. How easy for me to follow the narrow rocky trail of my New England heritage.

What has made the soil so rich is that my father and mother were not typical farmers, but brought to the life they built for us in the country treasures of travel and the world of art and a knowledge of the great museums. Like Bolivia and Maine this is a rare coming together. Not many small girls have the joy of growing up on a farm with a father who knows about Goya and a mother who remembers pages of poetry to recite as she lies quietly beside me when I am tucked into bed.

The fields that I have on my farm are wide and beautiful. It is only labor and care that will bring them to a full harvest.

Washington, Winter 1976

Benjamin Forgey, the art critic of the *Washington Star*, has come to see my work. I have read his sensitive critiques of art each week and value his skillful pen. He is admired by the artists of Washington, a rare accolade.

I rattle off in our '69 Volkswagen to pick him up. The sun is shining. It is in every way a felicitous meeting. He is slim, soft spoken and direct. He asks good questions, expresses eagerness to learn the vocabulary of tapestry making. It is a warm experience. He has agreed to do an essay on my work for my catalogue, "Textures of Our Earth," which Bowdoin College plans to publish for my show in August 1977.

I sense that my association with Ben will be easy. His direction is parallel to my own, a language of observation and expression; his in words, mine in tapestries. I base this singular first impression on a moment we spent looking out of our large dining room window into the garden. He said, "I would always like to live in Washington because of the light." A clear statement giving celebration to the beautiful skies as I, too, see them. The skies of Washington have a special quality. I feel that, after seeing so many heavens from different axes and hemispheres. Midnight blue is the purest here.

Washington, Spring 1976

Ben Forgey came again today to work on the essay for my catalogue. It is a pleasing exchange. We go back and pull out my earliest doodles and progress through the middle years of the *Ancient Images,* the pre-Columbian designs. He observes and ponders while I work giving him the quiet he seeks.

He is here—as the first time—for more than three hours, this visit broken by an interlude. I teach him to thread a needle and to do two basic embroidery stitches. Ben is a disarming and sensitive person. Rapport is easy because of my own irreverence for my early work and the knowledge that I feel I have much to learn.

He mentions that my early works are not only vivid in color but seem to be superimposed on natural material without interrelationship as there is in later works. Both of us like best *Surge I,* a gray sea picture.

Washington, Fall 1976

My woolly world flourishes. A helper is here each morning, sewing the pinned edges of appliqué, lining and hemming and leaving me free to do the detail, the creative assembly and to progress more rapidly with the ideas that spill out of my head in a constant flow. How long I can afford the luxury of an amanuensis is uncertain. I also need the hours, long hours alone to test fabric against fabric, to search my memory, books, photographs and the world around me for new ideas. The hundreds of brief, even five-minute sketches I have made are my principal source. Sometimes I use a written statement when there is no paper for sketching. I am always cataloguing and stuffing references into the corners of my desk and drawing board. A certain bark texture, a cloud, ice edging a brook, all take their place.

Russell Moore, acting director at Bowdoin College Walker Art Gallery, came last week. I dragged out from under dusty beds and from the lumpy pile in the upstairs hall all my more recent tapestries.

A woolly feast and a gratifying happening. He had no idea of the volume of work, nor did I.

I finish each tapestry and store it away for exhibit, hanging a few at a time to evaluate at leisure and to make changes. The rest go away to await museum walls in 1977–78. All my pieces seem to interest him. Only one, *Snow Boughs,* on black and white houndstooth alpaca seems out of focus. Both of us agree it is a maverick. He believes, as I do, that a museum show has a historical significance and should encompass some examples of early work, transitional pieces and finally recent hangings. This is a basic difference from commercial shows which delineate recent work and have generally a great sameness in production. Museum shows, for this reason, are more fulfilling. Less monetary, too, of course. Russell and I have chosen thirty-five pieces. There will be some changes before the final selection. I have at least three unfinished works that he has not seen. Between now and April, when the entire series must be photographed, I hope to have some new work that may surpass my present tapestries. Continuous involvement will bring new techniques.

Russell favors enigmatic titles. I prefer simplicity. I feel that a rock is just that; lichen is lichen, and rarely, as with trees in fog, do I say, *Fog Columns.* As we are in unison about nearly everything else I think he understands my decision. It has been fortified by two full-color pages of Georgia O'Keeffe's work in the November 22 *Newsweek.* While I was working in my studio I suddenly remembered that recent article and rushed to her titles. They are incredibly explicit; more precise and more like a first-grade primer than anything: *Shell on Red, Black Rock with Blue Sky* and *White Clouds,* and *Red Poppy.* I feel vindicated in choosing direct words. I will not use color words. That seems extraneous.

My titles are simple, unadorned, but like the title of a good poem they give, I hope, the key to the personal expression of the tapestries I create.

My last quest for a fifth museum for my new traveling show, "Textures of Our Earth," is to Akron's Institute of Art and to the Institute of Arts in Detroit. I chose Akron largely because I had heard it was a small museum with good exhibits, The director has done everything for me that you would for a middle-aged lady you did not wish to antagonize—almost nothing as a prospective exhibitor.

Apparently my relatives give a great deal of money. That accounts for his seeing me at all. The director came to Akron from the Whitney. He is reliving his years there; a show of antique crafts, this time from Ohio, and a quilt show. Dry ice burns my mind when I recollect his presence. Professionally it is a stone thrown into the sea.

From there I go reluctantly to Detroit, tasting my defeat in Akron and setting out at dawn over icy roads. The flight to Detroit over the crusted pollution of Lake Michigan is 40 minutes of disbelief and disgust at our avarice. The lake is dead, gray as the hide of a gutter rat. By 11:15 A.M. I am at the Institute of Arts, pulling my large leather sausage with six tapestries behind me through the block-long museum. "What am I doing here?" I think.

The institute is a museum worthy of an affluent city. It is several civilizations, one section piled on another, huge, varied, impressive. I feel inadequate. My appointment is vague and undefined. Russell Moore sent a generous, enthusiastic letter ahead. Stalwart ancestors push me to proceed. Dr. Neff, curator of modern art, has sent down word from his office to rise with the mighty. My heavy sausage bag still in hand I ascend to the curatorial offices.

Dr. John Neff is disarming. His openness and interest are startling in contrast to some of the cautious, tentative curators I am familiar with. He retains unspoiled simplicity. His specialty is Matisse. Matisse, who reveled in painting as a joyous pursuit, wrote that he wanted the world to be as comfortable with his paintings as with an old armchair. Never the agonized attitude; there is a significance in the artistic parallels.

I unzip my large, beige leather case and begin to pull out the yards of my art. First the gray *Rock Lichen* with its coiled wool motifs, karakul and lambs wool. Then *Mangrove,* the mohair hanging of white karakul and twisting alpaca on mohair lox from South Africa. Then *Winter Weave,* the white trunks and branches on gray alpaca.

Dr. Neff overwhelms me with praise: "So different than the poor quality of work we see here!" "So sensitive and beautiful!" At least he appears to feel that my work is worthy of an exhibit, and asks what would be the minimum number of tapestries I would agree to because of space limitations. I say twenty. He, as curator, must take the idea to the director and a committee. His wife also works at the museum and comes with another curator to exclaim. I stand in stocking feet on a large leather seat, holding wide my art, and show to my newfound trio of friends from Detroit *Orb*. It is a delicate embroidery of morning dew. Their understanding and appreciation of my hours of work is a balm.

Each time that someone who knows the measure of art is pleased I am humbled and grateful. I believe so deeply that my hand is guided and that by a mysterious confluence of work and celebration of gratitude I am led along paths that open. Of course, there are stone walls and storm-felled obstacles, but somehow I have always found a passage around or have been able to struggle past. For these insights I am also grateful.

When I used to paint I often felt a force between hand and brain over which I held no conscious control. This is magnified in my tapestries.

Perhaps something will come of my welcome in Detroit. Mrs. Walter Ford, a major donor and I believe a member of the board, owns two of my early works that she bought in 1972 at the Wingspread Gallery in Northeast Harbor, Maine. That should be helpful.

As I fly east the same afternoon the sunset at 30,000 feet is unusual and glorious. Rolled in molten hues of rose, it spins along the surface of the sky above clouds peaking and pulling like sea. I think I will do a sky hanging and call it *Borealis*.

Washington, Spring 1977

I have just been to Richmond to see where my show will hang in the Virginia Museum of Art, to talk with director, Peter Mooz, and to extend the olive branch to the curator, Frederick Brandt. He is friendly and receptive, especially in view of the fact that the exhibit was thrust upon him by the director. I came away feeling he is pleased. Either he is a thorough diplomat or my tapestries satisfy.

In all four museums my tapestries will be the first one-person show of a living textile artist. I already feel that some of my work is inadequate and am trying to look ahead and not back. I have pared the show down to thirty-two works, seven with organdy, my light hangings. I have eliminated anything doubtful. I sense that for some critics I am still too literal even though my medium gives a whole new expression.

The critique for my catalogue, written by Ben Forgey of the Washington *Star,* came in last week. It is sensitive and very perceptive, but very long, almost three thousand words. I am working hard on the catalogue to make it direct and also beautiful and to express the process and quality of my art. Bob has insisted that I include some of my poems. He feels they add greatly to the mood. I have not discussed this with Bowdoin College, but I will when I am there next week to put the catalogue together.

As these preparations near completion I am considering more and more the subject matter for my next series. I like to choose ground and then carefully explore it. I think of the patches of earth at Wheaton College which different generations of students nourished for over twenty-five years. Each class reported in detail on the plant life and biological phenomena of each rotating season. In a similar way I must, now that "Textures of Our Earth" is ready, begin to focus more fully on one single aspect of nature.

Boothbay Harbor, Summer 1977

This has been a week in which the details of my show that opened August 4th at Bowdoin College have consumed me. A hurried trip to Boston for one day at the Nimrod Press to check out the color proofs for the catalogue, another day spent in the gallery hanging the show, and then THE DAY.

It is my first experience with a "major" catalogue; forty-eight pages with nine color plates, three of them spread across two full pages. I have labored six months to fashion this slender volume, folding color sheets so as to get nine plates on two pages, proofreading, and raising funds from museums and corporate sources to pay for its printing. (I have added not a penny. I feel a professional should travel on merit or not at all.) One whole morning was devoted to the choice of print for cover. Now I am truly pleased with results. The Ben Forgey essay sets the right tone. Ed Born, editor of Bowdoin's publications, has been a careful technician. Bowdoin's three successive museum directors have all helped me; Peter Mooz to choose, Russell Moore for the long months of arduous preparation, and Kathleen Watson to add the finishing touches. I have wanted from the beginning to have a record that reflects my art and my view of the beauty I see. Five of my poems are included, inspired by ideas that also inspired tapestries. I feel the catalogue states with simplicity the essence of my art.

Openings are curious affairs. When I arrive Thursday night, walking across the campus to the lighted doorway of the Walker

Museum, I have the pleasant sensation of floating, floating into an elegant temple and along the flights of stairs down to the new galleries. I left the day before with the usual doubts, but suddenly I see everything goes together. As one artist commented, "This show looks as though it were created to hang here."

Candidly, I agree with him. The gallery could not look more handsome. The staircase leading down into it provides a stunning panoramic overview of the entire collection. The six large organdy hangings float in the middle spreading gossamer wings to the circulating guests.

Openings are fragile, full of discreet caring friends, but not something I look forward to. I know what I feel is good and where I am going. Ceremonies on the way are the occasional campfire to warm my hands.

Washington, Fall 1977

The commercial element of my work is a necessary adjunct. I find that galleries take forty to fifty percent of the sale price. I do not think that is my route yet.

I have talked with Grace Borgenicht in New York this week. She feels that I am getting better prices for my works than she could. The art agents are just not ready to deal in tapestries except, perhaps, Modern Masters in New York which handles cartoons by the most famous artists with no understanding of embroidered tapestries as they are one of a kind.

I am building a reputation, but my direction is always to do museum quality and show only in museums, not commercial galleries. I drive myself relentlessly for perfection by steady dedication to my art.

By cutting off the gallery route I know I limit my audience. If my hangings were suddenly to become available for $2,000 apiece we would probably sell out and my studio would be left empty. But I am interested in money only for the materials to do more work. No commercial gallery can operate with artists who have that point of view. Mrs. Borgenicht was gracious, available and wise. We understand each other and her sensible business approach clarifies my position. I am grateful to her.

Washington, Fall 1977

Today, October 18th, my show opens at the Virginia Museum of Fine Arts in Richmond. I drive down alone in the early morning, concerned and apprehensive. It is a fine museum with curvaceous opulence, not only in the serpentine walks, but also its fountains and its stupendous collection of Faberge and Dali jewels.

My apprehension stems from their total unwillingness to allow me any say whatsoever in the hanging of the show. Almost as disturbing is the sharing of the adjoining gallery with Duane Hansen, the Florida realist sculptor of human figures. They are life sized, with all their warts, fleshy wrinkles and vulgarity. This Madame Tussaud plastic exhibit makes my art the delicate sister standing next to her two-headed brother. Under these circumstances I feel that I have a greater prospect for longevity!

As I feared all thirty-two tapestries have been hung mopsy-topsy on the walls of the one gallery allotted to me. Three pre-Columbian pieces nudge the fragile *Orb Web*, teeter above *Nest*. The greatest travesty is *Surge*. Its black and white checks nudge *Wave* as though to swallow it. I feel as if I am reciting a nature poem while a brass band plays fortissimo.

Peter Mooz, the director, rushes through life hitting the high spots. In my case he has nervously hung my work like a new neighbor hangs her first wash, eyeing the adjoining windows for approval. He uses the word "nice" so frequently for my tapestries that I feel numb and empty. I am sure his honest evaluation would be less inspiring but still, like a dog with a bone that has some flavor, he gives my work a nudge now and then.

My lecture, "Bayetage—A New Art Medium," is well attended and enthusiastically received. Maybe one hundred and twenty-five came, both men and women; one engraver, some needlepoint people naturally, and friends of friends. My lecture shows needle and collage work as fine art. I trace its heritage from the Paracas caverns of pre-Christian Peru to its place in modern art in a mobile society. I tell them that *bayetage* provides an important new adjunct to art because of its greater ability to capture through its texture, folds and embroidery such subject matter as rocks, waves, trees or even clams.

Many bought my Bowdoin catalogue, which has captured as closely as possible the textures and colors of the actual work. From my catalogue, which I mailed to all the owners of my larger works, I have received wonderful letters from David Rockefeller, William Clements and Arthur Schultz as well as many requests from unknowns in Paris, Madrid and Canada. Today a letter from the Mordo Gallery has come expressing a desire to see me next spring in Madrid.

The day on the whole has been more positive than negative, but in the future I must have a hand, as I did at Bowdoin, in the hanging and final display of a major show. Each experience teaches me something.

Washington, Winter 1978

Richard Marcus from Neiman Marcus, Dallas, stops to see me. I do not know what will come of it. He is interested in work for new stores in California and Texas. I remember him as a bright-eyed young man with heavy black hair. He is now considerably more corporate in appearance but has a gentle manner. He stays for a good visit. Rick is home and comes to join us. Richard climbs the flight to my studio, enjoying the organdy *Dandelion* in my bay window and only shows the tension of his work in gulping like a Swedish schnapps the cider I offer. I have great respect for Neiman Marcus. Everyone who comes in contact with them receives, I feel, the same gracious welcome and high standards. I may be somebody or nobody but I will never know my badge by any sign from them.

Washington, Spring 1978

Winter this year has been a long period of walking artistic sand dunes in shifting wind. I feel no progress and great energy expended in futility. There are senseless interruptions and most of them I must resolve. Everyone wants to see my studio and would gladly allow me to unroll my acres of art, crawling over the hangings and leaving me exhausted and wrung out. I am resentful of even good friends who intrude on my mornings. It is a great dilemma for me as basically I am loving and gregarious.

Planning my trip to Europe is also time-consuming. I plan to visit six countries and each needs letters and arrangements. And co-ordination with the U.S. Information Agency which is facilitating the trip (although not financially). Starting in Madrid where I will see Juana Mordo in the hopes that her gallery will become my first European agent, I will move on to Zurich, Hamburg, Stockholm, Amsterdam and London.

In each country I expect to see modern tapestries and consult with curators and directors. There may be business sessions with organdy makers in the village of St. Gallen and with the International Wool Secretariat in London. With the assistance of USIA, I hope to lecture in at least three countries about my art form, taking slides and examples of my work. I anticipate that my work will measure up or even excel, but I may find that I am far behind European tapestry artists. Either way I feel my trip will be successful because there is much I can learn.

Seattle, Spring 1978

I am airborne again. This time as far almost in the westerly direction—to Seattle—to open my show at the Seattle Art Museum in Volunteer Park. There is less tension moving within the boundaries of one's own land. It helps explain for me also the expansive, even profligate personality of the American—especially the younger generations who are able to commute and live a life of two cities. Our land has solidarity—width and riches for the having. I understand it better for my travels abroad.

I particularly look forward to this trip because the archipelago of Seattle is so like Maine. I will have an affinity for its people as well as its place. People who like trees and birds and bright water are apt to like each other.

The atmosphere of Washington state is the clear air of my childhood. Faces are fresh and cheerful. The ride to Bremerton gives a clue to the beauty of Puget Sound. Flowers in May are in profusion, their colors seem sharper. The dust from the pines floats like a soft carpet across pruned gardens as well as wild spaces.

I drive by taxi directly to the Museum in Volunteer Park to deliver three tapestries that have been with me in Europe and to see how my show is being "hung." The Seattle Museum is art nouveau in every detail:—the entrance grill with its stylized chrome fretwork, the central hall with flights of stairs leading to a large center patio, more flights to left and right climbing to major galleries. The Seattle show has twenty-one pieces, cohesive, clear statements, but not as subtle and gifted as I would like; I always see ways to change and develop my style.

My tapestries are in a gallery visible from the entrance. Litter is everywhere. The walls holding my tapestries are full of nail holes and the abuse of title cards make a major distraction. "The head preparator"—a title for an Indian prince at least—is an agreeable, sensitive man, full of inexperience. The tapestries are hung although the lights are totally inadequate, but the organdy tapestries, instead of floating clean and starched are limp against the wall.

Now I've rearranged them into a central rectangle, two on either side and one at each end. The entrances at the far end of the gallery to the sitting room (dedicated "in perpetuity" to the Colonial Dames) are another distracting element. They apparently must not be obscured so we have tentatively hung two small organdy hangings—*Sand Dollar* and *Mussel*—across half the apertures. Everything seems a compromise: no platform under the central hangings (although now that the show has opened they have finally agreed to do so), insufficient light, no invitations to regular members for my opening, no sense that the tapestries either glisten or enchant. Everyone is cordial and I am grateful for their slightest help. I need to learn to be more assertive but doubt that I shall be; it is so difficult to move out beyond the years of accommodation.

Openings and the merciless detail of a show are counterproductive. There is an empty feeling that work does not measure up, that ladies with large handbags looped across their abdomens are my only supporters, that somehow I am middle-American, middle-aged, and middle-minded. I want life to be climbing mountains, to clear snow-melted lakes and not rods, poles and the paraphernalia of art. I am more and more impatient with the trappings of art but I realize the need to conform and to reach out for exhibits in order to see my work hung and give it my own appraisal.

The day of my lecture at the museum, the sun is bright in the park and the bongo drums are beating at an impromptu gathering of blacks at the end of the glade. I have lain on the grass an hour or two, looking up through the branches of a cedar of Lebanon. Willis Woods, the director, a gentle man in a tall western frame, introduces me. There are a few faces spotted around the auditorium. I begin but cannot catch the essence or proceed with facility. I am there but I am also out in the park. The slides pull my thoughts together and soon it is all over. A few questions; a sense of having done poorly when I wanted to be at my best. An audience is important. For the first time I developed no rapport. I see two women with their eyes closed before I have said six sentences. Perhaps that is why speakers look over their heads. Ho hum—I think as though I am Winnie the Pooh—"Ho hum. What am I doing here?" I want to be back in my studio, creating work that will sing even in a half-lighted room up two flights of stairs with dirty walls. I want to be beyond laborious, hand-written invitations to people who don't come. Tomorrow I go into the country and cleanse my spirit. I spend my last day walking in the Japanese garden of the arboretum. I revel in directing my own life, in being free in the best sense, to paint my own banner of living. So few my age have this opportunity. It is a product of work, work, work—and nerve. I read that on the plane. It was said by Georgia O'Keeffe. It is not talent alone. How lucky I am to have had health, work and courage all in good measure!

Boothbay Harbor, Spring 1978

Seattle is continuing my show for another month, to July 15th, because of interest and praise. I wonder if that is good or bad. I know many artists, the Motherwells, de Koonings, had originality but also skillful agents who helped them leap the barriers. *El publico* helps them. Their response is genuine and pleasing. Willis Woods, the director at Seattle, has written me so warmly I want to believe my work has merit even when I feel I will do better. The critics like my exhibit. I don't need their good wishes to continue but I don't reject them. I know I will improve. There is so much more I want to say.

Washington, Fall 1978

I am back in the city, my cheeks still rough from summer salt, my eyes bruised by the change. A whole new exhibit of thirty-eight tapestries now must be hung at the Textile Museum. Each museum has its own personality, charm and pitfalls. Hanging shows is hard work.

The Textile offers completely different problems. They have insisted from the beginning that I am to hang the show. I am just discovering how literal this is! I have only one assistant, a legend by the name of Barnes, surely seventy or close to it, whose wife is to be operated on for cataracts this week. He is leaving for two days and I am left alone to hang a major exhibit in the only textile museum in the whole United States. I think a book or at least a candid article called "The Museum Saga" would be appropriate. From the gallery in Scottsdale so many years ago where the "hangers" literally walked on my textiles spread on the floor to the white-gloved "preparator" in Seattle, I have had a whole rainbow of experiences. They require a core of patience, insistence, hard work, cajoling and doing it myself to shame them into cooperation. Most viewers, in fact all, who have found me laboring with ironing board and pail (for light hangings easily wrinkle in transit), or pushing nails into baseboard frames, teetering on ladders, think I am a paid employee, a female curator of uncertain ability. I flatly have none of the attributes of *l'artiste*. What delights me is the excitement and awe they show for my work. They are often transported, spending long quiet moments absorbing the work and occasionally saying shyly to me, "Do you know the artist? Have you met her? Isn't it beautiful!"

I am so humbled by the happiness I see in their faces as they move past the floating hangings and stand, as I have so often stood in nature, absorbed by the beauty of the scene. A gift has been given and I drive home jauntily each time from the museum thinking where did this all come from. And there is still so much I have to say.

Kilmarnock, Virginia, Fall 1978

A trip to Kilmarnock, Virginia, to lecture at the Art League at the Lancaster Women's Club, an evening gala for both men and ladies, is another experience; joyful, interesting, comical.

Tidewater country is flat. Flat as paper. Flat as Chinese noses. Flat as day-old beer. But fall leaves, the lacy edge the Chesapeake and a young eagle perching on the barren walnut tree beside our door are rare rewards. We walk to the pier to watch the tiny stinger jellyfish swim in indolent patterns everywhere, daring us to join them. Walking through the woods, I stop, transported by an exotic lemon-colored spider lifting his delicate, graceful legs to spin a web; the greatest of weavers, certainly the best in Tidewater country. His gleaming black, sophisticated embroidery is secured by seventy threads or more from edge to center to a far off branch and to a leaning weed stalk. He senses our presence and craftily climbs beneath a leaf to hide. The low sun glorifies his work. I visit his fragile home and lair at every hour of the day to catch different aspects of his intricate web as the sun spins out another day.

My lecture audience is varied, somewhat knowledgeable about art, receptive, conservative. I had thought to talk about the creative philosophy. Instead, I drew them as best I could into my own web of enthusiasm by careful examples, relating tapestry to art study, the need for the same artistic standards, and specific moments of inspiration. I have not yet become tired of sharing the beginnings and progression of my work, but I do see that these transitory periods for a lecture consume time. On the other hand, when I weigh that time against the view of the eaglet and spider's web I have received good measure.

Eaglet and Spider

Spin through the lodgepole country
down the straight macadam rivers
of brassy flat tide water land,
I followed the red line to cove
and cottage, turned the key, read
about the water heater, furnace gauge
where to find my bed. Throw down
my bags, light with necessity
and one outfit and fled into
the woods to see what gifts await.

The Chesapeake, profligate as a mother
hen with chicks running in all
directions, spreads wings to cover
the landscape. The Tappahannocks
and the Rappahannocks shared these
shores, feasting on the oyster, shrimp
and fish. They hewed the loblolly
for fire and frame, simple living
without coffee-master, scented soap
and polyester puffs; Man seems only
recently to have chosen to retire his
long present bones to clog these shores
        building one-story dreams

of ultimate comfort, close to martinis
and a golf course, a telephone
away from the best doctor and
undertaker. Into this stagnant
ruin about the tidal bay the eagle
still gives flight. Young birdlet,
large as a fox collar, perches jauntily
on a barren walnut tree unable
to hide one inch of tweedy brown
and white tipped feather. His head
touseled like an Afro, he waits
a field mouse. Slanting into
the woods before my fieldglass eyes,
he knows the spider's web I cannot
see and shifts his course, tucking
great wings between alder and pine
graceful as a folding and unfolding
fan. I stalk him, marveling,
his anachronistic presence in
this bedroom of flagging minds and
disappearing forests. The spider is
by his own design as fleeting
as the eagle. Only the sun
gives me an inkling of the shape
of corridor and room. Labyrinth
of silk tied by invisible knot
to weed and tree. He climbs
the ladder, curls beneath
a leaf, dismissing me.

Texas, Summer 1978

Texas is nearly as many hours by air and as many miles by
thought as London. The Texas currency is harder than the pound, the
dry earth rich as gold dust and the people carry their pearl-handled
pride in their pockets, smiling all the while. There is a physical opulence to their personalities, contrasting with the treeless level skyline
and the buff earth. Mental stimulation is predicated in terms of tech-
nical achievement, dollar's strength and a deep seven-minute frosting

of open-hearted cordiality. Everyone is addressed by his first name. At Neiman Marcus, where I have come to do an inaugural show for their thirteenth store—in Prestonwood—only Mr. Stanley Marcus, president emeritus—has the title of Mr. Stanley. Richard Marcus is simply Richard. I am immediately Nancy to everyone. But the courtesy paid me as an expression of my achievement is as wide as the oil slick rolling in from Mexico along the Gulf coast. My tapestries are an invasion from the foreign land of Maine.

Although I do not ordinarily show in galleries or stores I return to Neiman Marcus because they were my first public forum. I came here in 1970 with a paper shopping bag filled with my early pre-Columbian tapestries and pillows and bags made by the girls in the school I had founded in Mexico. I was sent upstairs at once to see the vice president. It all seemed so easy and natural. For them I did stoneware and even the broken pieces sold like shards from the mysterious past.

There is a special sense of belonging to a bright accomplished family when you work with the Marcus team. Yet hanging these tapestries has again proven to be a test of patience and will. The chief decorator does not feel I should use any of the windows for the organdy hangings. Currently they line the walls like a drab clothesline, hiding behind the double row of salivating shoppers waiting for lunch in the NM restaurant; black bread with raisins, salads with kiwi fruits and other exotica and walls of spathiphyllum bursting roofward laden with spatulate flowers.

The high chief decorator and I have engaged in a battle of wits. He feels my large organdy hanging *Dandelion* would be too conspicuous in the restaurant window and, above all, would appear awkward from the outside. My conviction is that nothing is worth showing unless properly hung. I do not believe in shouting or even raising my voice; I do believe in perfection. I am here to hang my work to maximum advantage, to glorify the NM name, to persevere with New England tenacity.

I walk down the escalator, seek the guard with the keys and am soon outside the new store—ready to open in an hour! I see the restaurant window is made of tinted glass; no one can see in! Back I rush, stumbling hastily up the magic carpet of the escalator, bursting with courage. Hoorah! The organdy hanging goes up. Monday, more will be hung.

The salesgirls are all thrilled. NM still maintains the old system of percentage earning. Some of the skilled, older sales personnel, who know their clientele, will earn as much as $50,000 a year! They all see the potential of a product that sells for $350–$500; the commission it offers. We part with handshakes of accomplishment.

My last day; I visit the beautiful collection of Spanish painting at S.M.U. There is an early cubist Picasso on a rose brocade wall that haunts me. The Spanish dignity and pride is everywhere present. I walk with the curator, uninterested when I ask about twentieth-century art and confide I have friends who have the largest contemporary collection in the United States. He doesn't want their address. He has found his special mat before the hearth of the Spanish past and although the flame and heat are only what escape from the olive pits in the brazier, he is content.

Returning to Maine is a visual relief. The cool green rolls in on every side, sun slanting through the leaves, glistening on the water. Even with a return to the beauty I know and treasure there is a letdown. I am no longer the professional, admired and entertained. Suddenly, I am a housewife with guests who have already come. There are needs to fill on every level. Bob is on the tennis court. I see the garbage can, a stack of mail, and no one to greet me or share the first moment. The instant of arrival is so precious.

Housewifery and Art

Like
- a royal guardsman on parade with a Pekingese
  nipping his heels
- eating caramels with braces on your teeth
- Niagara without Houdini
- sailing into the wind
- broken rubber bands
- a kite with sinker
- too much to eat
- a reversed escalator
- love with a broken rib
- mussels with barnacles
- eating a sandwich through a plastic bag
- a five mile hike on your knees
- eternal snows

Norton, Massachusetts, Fall 1979

Tuesday, I drive the long miles from Maine to Wheaton College. A small exhibit combining twelve of my tapestries with eight of Amy Gray's, my student for this summer, is opening. The Watson Art Gallery given by Nancy Watson (IBM) has limitations. The ceiling is scarcely nine feet high, the room is full of folding doors so that only my large horizontal tapestries are appropriate. The show is well hung; entirely monochromatic except for two early tapestries of Amy's. She has grown in color perception and in dealing with composition these months together.

Alice Emerson, president of Wheaton, lives in a wedding-cake house. Past the picket fence, white as alabaster, are tall pines and a walk leading into a spacious hall that glides with the eye back to a shaded lawn of apple trees and bursting flower borders.

I take my white grape tingling with ice and stand alone on the screened porch capturing the light on the zinnias, the faint red on polished green fruit. I can be alone in nature in a sea of tranquility while the guests rise and swell behind me.

Amy looks exuberant. Fresh and peach-polished in her flowered bertha dress and amber rose corsage. She is an old fashioned girl. This is her moment of triumph and all her family—parents, blond sisters, her cozy grandparents—are about her.

Wistfully I wish I might have claimed an extra plate at the buffet for my mother and I know without rancor that there is more than art and our joint achievement being celebrated here. The Board of Trustees is the lord high executioner at any campus. I can easily afford the generosity of singing the chorus, "Defer, defer to the High Executioner." It amuses me as the guests, the art department, bring their words of incense and myrrh. Art is being used. I accept that but regret the lost hours.

Chicago, Fall 1979

Years ago I traveled to Chicago to meet my own true love. We had been separated for eighteen months of a Pacific war bursting like boils from one atoll to another until the word "Pacific" became a cruel taunt. The holocaust over, Bob took the train from San Francisco and I from Boston to meet him here. Even for people whose knowledge of each other held such deep understanding it was a strange time.

Bob had fought on Iwo Jima and saw so many maimed and killed. He knew the gut terror of strafing bombs with a thousand feet of beachhead. My own adventure had been bearing a first child alone. Mine had a fulfillment, his futility.

This time we are here to share the beautiful fall days with friends, to enjoy the museums and concert hall. I visit Dr. John Neff at the Museum of Contemporary Art to arrange a show for 1984. We had met before in Detroit, three years ago. Each of us will remember because he told me jubilantly that he had a brand new daughter. I liked his humanity. He liked my tapestries, using the fateful word so hated by twentieth-century critics, "Beautiful!"

Our second meeting is a felicitous extension of the first. We are now friends. He has seen my catalogue. He is willing to save me a space in 1984 and I will return in 1982 to show him my work. I plan to do the same in several other cities. His secretary intervenes. I am a boring, older lady taking up Dr. Neff's time. John politely and explicitly makes it apparent we are enjoying our visit together. He plans a major exhibit on advertising. That brings us to Uncle Bruce Barton and my friend, Ray Rubicam. It is fascinating how our interests crisscross.

From the Museum of Contemporary Art I dash to the Art Institute where I have already left my bag bulging with two large tapestries. I have an appointment to see Christa Mayer Thurman, curator of the textile division. I know her only through distinguished catalogues she has produced and am eager to meet her. I have reasoned that in such a large museum the director is a business and public relations man and that I should head for my own department, textiles.

Christa Mayer Thurman is restrained, attractive. I unroll my tapestries along two large white tables and watch as she quietly and delicately touches them. There is no conversation. She examines them with candor and determination, then asks "Are they for sale?"

The question catches me like a battering ram against a fragile structure. I collect my composure despite racing pulse. I answer quietly "They could be."

"How much is this one?"

In ten seconds I think of my tapestry *Elements* conceived in a long summer of rowing to and from my island. I think of the walks across the fields of wild flowers, past the empty cottages to the rocks, the veins of quartz and the grooving granite patterns etched by sea water that are my inspiration. What price does this tapestry carry in my heart? I answer honestly, knowing where it belongs. This is a home for rare art and I am overwhelmed to be chosen. Tomorrow a board that meets semi-annually will convene to choose acquisitions. Christa says softly, her poise unchanging, "Your work is very beautiful."

I want to laugh and weep; laugh at the surprise of a sharing soul, cry for the mystery of a gift that is mine. I ask simply because I cannot quite believe, "Do you do this often? Buy a tapestry without knowing the artist? There are people I can suggest you speak to who know me."

"That isn't necessary. We know. We rarely buy a work so unexpectedly, but occasionally. . ."

I return back down the long corridors past the twentieth-century names we all know as thoroughly as Mother Goose rhymes: Oldenberg, Diebenkorn, Still, Davis. They are all there. I am not one of them because I am a woman and a maker of tapestries. It is as though I speak Guarani. Even in tapestries not many speak my language. But today two wise, knowing leaders of art in a single day have touched me with their wand. I cannot tell anyone until the committee has decided. I think suddenly of one of my sons who needs success more than I do and pray that he be chosen, not me. I have never been able to ask for myself and so in the end it is even a little bittersweet when I learn that my tapestry is chosen. I feel saddened by my whirling good fortune when others of equal talent fail. The exhilaration is May wine and rue.

The same son calls unselfishly to share my joy. All my family is generous. They believe I can do anything. That often stretches me to the brink. I feel the same for them. With all of us first is love.

New York, Winter 1980

What better way to start the New Year than to visit the pinnacle of art collections, the Metropolitan Museum of Art of New York. It occurs to me to stop here on my way to M.I.T. in Boston. I had made a firm appointment with Jean Mailey, a comfortable, unpretentious lady and curator of the magnificent textile department's great collection, to see if the Metropolitan would like to acquire one of mine. She greeted me at the south entrance where son Bradford had brought me with three large bags of tapestries.

Jean Mailey's attitude is so solid and sympathetic that not even a mouse would scuttle from her. She seemed genuinely enthusiastic about the tapestries but, alas, no money. The associate curator of contemporary painting, Lowery Sims, a widely smiling, black woman both graceful and positive, comes to look. I feel they would love a tapestry as a gift but I cannot play favorites, giving to some museums and not to others.

Jean Mailey's favorite among the tapestries is *Fog Columns*. I have with me *Aqua Lapis VIII* ten feet by eight, *Elements II* in brown and red, *Rock Lichen* and *Borealis*. But she says wistfully, "Of course, this museum will want one of the grander pieces. That seems to be policy." Speaking curiously like Alice when the Mad Hatter seems most overbearing.

The humor of it all is to think I can now walk with confidence into the royal circle of museums and feel no uncertainty or torture.

Cambridge, Winter 1980

Today I want to be accurate and wise and hope the right choices will surface. I am on my way to the house of M.I.T.'s president—111 Memorial Drive. Flow gently sweet Charles before these great doors!

The rooms *chez le president* are impressive:—a great center hall in dark paneling, a long dining room to the right and a reception room to the left, each room lapped and cosseted on the east by the Charles River. With two men with tall ladders, two decorators, an administrator, a housekeeper, an architect from the M.I.T. department and Priscilla Gray all gathered, I feel a bit like Houdini, ready to roll my barrel over Niagara with me inside! Here goes—up against the dark walls, first one and then four pieces in lively succession against the mellow surface of the reception room. All of them looked well there. My new family will make the grade. My big children are men casting their own shadows, and these new fledglings have power in their wings. Tapestries that have been held lovingly in my arms hour after hour and received my fingertouch with caress and care are now my family. This ultimate extension of myself is exhilarating, the development, the patience come easily.

San Francisco, Spring 1980

Bob has accompanied me to my meeting with Henry Hopkins, the director of the Museum of Modern Art of San Francisco. With his assurance and grace I am greatly enhanced. Mr. Hopkins meets with us first professionally and then as a friend. After the initial discussion about a show for 1984 I suggest the collection will probably contain at least twenty works, most of them organic forms. He is interested in my long-range plan and voices his wish that other artists would plan so far ahead. His large white sheets of projected shows stretch like a shopping list along one wall of the conference room. Nearly every space is already assigned as far as 1982. It astonishes me that other artists do not understand how museum shows unfold. In the ten years I have been involved in them it has always been this way. Hopkins says many excellent exhibits must be turned down because of earlier commitments of a museum.

My visit should preclude this. We discuss fiber art. The San Francisco Museum of Modern Art has never had a fiber show although he plans to have in 1982, a group exhibit now being organized in New York. Hopkins says some tapestry artists are thinking in terms of fine arts and others prefer to associate with the crafts. He notes that especially here in California the craft association is very strong.

Washington, Spring 1980

David Yerkes, the architect, called me in California to come to Washington as soon as possible. Time, Inc., has leased a suite of rooms in the Hay Adams Hotel. I am asked to present a tapestry or two for consideration. The corporate world is not my first choice for I see clearly that decorators move in to display their own banners that subsequent decorators will destroy. But now we are here together in the unfinished room. The air conditioner gapes with a sneer along one wall. Boards and plaster are looped around the unfinished area, all of it unimportant because the view is incredible.

As I step over a pile of lumber I look straight across the greensward of Lafayette Square to the White House. I see only sheltering trees and the foundation and pillars as though we are neighbors. No city exists. Who discovered this suite? I am fascinated that such privacy and proximity are possible.

From the east windows the gold dome of St. John's looms in opulent grace. Two extraordinary and symbolic views. The north wall is for a tapestry. Seventeen feet long and eight and a half high. What can complete this circle of presidential elegance seen through towering trees and the spire of colonial Christian faith? Does the tapestry need to be a third statement of strength or should it be a self-contained world of its own? I favor the latter; something that suggests reflectiveness and simplicity.

In my studio I review a list of tapestries, discarding all the verticals. Five titles surface: *Spruce Fall, Surge I, Epiphyte, Salt Veil* and *Salt Wash*. I choose to show five although I know *Spruce Fall* with its strong arrow of color is wrong. It will allow variety and choice.

I carry three heavy tapestries down from my attic studio and retrieve two more from Security Storage. I cram the first three in their limp plastic bags into a black limousine. At the hotel, workers in paint-stained overalls drag them to the sixth floor to be hoisted up like wet laundry. The effect is atrocious. How can I show tapestries with style here? Paint rags litter the floor. Three barrels full of fragmented plaster sit below the edge of windows framing St. John's gold dome. I have placed sheets over the dust and removed my shoes, but the workers blunder carelessly onto the sheets, hauling the tapestries one at a time up tall ladders at either end of the seventeen feet. Inevitably the heavy hangings sag in the middle like an errant hemline. I sense "pure art," even a work that has taken months to fashion, may not appear like much in this debris. An expensive chair has more merit because it can be sat upon. It has practical function. To complete the circle of visual beauty from White House to church to nature may be too long a trip.

From the hotel we proceed in two cars to my cool Georgetown home. It is a country house in the city. It is a house that smiles. Two of my large tapestries of the sea hang in the living room, one on the walls, another in front of the Victorian bay window. I show Mr. Steele, Time's vice president, *Salt Veil*. The pale wool with tracery of linear yarns and appliqué of organdy is a restrained white on white. Mrs. Steele, sensitive and quiet, brightens. They both respond to the delicacy and nuance. They mention the quality of purity and speak of weddings, a strange coincidence because of my poem written for *Salt Veil*.

The last adventure is up three flights, holding the polished turn of mahogany rail, to my studio. *Surge I,* the gray squared Irish wool study of strong sea motion, is my last suggestion. People like to visit my studio. They seek it like a mysterious hiding place. Although the shelves are covered with shrouds for the summer there is a sense of discovery, of membership in a secret society as they cross my studio threshold.

Perhaps some visitors capture my lift and exuberance as I open the door to my attic workshop. It has five windows facing east, south and west that catch the light and delineate the progression of each day. I see west and south to chimneys constructed at the time of the American Revolution. Gables and peaks lift like a mountain range to touch the few remaining elms.

My ceiling slopes in, pressed beneath a mansard roof. It offers few spaces to tapestries. Two by four uprights stand in the center of this square, naked and unplastered like thin saplings. Yet I can use them to hoist work in progress and see a vertical view that is so important, so different from seeing the pull of wool across a tabletop.

As my visitors move from one wall to another to see *Surge* and *Rock Lichen* and on the small wall near my narrow closet *Wood Lichen,* they step quietly, thoughtfully. There is the atmosphere of a museum or of a baby sleeping. My throat is dry. I feel vulnerable to their gaze.

And then they are gone. I am surrounded by lumpy mounds of tapestries to be rolled and tissued and carried back up the long flights, around and around the tall, narrow staircase to my studio. A great tiredness overwhelms me. I fold and roll mechanically, feeling somehow I have failed to communicate what I want to say.

Time, Inc., will decide in a faraway office in New York if I am worthy. Will they ever know my exuberance on the beach in Seabrook, South Carolina, running the miles of untouched shore, touching my hands to the wings of the plovers skimming the sea? Today as my visitors look at *Salt Veil* they could not know that my life "beautiful and bitter" is traced in a poem, but the intuitive thought touches me that perhaps I have reached them.

It is not just solitude but honesty that brings the creative moment to fruition. As I watched the Carolina sea curl in and knead the white lace and foam, sewing it with pearls, I thought of my relationship to it. I rediscovered myself. In a single, direct way I re-member fashioning my own veil from ancient family lace. Pulled by the same inevitability of tide and wind I chose marriage, accepted the flow of life, the assault of tide change and the parched times. Always the sea has refreshed me. Over the years I have learned "to seek the delicate change within my reach," the bowl of wildflowers rather than the long-stemmed roses.

Do these visitors know my depth of feeling? I hope, whether they choose a tapestry or not, that some message of delicacy and strength is shared.

Para acordame de porque he nacido	To remember why I was born
Vuelvo a Ti, mar	I return to you, Sea.

— Juan Ramón Jiménez

Washington, Spring 1980

Washington, after all these months away, seems somnolent. My green garden sways and shades like a heavenly umbrella. No one has been to prune or cosset. Weeds seem miraculously discreet. Mock or-ange and the Chinese dogwood (*Cornus kousa*) are the white of fresh snow against foliage. Today a wisp of a chipmunk has been chasing up and down the mulberry close to the dining room window. I have had gray and black squirrels and sleepy, pregnant raccoons in that tree, but never before a chipmunk.

What are people talking about?

Washington is in the eye of a sculptural maelstrom with works on the Mall, in the major museums and being discussed in panels. I would like to see the sculptors at work. Noguchi on the Mall with a hammer and chisel would confound me. Perhaps sculptors are bet-ter at works than other artists. Like the titles of paintings I find an obtuseness, a camouflage of words, neither one color nor another, certainly not black and white, whenever artists gather to talk about their work. We seem dyslexic, reading from right to left, when words are our pictures.

It makes me wonder why it is so much harder to pick the right word than the exact shade of color. Both require a mental agility and the color sequence suggests an even more complicated range because of intensity and value. I have missed the WORD on sculpture but go tomorrow in rubbers or straw hat to see the images. Ribbons of steel are everywhere. Abstract forms seem to be scribbles in metal; not the substance of a Maillol figure or the humor of David Smith. There are legions of Smith copyists without skill or subtlety. It is hard to evaluate a mangled arc of copper or aluminum when an elm tree spreads maternal branches above like a mother sheltering her ugly duckling. I cannot feel that in these visceral sculptures there are future swans.

Boothbay Harbor, Summer 1980

Today David Yerkes has called to say that Time, Inc., wishes to buy *Salt Veil*. I am totally surprised. Almost too much good fortune overwhelms me. *Salt Veil* will be an island of calm, a sensitive foil to the wide White House view and the sculptured dome of St. John's. I am pleased that they have found it worthy. I know the tapestry has unwound from deep inside me. I think I will do many other works as good or better.

New York, Fall 1980

The Metroliner ride—New York–Washington, is my time capsule. Each day in New York is like a week. After the careful telephone preparations it is fascinating to fit the squares and angles of a frenetic montage into the pattern of available hours. Today is rain and wind and weather, but the yellow lights of the waiting cabs glow for me outside each building. I treat myself to this rare extravagance wondering about the lives of the silent brooding drivers I meet one after another. Only one is a voluble Israeli who feels we should fight nearly everyone, the Iranians, the Italian and French Communists, et cetera. We are weaklings because we do not punch the fragile bag of peace or crush the hornet to our lips.

Mary Jane Lightbown, editor and architectural specialist, has worked for the Museum of Modern Art for a round season of years. We have met often and talked museums. She has urged me to come to MOMA. It seemed so far beyond me but then by chance we have met again passing through the revolving door of the East Wing of the National Gallery of Art in Washington. This time the invitation, always warm and friendly, made me understand I should grasp it or offend.

She arranged for me to meet Stewart Johnson, head curator of design at the Modern Art. We have talked this rainy day. He has seen slides of *Elements* (about to go to the Art Institute of Chicago). I have given him a catalogue and press clippings. His response is all positive. He, too, likes the idea of my four-year work plan and wishes me to return in 1982 to talk again. He finds from even the slides and pictures that the work I do is different and interesting. I am again gratified to see that at the top there seems to be more decisiveness. A silent hand surely is guiding me up the long slope past the gaping galleries and to the very heart of the great institutions of art. Mr. Johnson says of *Aqua Lapis*, "A great title! I like it!"

Stewart Johnson is urbane with a small gesture of sadness that scarcely touches him. His respectfulness and apparent acceptance of my age and sex warm me. They appear to be no subject for special consideration yea or nay. He has come to the Modern from Cooper Hewitt. I compliment him on that because I feel he will be more receptive to tapestries. He assures me he is anyway. I notice he seems to refer to my work as "hangings." I agree except to say that in Europe they call them tapestries. "Hangings are a product of the French Revolution." We laugh together.

Then to the Wool Bureau and a brief meeting with Thomas Haas, vice president for public relations and advertising. After four years of working together we are real friends as well as colleagues. A sense of ease and understanding make our projects a special satisfaction. Tom sees me as a good potential figure for the promotion of wool. He says the article about me in the *Washington Post* by Sarah Booth Conroy is the best publicity the Wool Bureau has ever had. "Phenomenal!" to use his word.

Right now, under their sponsorship, two tapestries are still traveling in South Africa. From Pretoria, Anna Viljoen has written that the *Tipi–Waterfall* is much talked about and was easy to erect from the instructions we included. She is sending catalogues of the entire show. Tom is pleased and promises future collaboration.

I lunch with a young friend. We talk about careers, hers in public relations, mine in art. There are so many messages I want to share. Sometimes I am appalled at the first person singular of living after thirty years of first person plural. I find no greater joy in shifting to the solitary "I." The "YOU" becomes each created and completed work.

Artists often speak of their paints as their "children." Each birth is an agony and exaltation. Each springs full measured, complete, findings its way into the world to face acceptance and rejection on its own. How close the parallels are in many ways. It explains my headlong absorption.

Washington, Spring 1981

How does it feel when the Metropolitan Museum of New York asks for one of your tapestries and comes to pick it up?

First, there is curried lamb and emerald broccoli and raspberries on sherbet with which to get acquainted. There is no time to think back to the beginning. When was it? Long before the narrow room in Bolivia, before the days of the 5 A.M. watercolors, before remembrance.

Instead, four of us are climbing the three long flights to my attic studio. The curator has a whirlwind of hair caught in a brooch that is plastic and popcorn and penny candy. She has an easy happiness and comes with a friend called Daisy.

And Bob to "hang," with no need for a step ladder, unrolling tissue and tubes. *Moon Web* and *Borealis*? Sorry, they have already been sold to Seattle and M.I.T. How about *Frontanella Web*? "Bob, dear, that's under the bed in your study." Up it comes, a rainbow of whites, lace, string and yarn on white wool. "Not right?" New works: *Declivity* and *Basalt*. That's more like it. Finally, folded on a trunk in the hall *Aqua Lapis VIII*, the introduction and original statement of *Flow of Inner Seeing*. Gray-blue to white like snow falling at daybreak, it has bold appliqué and yards of twisted yarn caught and knotted and embroidered. I remember many six o'clock mornings embracing that cold beautiful snow as it fell beneath my fingers and the steel of my needle. The silent flakes of discovery and patience and repetition. Each pull of yarn a footstep in snow nearly to my waist and then, as the thread caught and shaped, a footstep only knee-deep. Finally, the firm crust crackling under my feet, sustained by a thousand stitches.

The Metropolitan Museum! I sit by the limited glow of a single bulb in my studio and think of that great, gray edifice. I remember that I will be breathless if I try to run from one end of the building to the other. I remember that I am breathless with the fragile beauty of what I have seen there. The great wrought iron gates of Valladolid seem to swing open and I stand like a child scarcely believing. I feel small and wondering but comfortable in myself.

When we have climbed down from my studio and the curator and her friend have gone, carrying the photos of their selection, I go back to roll up the tapestries I have shown them. I am down on my knees among the tissue and plastic bags; a time for quiet.

I would like to celebrate this moment, fling myself out of my turret to dance. "Let's go to a disco! How about a red rose and a glass of wine?" Instead, four games of backgammon, a few salted almonds from a silver plated bowl and supper to make.

How does it feel to sew a tapestry for the Metropolitan? It feels everydayish and normal, also outrageously thrilling and even a little lonely. No one else can feel quite like I do, skipping on silk and riding the foam of the cascade from the top of the cliff. It is all against the current and yet as smooth as a lemon leaf. That's how it feels.

If I had gone to the disco, laughed and danced I would not have sat here in this soft circle of light from my lamp and written my thoughts.

New York, Spring 1981

Two days in New York. I have appointments at the Modern Art, the Metropolitan, the Wool Bureau Foundation, and a sheaf of papers to leave for the high priestess of the MacDowell Colony.

"Just drop them at the desk downstairs." Personally, I would want to see the shape and smile of anyone I chose to come for a month of solitude and work in the soft hills of New Hampshire. They only want slides of my work and letters as cold as February hands telling them what I do.

The MacDowell Colony is the least of my concerns. I flirt with it for two reasons. First to have closer contact with other creative writers, artists, sculptors. All my adult life I have had few art friends due to the isolation of my diplomatic life. I want to observe and see what goes on, if indeed anything does. Peers are important. I learned that at the Art Students League. I also want to be alone one whole month, fed and housed and left alone to see what I can do with it. Not to create tapestries but to draw and think ahead, to walk the fields and count the stairs alone.

The visit to MOMA is lumpy. Stewart Johnson, who saw me a year ago, suave and polite, somehow feels he has been trapped and that I have returned to talk about the show "he promised me." I reassure him that nothing has been sealed and that we proceed only at his command. Curiously, I find myself with the upper hand. I came only to show him where I am going in my work, to report on progress, to congratulate him on the slender volume about Eileen Grey that he has just published.

My slides come out in disarray. He shoves them into a machine, upside down, sideways. I should know better. I had not meant to show them, but like MacArthur, "I shall return." When he suggests a vague future date I say, "Stewart, I am sixty now." Said as a train conductor might shout, "Watch the tracks ahead."

The Metropolitan is a different adventure. Somehow, in an environment that deals largely with history, a mellow quality abounds. Jean Mailey, curator of textiles, asked for a tapestry the first time I came to see her in her narrow corner of this great museum. We have had a year's duet. Bob and I have dashed through the rain, splashed to our knees by Park Avenue traffic on our way to the Met. As we enter the museum, umbrellas lie about like the spring tulips, and two gazebos, complete with grass and benches, grace the majestic entrance hall.

Lowery comes in shaking her umbrella, her black hair parted down the middle and flying out like wings. She is smiling and warm. We hug each other in fresh greeting and she confides, "It is all set I think." That is it. Without a backward glance my large tapestry eight feet by ten feet, *Aqua Lapis VIII,* has moved from my studio into the arms of one of the greatest museums of the world. Like the Art Institute of Chicago, where I have shared the same experience, there is breadth of knowledge. Those who believe in themselves can believe in others.

Boothbay Harbor, Summer 1981

Tuesday I floated on a new wave that has lifted me with frightening exhilaration. The Portland Museum of Art has just laid the cornerstone for a large addition. Now the museum is in two handsome old colonial houses. By 1983 it will have a sweeping airy partner designed by I. M. Pei Associates. Tuesday I visit John Holverson, the director. The museum is closed because the renovations are so extensive. I ring the bell on a dusty colonial door and wait. I can see through the faintly tinted glass, the heavy white moldings and a long staircase climbing to the director's office. We sit together, John Holverson and I, in a puritan white office and talk. The Museum will be a jewel in a revitalized city. From the top levels the intricate tracery of Portland harbor and the coastal islands will be stretched outwards and beyond. This is the future cultural center of New England's three northern states: Vermont, New Hampshire, and Maine. Only Boston, Portland and San Francisco have such beautiful harbors. Only Portland and San Francisco have the promontories and the long view from the water's edge. The museum rides the crest.

As John and I talked I unfolded a small swatch of mohair fabric, handspun and handwoven, that has been woven for me in Swaziland. On the top of a mountain in the green velvet landscape of Southern Africa I saw the mist of clouds fold and ruffle among the hills and asked the weavers of mohair to catch those clouds and pull them through the loom.

I have the sample to share with John and we agree it is very beautiful—a tangible cloud one can hold in her hand.

They want for Portland a huge tapestry, twenty by twenty, to float in the light-filled great hall of the new museum. Something transparent with no wrong side. The piece suddenly emerges from an idea that started three years ago called *Nimbus*. From that beginning the creative germ has traveled with me to Africa where I found my weaver, and now the great hall at the Portland museum where it will hang. I feel the idea taking flesh and tingle with excitement. This is not the first time a design has taken shape and found its place. I believe in inevitability and fulfillment. There are still long hours of thought and longer months of work but I already know the motion and the quality of place.

For the first time a director of a fine museum has said, "We hope you will consider us." It has always been the other way around. His gentility is moving and gives me courage. It is important to move into a new piece with a sense of empathy, a happiness for challenge.

Here where Winslow Homer is enshrined and John Marin and Marsden Hartley are the deacons of the world of Maine, I too, will have a voice. I am not frightened but immensely grateful and full of joy.

Boston, Summer 1981

The Museum of Fine Arts in Boston has just opened its new west wing. Everyone refers to it as "the new I. M. Pei" wing. The east wing of this same famous architect is in Washington, D.C., the tiny oriental with the genius of imagination that has given him great buildings. How did he know that he could create such visions and clothe in steel and glass the air around us and the glorification of art?

In this new wing Morris Louis is splashed on the walls of the fresh galleries, his rivulets of color pouring on the canvas. I am struck by an oblong painting of his that is a burst of color with a dark shape, a rain cloud adjacent to the bright streamers. It is the foreboding depth of the cloud that holds me. The sheer audacity of the juxtaposition on a single canvas. Lewis speaks to me personally with his knowledge and confidence. Everything is intentional, cerebral in concept, sudden in accomplishment. That is the canvas among many large works that arrests me.

Paintings by Pissarro are also gathered like clusters of wildflowers in the new rooms and spread into the old corridors making a bouquet of the French countryside. Green is the color, in every shade and combination. As detailed as pincushions, often as buoyant and gypsy as spring, but nowhere the icy independence of Morris Louis.

While Bob wanders through a collection of Chinese bronzes and life-sized clay figures, recently excavated from ancient oriental tombs, I choose to stand in the vaulted hallway of the new wing and absorb its dimensions. It is a graceful capping of the sky under a barrel vault roof of glass reached by a floating staircase. A grand concourse leads to the upper galleries.

Here I can learn the patterns of the sun and the quality of light that will be similar, but thrice repeated in the new wing of the Portland Museum of Art. Another wing, a hydra-winged bird for the flight of I. M. Pei. With this new work there is an opportunity almost to touch the stairs, surpass anything I have imagined in a transparent tapestry for the new galleries in Portland.

The Portland museum, founded in 1908, was a gift from a donor with the unlikely name of Mrs. Lorenzo de Medici Sweat! In Maine it is the name Sweat, not Lorenzo de Medici, that is aristocratic. Old world culture and new world initiative. Now a mandarin Chinese architectural firm will add the finishing touch for another one hundred years.

In such varied company I feel totally at ease. From Boothbay Harbor to Bolivia and back. My great great grandfather, Moses Hemenway, who was pastor in Wells, Maine, for fifty years, might be amazed to see a tapestry instead of a religious tract bear his fine name. I like to imagine what might transpire three generations hence.

I am filled with the excitement of a new challenge, by far the largest tapestry I have yet tilted with, but an idea that has been gathering in my imagination for several years.

I am confident now that I can achieve whatever I promise, and what museums hope for. Hard work and imagination are spun tight together in my artistic center. Sometimes it is hard to show these qualities to a casual interviewer. A museum director who sees a slide does not catch the intricacy of the work; he sees only a flat outline and an average middle-aged woman.

Artists, like actors and actresses, are average people who frown and smile and shop for milk and eggs just like everyone. When the lights dim and the curtain rises we are conditioned to a state of awe. We are the suspended audience caught in the actor's web.

With art the electric connection, the curtain rising never occurs. Somewhere in a loft or an attic studio, or perhaps ignominiously in a basement, a work of art is conceived. It flowers quietly. There is no audience in a room with paint blotches or a shelf full of yarns.

Artists are supposed to be slightly seedy, not just because they are poor, but because they have no audience, no sense of self-importance. All their desire and creative drive flow from their minds and fingers into the object before them. It is an electric charge strong enough in some cases to illuminate a stage. But who looks at the electrician?

Louise Nevelson has taken to wearing eyelashes that dip like pine boughs, heavy with dew. I know a tapestry artist who dyes her hair the color of sumac blossom and wears extravagant clothes of black and purple, another who parades in capes and oddments, but most of us live totally unconscious of self. A few of us have someone who shares our world and whose presence says, "Stop and get acquainted."

Occasionally to keep me patched and presentable Bob takes me shopping. I loathe the wasted time, looking at limp racks of slacks and blouses—ten years ago I gave up wearing dresses—that is entirely too complicated. I submit to new blouses and a suit or two, searching always for pockets and comfort, suffering the lost hours in my studio or the time to walk the fields and woods.

Mother has left behind a whole stack of wide-brimmed hats that she wore when she rode, stately and erect, in her twenty-foot Surf Rider. Under a Mexican lace or a floating Panama her straight back and strong stem flowered to shade her blue eyes. Now I have her hats, all stacked like an open umbrella on my bedroom lamp. I plan to take two or three to Africa, as a way to say, "Here I am," "I am an artist" in a sense to not disappoint them by being so totally average. My hair still shines forth blond as I turn sixty. It seems wise to accentuate my own heritage.

Each of us has her own color and song and amid the handsome black people I will visit, I am meant to be white. I am easy with the idea. In Mexico I always referred to myself as *la gringa*. It was natural for the village people to know I accepted the appellation. There is no way I can suddenly be like them visually in Benin or Madagascar. Spiritually I have always been at ease pulling lobster traps, visiting with the Queen of Bulgaria and her daughter, or just curled up with a book at home. I don't plan to try disguises. I have one trick in my satchel, the agelessness of creativity.

Chicago, Fall 1981

Two short years have elapsed since I came to the Textile Division of the Art Institute of Chicago and laid my two tapestries on the tables for Christa Mayer Thurman to see. I came first just to make her acquaintance, inspired by her catalogue of church vestments which had far surpassed other textile catalogues I had seen.

Again I have stayed to learn and form a friendship and to grow from the knowledge and expertise that I find here. Christa has walked with me through the Fortuny show this morning. In a gray Gothic arcade are slender figures encased in a waterfall of pleats, the Delphos and Peplos of the Venetian artist. The pleats falling to touch the ground and circle the feet are spring water and color slipping over the female form in a delicate and sensual wholeness. Fortuny borrowed from the classic statutes of Greece but went on to add color in subtle hues of Venetian reds and ochres and black and gold. The intricate hand-painted velvet robes and yardage of cut velvet are works of art. The Art Institute has courage. It originates many distinguished shows. In textiles they have done only two living artists; Jan Groth and Claire Zeisler.

The prospect of being the third seems another wonder in a life of miracles. Christa says, when I ask for criticism, that my work is fine, that is has no faults. I feel that much of it can be improved. I accept her praise because she is straightforward and has integrity. She chose my first *Aqua Lapis* tapestry with no knowledge of me or my work. I can move not because of praise but because I have a sense of future direction. Christa in turn shares her independent spirit and her expertise without measure. She is a perfectionist prizing herself the least of all. The Fortuny show is a testimonial. A handwritten note to her from a distinguished Chicagoan says, "It is magnificent."

Chicago has been a watershed in my life. Here to my surprise I sold my first tapestry to a great museum. Today in Christa Thurman's office in this same museum I have stretched a white streamer with the shapes of my *Aqua Lapis* tapestries across her wide floor. With the light streaming through the high louvered windows, I lift my head straight at the light and beyond to infinity trusting and waiting for her verdict. I am ready to accept whatever she says.

Photographs of completed works are open on the small table in a large folio. There is a moment of peace in the protracted silence as she looks through my photographs.

Where am I and where am I going? I wait with my eyes upon the window "whence cometh my strength," feeling peaceful, relaxed.

The answer, thoughtful and quiet, is reassuring, clear in stating that Christa feels my work has merit. She says she would like us to do a show. The nagging image of hundreds of lady embroiderers storming her door and the need to support her choice to many is difficult. That must be resolved. Am I old enough for a retrospective? Can Chicago accept an artist from faraway Maine? Christa feels that merit is the only answer. I like her courage and acuity, and I am grateful for it. If we do this exhibition I would like to start here in Chicago because I know it will be perfect.

From the Art Institute I go to talk with John Neff, the director of the Museum of Contemporary Art in Chicago. He is already a special friend from Detroit and earlier visits to Chicago. I learn that he is the person who recommended that I go to Africa. A visit with him makes me feel full of ideas and enthusiastic about art at every level. I tell him honestly that perhaps the other museum wants to show my work. His generous response is just what I knew it would be. I think I will do a special show for him at the same time—maybe the tipis. We half agree on that and part with ease and reassurance that we will meet again and share ideas. Why should all this happen in Chicago, a place I hardly know?

Walking out into the street again I feel so full of excitement I want to do something outrageous, to say out loud to everyone on the sidewalk, "I love your city, all the new towers and the wide lake and the wide open eyes and minds here." At the corner I see that a very new store has opened, full of lush wools and some outrageous hats. That will be my badge of recognition. Like the red straw that I wore all through my African adventure, I need a new hat on my average head that says I am an individual and have a small importance. It is burgundy, soft as a rabbit's fur. Within my average flesh and bones leaps a flame. That is what I want to say. Through my tapestries the fire spreads and gains strength. The red hat is a sign. The hat is from Chicago and along with the memory will warm me all winter.

~ 6 ~

God Is My Song

So much is written about beauty. It begins essentially with nature, whether it is the human form or the smallest molecule. Nothing written quite reveals the optimism, mystery and transcendental perfection of searching nature for its messages.

I am learning in art to express only a small portion of what I behold. So much must be eliminated and only a fragment, expressed in essence, can reach my finished tapestry. The process of distillation reminds me of spring sugaring off in Vermont. I tap my tree of imagination and the sweet liquid fills my waiting pail, but it must be boiled down over and over again before an idea crystallizes. Each successive work is more demanding because I am always trying to surpass my previous tapestries in imagination and originality and skill.

A bivalve keeps its beauty no matter how much it eats. Its curved surface grows proportionately and its silhouette never varies, whereas humans pop and bulge like weak balloons. A tree missing branches has grandeur but we turn from the lost human limb in disgust and shame. Nature tears and mends and evolves and burnishes. I should like to have someday the sturdy uncompromising look of an ancient tree, to feel that the changes and shadows also have grown.

Solitude

Deep in the forest
the bow arms of the pine
strum to the wind. Birch
rise to puncture the sky,
cutting clean shapes.

Cross-country skiers flounce
and swerve across sloping
floor of the snow. A few
lift their eyes to the presence
of Bigelow, the massive white
dome, married everlasting
to the cone of ice.
The same royal couple I see
between the fingers of birch
as I lie in my bed.

I think of the Kennedy Center;
the bend and stretch of dancers
and the words and gesture
of plays. The sound of feet
on the gravel path, walking
beside the Potomac. Past
the columned cloak that holds
Lincoln. In these buildings
of powers, built from the core
of the forest and rock shelf,
there is no beat. Nothing to keep.
They are rattling names
of great men. That is all.

My blue and white garden,
with silken peony, in its
five-day glory, are speech
of the parlor. Seasons and seeds
sewn for garden clubs and my pride.
Grasses are clipped, never fruiting.

In the woods, as I move close
to the trunks, cutting least path,
trees sing the round of the forest.
I remember the curve of each bough,
watching their bark uncurl like
my flesh, accepting the mutilation.

Alone I share the deciduous living
both marble and bark bound.
Threading the paths of two forests, feel
the continuous sky holding
pillar of rock and of birch, as
I move, scarcely tracing the snow.

After gas rationing, abortion debates and women's rights there will still be trees shedding cadmium tresses, standing stark to pearl winter sky. There will be rain and sun and love. That is what I want to say and can in a lifetime reach so few.

A phrase from a Psalm that I want to remember is, "God is my strength and my song." I heard "salvation" before, but "song" is so much better for nature is God's song—our song—and our strength.

Mouse Island, Summer 1977

This is a beautiful day, wind-swept and open-armed. I am speechless with joy as I begin to drift into my work, not pushing but observing and tasting as I go. Mouse is my island for this summer and on a blue-blown day a secret world. The narrow cut paths to the beach through bayberry, alder and spruce, the raspberry fringe, the sheer wonder of this quiet place overwhelm me.

I remember so much about Mouse Island, watching with clear eyes as owners and visitors came and went, leaving their touring cars in the shanty barn next to my home and loping down to the Vagabond if you were Fosdicks and the Puff o' Wind if you were Huggins. Gurry Huggins needed only an H instead of a G to explain his intense forward motion. He was tweedy, distant, preoccupied, but Marian, pacing behind, always wore flat crepe-soled shoes and clothes cut from Girl Scout patterns. Dr. Harry Fosdick was jolly, his round face trimmed in wiry hair like a bayberry bush. Florence was our favorite because she noticed us. Her musical voice and shapeless felt hats made her as much a part of our world of fairy tales and tree houses as any adult could come. She had time.

Sometimes I watched through the rusting screen as guests and mounds of groceries were carried to the dock. It was a world of imagined splendor that I saw as one might through the glass of a favorite shop window. We swam to Mouse Island, rowed around it, watched the flag to give us the way of the wind for our sailboat, but rarely went ashore at Mouse Island.

Scrambling between the piano and cello, I played trios with my sister and David Huggins in the wide living room of their brown-shingled mansion. The fluted music stand we used still teeters like a heron in the barren house that Uncle Gurry built.

Over the years I discovered that the first surf scoter and the least sandpipers preferred the Mouse beach. Early and late, I headed into the cove in my rowboat to watch them. Occasional sand dollars that I could not find anywhere else lay below the tide. I came once to paint a spruce on the southern point, caught for life in the curve of the south wind.

Something about island living makes people secretive and self-sufficient. I feel it after only two summers here. My new friends are nesting yellow warblers and the fringe of sails ruffling in the harbor. I watch and think without taking part. Timelessness fills me as an island dweller. There are no contacts, abrasive or beautiful. The day circles back on itself like a line on the carapace on the beach calm. I am alone but never lonely.

Suddenly the last of my island friends is gone and I walk by myself on this beautiful island. I am full as from a feast moving along the grass-shaded paths feeling as young as ten—still barefoot in my one-piece swimsuit. All of my Mouse Island friends who move in a *son* and *lumière* stage behind the windows of the large empty houses are with me on the beach. They are never close, always removed as they were in life. None of them could have guessed that I would come along to polish their lost presence. But the single talent of brush and pen and needles I sit quiet and steady in the studio where so many words of guidance and love have been written.

Mouse Island, Summer 1979

What is a morning in my studio at Mouse Island? It is like today, a racing blue, fresh and untried.

I finish my bowl of hot cereal and swing out into the bay to row to the island. There is one lobsterman in a small whaler skirting the far shore. None of the corporate fishermen in their superchargers are about. The sun glows from the east, catching boats and low rocks at a full tide in drapery of silver. Seals and the great blue heron are hiding because it is August. The rickrack patterns of the crested cormorant slant across overhead, coming and going like secretaries in official haste. They always seem a flight of urgency, never the wheeling casual glide of the herring gull.

I have in my small skiff only the stark necessities. A new painter, unmatched oars, a large square of toweling to wipe dry the heavy dew on my rowing thwart and my quilted bag with fruit, a drawing pad and my camera.

In the six-thirty light I want to walk the rocks and make a record of the overlapping layers of granite that shelve down to the low tide edge in *mille-feuille*. I know Mouse Island now like the lines and curves of my own body. There are special rocks for beautiful cadmium lichen. One rock has patches of ovate green as tender as velvet; each year some new detail assumes importance. Now I see as sculpture in wool the composites of shelving and thrust. I have learned that the heavy winter seas change these shore patterns and that clusters of rock of special beauty to me that I thought would be there forever are suddenly gone.

The key to my square, gray studio with six windows to the sea is hidden beneath a stone. I open the door with anticipation and stand there for a moment. All the shades are up and the sea is hot with light. Quickly, while the island sleeps, I gather my camera and start along the path to the outer fringes of land near Burnt Island light. Dr. Fosdick, who built my studio, later had a more reclusive study away from the harbor-side on this narrow ledge. We understand each other in a new way. I wonder if I will know the last day that my foot will touch this island. Did he know? I think so. I want his courage.

But this new day is mine for five hours and I walk like an Indian, not breaking a twig. The door of the studio is slightly ajar and as I slip to the water's edge, I see innocent curls and the curve of the head, lumpy in a sleeping bag on the floor. Other island children curve in masses beyond. A sleep-out, an adventure away from the hearth. I reach the reefs with their curling edges in strong light.

On the way back, crossing the crescent of the beach, a tiny plover with his black tie stands his ground silently. At the edge of this beach are the granite and quartz of my first rock tapestry. I like to return here, and now, without thinking, I begin to whistle "I Lift Mine Eyes Unto the Hills." And then I stand in wonder. Remember, store, remember. Remember grain, angle, color, sweep of wind that has bent and sustained. Know footsteps as nothingness, only here between each tide. Even rocks will shift and hone in the sea.

Mouse Island, Summer 1979

What thoughts wash in as I sit at my art table in my island studio looking over the still, quiet bay? The gray light of this foggy summer hangs in tattered strips along the spruce, fishermen weaving their Maypole patterns, catching threads of fog, pulling free and rocking forward into the next pattern.

Last night Katherine Hepburn spoke on *60 Minutes* about old age. She leads me by only ten years. I learned much from her twenty-minute interview. She is courageous, wise, and forthright. I want to emulate her strength and wit. She is still involved. She spoke of the "gas chambers of America," the homes for old people, now an enormously lucrative business. She called them hideous and worse than murder. I told myself for the first time that probably I will end in one, not in resignation but learning ahead of time to accept the eventuality after a full life and possibly create even a small garden of pleasure on the ice-floe of old age.

Katherine Hepburn said last night she is not an actress or person of importance to her friends except she can mend a window, cook a meal and relate to life around her. This is reassuring. The creative process, whether the art of acting or of art itself, is a compartment of my life totally removed from daily living. I am reassured by her declaration for she has learned to live the two halves of her life. She lives in the house she has known as home since 1934. That is also a message of importance. This summer I have come to the same conclusion. I cannot start again in another spot. Often I think of moving further north to a wilder Maine, but I know I will not flourish in other soil. The roots are too tight around these rocks.

Washington, by contrast, is a stage. I have no deep feeling of belonging there. I quest for a winter home and hope to go to Oregon or northern California. I am counting on this winter to find a new spot of beauty that I can study and absorb the last long adventure of my life perhaps.

In my studio, I shift this day's discoveries. On my long flat table, I have already laid two lengths of alpaca, one gray, one shades of brown and white. They are two vertical rocks. With fine thread, I need to vein and surface them. One lifts over the other and sweeps at an angle. I tie them together visually with handspun mohair and lambs wool. The ideas pour into my consciousness like tide reaching a hidden pool. I must retreat and select.

Underneath my table is a stark cot stretched like a hide across its aluminum frame. I can just crawl in and lie flat if I twist my body and flatten my spine in one movement. With eyes closed to the still low sun I collect and sort. Turning my eyes away from the sun gives another series of impressions. Light and darkness are a counterpoint that carries new designs.

How will I hang these new angular tapestries? I am experimenting. Wood? Carved, or unseen, an armature, no more? Lucite, pristine and discrete? Foam flat sheets as rigid backing?

Mouse Island, Summer 1979

Boats are racing out of the harbor. My keen anticipation of a cruise on the Penobscot has come and gone in a day of storm. There will be another and another—if only in my mind. I will buy a chart and trace voyages along those granite shores. Even here in the harbor I know coves and trees and the woven lengths of rock that are unknown to others. Perhaps the infinity of the Penobscot is too much. The infinity of my own harbor and my island still beckons.

Yesterday I stood at the window of my studio watching a covey of myrtle warblers in the bayberry bushes. Just beyond the glass they gobbled seed, found nutrients along the branches, young and mature, some with a few dozen feathers, others seasoned travelers, all undisturbed by my presence.

Eliot Porter told me once that when he photographs the nests of birds on Great Spruce Head Island he allows patient hours of discovery simply sitting close to the nest. Like a giant mushroom, he shows no animus, no haste and soon the birds come to accept his presence. They go about their ritual without restraint.

This has been a fruitful summer. Besides the *Tipi–Waterfall* that has gone to Africa there are six *Aqua Lapis* hangings well advanced. I am designing new rock tapestries combining wood and wool.

The handwoven yardage for the *Flow of Inner Seeing* will not be ready until October. The weaving is fraught with difficulty; a rare problem for me as usually my relationships are splendid. The results so far are acceptable but undistinguished. I hope I can make a sweep of free rhythm. There is the taste of green persimmon in the weaving. I bend my head quietly asking for patience.

Mouse Island, Fall 1979

Rain, gray, sea-hazed. Another season is folded away. The tiny drawer where Dr. Fosdick kept his pens and pencils is emptied of needles, pins and sangria chalk. The faded yellow pillow from my cot beneath my worktable tucks into the corner bookshelf for the winter. I leave a small pile of sketchpads and my cup for drinking water. Already the heavy bags full of wools have gone ashore on the prow of my whaler brought to the ledge beneath my studio. Only a light roll of organdy and the drawings for the winter await me.

This has been a "rock" summer. Last year I sewed as ardently as Penelope completing the organdy tapestry *Jay* and *Salt Wash*. I have agonized over *Salt Wash* and finally seen it hung. I realize it is a bridge to the rock tapestries of this season.

Last year I drew a clam in its many clear poses—hinged, cracked, glowing white. This summer I have scarcely drawn, instead cutting and pinning furiously, ideas surfacing easily, faster than their freshness can be savored. I have reached a slope and climb full of fresh enthusiasm. I leave confident and eager.

Boothbay Harbor, Fall 1979

At last a studio! Searching the sharp coast, the classified real estate ads, talking with brokers, then finding the secret along the ledge, just east of our own cottage. Casually, I thought, as I rowed each early morning to Mouse, "the Kimball cottage is hidden by spruce, perched like a seagull, eyeing the wide expanse, even to the White Islands. That would be a perfect spot, but surely it will never be for sale."

And then I learned it is to be sold; the next frantic hours consumed with need, the fierce dollars, the agony of knowing that beauty has its own extravagant price. The view is a cliffhanger. The first night, knowing I have bought a ravishing front row seat to the world of Maine, a hurricane, followed by a north wind sends the clouds in a scarf dance across the path of the moon. I am frozen in the path of gold, it is so magnificent and clean. I feel caught in a great searchlight that will delve the depth of my creative drive. I will meet its measure.

Two tiny bedrooms and a bleak porch will all be thrown together to make a room twenty-five feet square with the sun and sea pouring over my shoulders. It is a blue and white world that lifts my spirit.

Long ago, twelve years back, I begged to add a small studio to my farmhouse. Mother refused because she did not want the field it stood in changed or reduced in any way. And then in capricious willfulness my brother burned the house, my Joan d'Arc, pristine and unresisting, and built a suburban pretense sprawling along the greensward, lopping branches from the ancient cherry and spilling out into the field far beyond the boundary.

The little rancor I felt has all these years been far exceeded by consideration for Mother. But I am wistful at the years of my own work that must now sustain a studio born in expensive times. Perhaps these turns of circumstances are the momentum that challenges me. So many with small stipends and bequests sink into dullards.

What has been bequeathed me in this house? I remember the family who built it for a charming daughter, Nancy Kimball, whom I watched with awe and admiration through the tufts of goldenrod and the movement of low branches of spruce. Where is she now? Does she remember her perch above the deep harbor of Boothbay? She seemed to me a sophisticate as smooth as porcelain. I heard once years later she had married a man named Stone and had been divorced and I hated him for the cruelty and coldness of his name and character. I wonder now if through the years other innocent eyes have charted my course and seen a meteor where only a glint of sunlight passed.

This house will be my Loft, the second or third story above the rocks, high in the tips of trees. It is also my own loft of the mind and creative passion. I will leave the folding of daily chores behind when I climb into this tree house.

Blue sea is cleft below me, parting on either side of Mouse Island. I can nearly see the tiny studio that on the east shore has been mine for five years. In the farthest view to port lie the White Islands and Ram. Both the Whites are open and ravished by winds and the burning ammonia of gulls and cormorants. To starboard Mouse, Burnt, Squirrel, and a fringe of Damariscove stretch like warm animals at the sea's hearth. They are heavy with coats of fir. The shore, steep below my window, laps and folds in a wind blown straight from Spain.

Expanse and height are an ideal creative site. I feel here I can stretch my arms to all the elements and pull them together to my choosing.

I imagine that others, who poked through the carcass of this house, testing beds, checking pots and pans, saw a totally different structure. Where they counted beds for warm wriggling bodies and spoons for cereal, I intend to fling, to fling hard, the housemaid out, to tear down the multiple walls, closets and clothes, scarcely room to crowd between the docile twins and make a space to match the view.

The covered porch, heavy as a grand piano, with false posts and visored roof will all come together under a single slanting roof, a wide smile of a room where tables can be stretched for a banquet of tapestries in any direction. I will topple the wall to the sea so that only the quickest eye will catch the transition from endless space to confinement. As I come each day to savor the low sunrise across the water at Mouse Island I can exult here for I have not only sea but the levitation of an osprey. The distance lends the mind an opportunity to distill the elements and catch their magic.

Each time I find a new creative nest there is sudden growth. The roots of my imagination move into the new space and fill it, seeking the edges of a larger mold. First there was N Street in Washington where I labored at the living room window and sacrificed my piano to needle and thread. Then the move to our Queen Anne castle with eleven-foot ceilings and staircases, sliding up and down like a roller coaster, allowing me to create without fearing my limits. There large organdy tapestries can float on a casual bamboo pole in the Victorian bay. Passers-by collect in groups like carolers, sharing with me the glory of a dandelion seed crown, or the humor of a clamshell with flaming tide line. Sometimes strangers ring my bell, eager to touch the pale threads and run their fingers along the woolen tracery. My message is clear—almost too ingenuous—and sometimes I crave their scorn or indifference. I know that instant recognition and empathy means that the deeper interpretation still escapes me.

While I studied music at Harvard I chose a course in Stravinsky, which he was scheduled to teach himself. He never came! I chose the course because I disliked his music. I understood my own lack. I did not comprehend his musical pulse but I wanted to. I knew instinctively that he was composing beyond me. And now, of course, I am as comfortable with Stravinsky themes as I am with Bach and Brahms.

Art is like that too. It is best when it takes time to know.

Winter 1980

Today we are traveling west to Mendocino, California, crossing the Rockies at thirty thousand feet.

So much is made so easy—no oxcart or mountain passage delays my voyage. Within my silver rocket, my eyes can follow the patterns of earth below. I see the salmon and Venetian red earth, again the doeskin ground; the snow creates patterns my needle would trace, the gullies and rivulets of the Colorado.

Colors of beige and yellow buff beneath snow on the western mesa, the deep rims of earth clinging to flat pinnacles and small flats in soft pheasant hues with the gray-white stubble of trees, their snowy roots clinging to arid earth.

The fissures of snow, deep shafts of snow down sleek mountain-sides, the puncturing of the earth's white face by red stone, home of the Colorado. Tree patches and forests move from jet black in their populated centers to the soft edges of mouse fur as they are engulfed in snow. To duplicate the earth's design from the Smokies to the Pacific would be a monumental project, always a sense of westward motion from the geometric fields of cultivation to the Rockies and back to the squares and rectangles of farming. This is my first air trip coast to coast in one gulp, a moving, visually charged experience.

Little River is just one of the tentative series of small towns clustered above the surf and angry rocks north along the Pacific coast above San Francisco. Here the Indians fished and hunted in some of the most ravishingly beautiful country. It is easy to understand their potlatches, orgies of eating and giving, for the forests behind them held a limitless supply of food and shelter. The redwoods, now diminished to second and third growth, still stand straight and enormously tall. Their feathery foliage hangs lightly like mourners' veils as they cluster around the stricken stump of the mother tree.

Each scattering of white houses on the moors and cliffs must look like random gulls to the tankers passing far out on the horizon. The redwood cottages that have filled in among the trees in later times are almost hidden. The early settlers to this area came from

Maine—around the Horn or dragged across the steaming width of Nicaragua. Their nineteenth-century homes are modest and Victorian. In Mendocino they already form an Historic Area. The sweep of moor and cliff have become also a landmark protected against new construction. Harbor seals bask on the rocks at low tide. Now in February the gray whale is swimming north again, returning to the Arctic from the Sea of Cortez, skirting the coast well within the outer reefs to protect her newborn. Nearly daily this month I see them puff past, spuming their salty breath, while we eat our ham and rye on our front veranda.

Each day here has depth and poise. The trees and hills need not preen for they know their beauty. Boats are scarce, two or three tiny fishing craft in a month, but the sea swells and uncurls, flattens like clean sheets and ruffles to the wind. Every sunset is painted with fresh watercolor. The air sweeps frosty from the bowl of the Pacific. I touch my shoulder blades, one against the other, filling from my toes to eyes, filling like a parched traveler the wineskin of living.

Nights and stars worthy of sleeplessness. The evening stars, then Mars and Jupiter and finally Orion, at first pale and vagrant, one, two, three growing as the night deepens until his belt is three burning coins. The Big Dipper is far down the horizon, his seine heavy with midnight sky. There is a song:

> Stars of the summer night
> Far in your azure deeps.
> Hide, hide your golden light!
> She sleeps.

—Longfellow
"The Spanish Student"

On our terrace are flat, succulent jade plants. Whatever the weather, a month of rain, a week of sun, they flourish here. In their heavy redwood boxes they are as beautiful as the best bonsai, standing three feet tall or more. The fields are dotted with delicate stalks of zinnias and jonquils, two plants the deer will not touch. All gardening seems built around plants that resist gophers, deer and rabbits.

The impact of the Pacific Northwest lives in me. The relentless cruelty of wind and sea holds a fascination as macabre as blood gushing from flesh and bone. Each wave upon the rock at Little River spreads below me, wide angled from our long porch. The anger of the wind and the full mane of the charging sea will all affect the new work I do both in tapestries and sculpture. There is little fragility. The foam is knit like an Irish sweater and even the western humming-birds have brassy coats of cadmium and olive that turn black in the sharp sun.

Pacific

Raw boned rock
fractures the skin
of sky, pointing
wet agony above
the ruff of salt.

With her scalpel,
water lifts, bursts
and recedes, leaving
the ravaged stone.

And while I sleep
the rupture of the waves
goes on. Moon cuts
and rock coils the rock.

Pushed by sea pressure
the pitted lace, laved
and wiped clean
weeps the new day.

The Loft, Summer 1980

To have a studio has been my absolute. More than inner space or the convenience of shelves I have been searching for a high perch above the sea with a long view out to the farthest rim of islands. Almost any platform with solitude and view has the potential and here just two minutes through the woods from my cottage I make a discovery.

The path from our house rises into the woods, up stone steps between the balsam firs. I tread lightly on a scattering of lily-of-the-valley and a carpet of clintonia. Making a path means that some green stems will be crushed. I think of it each time I pass but hope the spared fringes will thicken to define my way. The path borders a narrow dirt road that I take for only ten paces and again turn off, over the granite ledges, to drop into the hollow at the edge of the sea cliff where my loft nestles.

Today it is all raw board and bruises. The inner walls of the two minuscule bedrooms are gone and half the narrow bath is torn away. The chimney that once defined the outer boundary of the living room stands alone. There is dry rot in the porch sill and a crack in the fireplace. What I have purchased is a ravishing view and some square footage so that I can build my sea studio in a spot that lifts and carries my eye and mind as free as tide and wave. There is nothing to stop me. No stone walls, no city buildings, no suburban life flowing around me; only elements, rocks, trees and azure. Looking out and beyond with a sense of belonging, I have won all of the sea. Five, even six miles of blue space, a grey fog or moonlight that will change every day without ceasing.

Water is a magnet that compels most of us. Even a pond or a brook is enough reason to choose its company, to build houses or cut paths to watch water.

When the bay is lively with boats I feel comforted, increased and reassured in my solitude. Life goes on about me and I can snare or evade the net of activity at will. But always there is a sense of levitation, of not quite touching the earth as I pace around the yawning frame of boards and imagine my finished workshop. I am stretched from the palest wisp of cloud to the ledges that hold my new loft tight. They meet through my caring, are held together by my vision and what I propose to create here. I am even wondering already if it is too small and I need more space.

Perhaps the basement should be my place not only for my yarn dyeing, but for stone cutting. Slate excites me as a medium for its brittle edge and basic hardness. I know it takes paint well. It has been used by the Italian masters as a canvas. A series of stone sculptures builds in my imagination. I have been to two slate mines and hope to return this summer. This is a level that tempts the rim of my consciousness.

But it is not all dreaming and blissful creativity. There are electricians and masons and carpenters. The parade of shovels and hammers comes first. I know something about that, too, and precious hours will be lost or at least spent to clear those hurdles.

While the Sunday sailors spread out across the cerulean bay, I am becoming acquainted with my new land. The voices of children and amused parents float up past the pine and spruce between my door and the house on the point. The quiet of May and early June is gone. This is the second day of summer and already the ocean is crisscrossed with the white pique of sails and the slashes of power boats. I wonder if I will live and work here into my old age. Will I expand beyond this spot? I watch the black ants scurry across my lap and see that the trail leads to boards underneath the house.

I think of the great white farm that is the studio for Leonard Baskin. It has more room for growth than anything I can achieve here. But artistically he has not grown for years, I find myself thinking. Does he still see the beryl grass running in fat brush strokes to his stark barn? Does he see the point where water and earth meet, the line of definition?

Even with the edges of demolition about me, I feel I am working into the life I wasn't to lead in my loft. I want it to be clean and sparse and basic, to be full of light and to be uncluttered of all things except my work. I want to function so simply that all my energy will leap from one idea to the next.

The Loft is to be my country of third language. Not the English of my childhood or the volatile Spanish of travel. The consonants of my tapestry art and the bright liquid vowels of color will come together here. This platform above the sea is a private vision I have carried about, tucked away for years on many voyages.

Virginia, Fall 1980

Winterhouse is my new studio for fall and snow and the first crocus. One large airy room, it hangs in the woods between the forest of tulip trees and the deep wide gash of the Potomac. No river I know in the eastern United States has the grandeur of the Potomac, particularly above the city of Washington as it rises steeply to Great Falls and on into the Blue Ridge Mountains. My first morning here, as I wield mop and broom, the Carolina wren drops liquid notes in a rush of joy into the filtered light. I came at seven to a sky soft pink and gray airbrushed and stippled.

Winterhouse has many of the attributes of Mouse Island. It will be isolation and natural beauty as I fold into the green world of the river's edge. I move with the same quiet and discretion, hoping not to disturb the forest patterns. The privilege of such a place of quiet is broken only by the repeated roar of jets, cruising the same broad river like a school of sharks.

I plan to wander the hills here, to know the configuration of river stones and wait with anticipation the ice and snow. If I can come upon the miracle of lacy ice gradually, acquainting myself with candor and caution, there is treasure to be found.

A river means water, bringing with it a greening world quite difference from the salt cover I know. There is a tropical lushness, an unleashed embroidery of leaves, woven like an enormous basket into the sky above the watercourse. The very extravagance of the green is emphasized by the narrow artery, the life-sustaining river, nurturing a grandscale landscape. Where the sea is infinity, the Potomac is contained. Not tidy but encompassing even in the spring flood. The eye and the imagination can deal with it. This I mean to do.

The hunter knows his prize by violence, destroying the pulse to touch feather and fur. He holds the limp prize, catching a brief moment of warm blood to quench his own hunger. Art is just the other way. The approach is equally guarded, but the questing eye shoots unseen arrows to the brain, along the nerve ends to arm and fingertips, to a pencil or brush or needle. There is no clammy pulse. No endings, only beginnings. Hunting a stone, or a leaf or the fragile seed pearls of ice is a living experience. Gently, the discovery can be distilled and creative strength found. Until I hold the knowledge firmly, I will sleep softly, building a friendship with my new world.

Virginia, Fall 1980

The first day is not for Elysian prose. My faithful Bolivian friend Jesus and I have come with buckets and mops and all the rainbow of Windex, Tide and lemon oil. Winterhouse has white floors with a black checkerboard center covered until today by an oriental carpet.

The drive from Georgetown slips like a satin ribbon along the Potomac, a view brushed with oarsmen in the seven o'clock light. The leaves have turned and fallen while I was in Africa. I am lifted as though coming from ether and suddenly revived. I scarcely remember my departure from Mouse Island. I wonder now if this will be another island to love with the same knowledge.

Joanne and John Bross come to tidy up and consider. There is no reason, only kindness, that offers me a haven here. I want to be unobtrusive, to have this spot as hidden as the squirrel's winter treasure. The sun climbing east warms my back. Unrolled along two tables are the open leaves of our African adventure in my oriental watercolor book; the dancers of Abomey, the candy striped cathedral of Cotonou, three pages of the floating village of Ganvié.

The Japanese temple books are visual poems for me, printed into the folded pages as swiftly as the passage of two sailing ships. I draw almost without contemplating the page, straight out—a brush recording lightly as the eye watches the passing panorama. It is a secret memory that Bob and I return to. Better than photographs, the continuity is a color poem reciting the whole adventure, the Masai of Kenya and the incongruous Victorian brick houses of Madagascar.

At home I am a dervish and cannot stop. Here in Winterhouse the tension drops away. There is a lumpy chaise of feathers where I can slump like a lazy princess and fall asleep if I wish.

The Loft, Spring 1981

The fog curls and pulls like a dancer's scarf across the bay this first morning that I am working in my new studio. The heavy drawing table with sturdy black knobs and a half moon brace of iron on either side belonged to my father when he was a student at the Museum Art School in Boston before the First World War.

Now it slants against the balcony wall of my studio, the Loft, and as I work, lifting my eyes up and beyond to the rim of the harbor I see the white froth of fog settle and stretch, lazy in a May breeze, and part like curtains on a stage to reveal black conifers, wiping them out again with the same whimsy.

This is the first morning that creative current has taken hold for me. I have names and ideas that have jostled like brook stones in my brain for days: *Wave Length, Talus, Rock Bloom,* and a nameless area of rock shelf I am eager to transpose from Mouse Island into organdy and embroidery with strong colors of rust and rose.

These four tapestries are all aborning as I sit quietly, turning each idea over, sketching with my pencil, searching rhythm and form first and then texture, and last of all color. There is no urgency. Forms will surface and shape while I am here, perhaps not be finished as I move along but partially complete to fill the winter months when Maine is only a memory and a need.

Creativity is the revelation of solitude, the flowering of nature in a personal vision and an artistic odyssey that is limitless. Where nature has been spared and left to her own housekeeping of washed rocks and purifying water, ideas of beauty flow. I could as easily stop them as hold my hands against the fog. They will surround me, gently pervasive and consuming.

Today is my first opportunity to visit the rocks below my Loft, to acquaint myself with the curves and striations that hundreds of years of full and neap tide have wrought. I find a rock shelf in the sun and with my stocking cap as a pillow stretch out to feel the warmth of the granite plateau. Here are the curves and pull as clear as new ribbon.

Possessively I think eighty feet of this shore and these rocks are mine, but I laugh softly at better memories for all of this shore in and out of the fretted curves belongs to me. I have known its planes and angles since I climbed back and forth along these declivities from the age of four. They are part of me even though I see them each time washed and polished in new ways. My possession of these rocks is visual and emotional. There is comfort in knowing they were there before I was born in the tiny hospital a few coves north and in the certain knowledge that when my eyes close for the last time the stones and the lapping waves will go on and on just as they are today. Very little will change.

The feeling of eternity is wings, not weight. The continuity of natural beauty more even than the flow of life of family is a deep need that the line of sea and the massive rock complete for me.

Cruising in Maine, Summer 1981

An azure day, the blue of exhilaration. What Ramón Jiménez thought of when he wrote, *vuelvo a ti mar, mi cuna, mi sustento*. It is the nurturing color of sunlight, the buoyancy of clouds.

We are floating in a breeze hardly strong enough to tickle the feet of a newborn, out past Fisherman's Island with its stone castle, heading straight for Pemaquid Light and the sweep of Muscongus Bay. I am somnolent with satisfaction. Dreaming and reality merge in delight.

A weekend of cruising with friends on a lighthearted voyage to the islands. A perfect chance to watch water patterns. Rounding Mosquito Island at the western cove of the Penobscot, the wind blows hard and hot, pulled by a pale moon rising east. There is always wind at night in Maine when the moon is full.

I think of titles of tapestries; sometimes I choose a title to fit a particular design and then look for a series of designs to match the title. *Wave Length* is such a choice. A long, sparsely folded tapestry in white on white. Now I watch the waves closely, see the horizontal roll of water cleaved by the deep keel; perhaps another *Wave Length*?

Sails ahead of us point north up the river like ninepins. The breeze is ready to topple with the strength of a bowler's ball any unwary sailor. The air whistles as we lean north, caught in the balance of sea forces.

A greedy sailor, his face the color of roast beef, eyes caught in folds of dissipation, sails close, throwing spray and heaving the shining carcass of his boat between our sailboat and another, running with us along the stretch to Tenants Harbor. The sparkling moment is lost in brutality. I know him in the ten seconds it takes to pull away. While we have floated buoyantly forward, seeing osprey, he has finished a six-pack. Each of us is incorrigible in our tastes. How fine that the wind has separated us like chaff in a field of fresh harvest.

Last night we anchored in a tiny funnel of harbor with a Cape Cod house set among wild roses. Birds sang in abundance; a solitary island deeded to wild life with rugged rocks like Mouse. What is different is the great wildness—no habitation—whole bracelets of dark islands, circled and tied by quartz ribbons on granite shores. Pot buoys in new plastic colors are handfuls of confetti on the water's surface.

Bob and I want a small boat to carry our grandones to picnics and for visiting rocks and coves of the Maine archipelago. Here in this tiny cove is a lobster boat with a cuddy that suits us. As we row from the boat to the beach we have a chance to see if this is our kind of shingle. Will Bridgit, Robert, Lisa and Sasha fit into this cockleshell? But most of all can I travel silently with pencil and camera to other islands to find inspiration?

The rocks of Muscongus Bay are different from Boothbay Harbor's. They are like the heavily wooded islands, rougher, deeper-textured, more wanton, almost as though civilization has washed and ordered the areas of population. It is essentially the difference between protected harbor areas and the rock edge of open sea. As one moves along the coast toward the Penobscot into granite country, huge piles of talus from the years of great public building, millstones and massive foundations lie strewn about and piled in cones rising above the spruce. White veins of quartz thick as bread dough ooze and trickle down the face and fill the crevasses of the grey stone.

We sail past the south face of Monhegan Island twelve miles at sea, and even there the fissures of white stone are laid precisely from cliff to sea down the grey stone. At the southeast corner a waterfall of stone, wide and convoluted, sweeps over the ledge. For six million years this beautiful south face has risen here; long before there were trees. Now the woods are full of deer. I startled one recently as I walked alone through the forest at the eastern end of Monhegan. In the evening, the deer come to savor the vegetable gardens and nip apples off the trees close to cottages. No one knows their antlered origin on this remote landfall.

Reefs along the coast run north to south; the glacial sweep is as apparent today as ever. Veins of white among the rocks tumble and twist, but the grand design is clearly rock ribbons that stretch south. Monhegan shows this pattern.

Boothbay Harbor, Fall 1981

September is pulling away. The tide of Maine summer, easy and strong, lifts me out of cover and cottage. It pushes me to rearrange myself for the cityscape of Washington. I am full of the saltwater views, the seven o'clock confluences as I swim the bay and the all-day drinking up of beauty. I know the parching that awaits me as these images evaporate. I want more than anything to stay, to seal the fragmentation of my life, the travels and changes, and to have continuity.

Living in many houses is an illness for creativity. There is no depth of knowledge, or friendship, no savoring of every dimension when you must move on. My Puritan forebears have left me with a need for unceasing industry. In a changing landscape it is hard to find the right tools and the chance inspiration before I am packing again to start over among the chimney tops of winter life. I feel I am running the antic wheel hour by hour seeking an escape, knowing its futility.

Yesterday as a farewell, I rowed again to Mouse Island in a breeze as gentle as June, to peek through the vacant windows of my abandoned studio and enjoy the crop of fall raspberries held still by the balm of summer. The table that filled my studio is gone. I could see as I pressed my forehead against the glass that someone had bought a garish rug, azure and lime, braided in a self-conscious coil. There is now a small white lambskin before the hearth and the writing desk where I kept my scissors and tape, where Dr. Fosdick wrote his sermons, is flanked by a canvas easy chair. It seems like a page from Sears and Roebuck, a cheap opulence. I hope the young wife who is a poet will have this space, but I sense this is not a poet's corner. Intuitively I see it being used less and less frequently and finally abandoned with the door swinging like a forlorn child waiting a playmate.

The rocks are the same. I know them, stepping softly as I walk from one shelf of granite to another, acknowledging their grandeur and the detail of ribboned quartz. I stop at the ledge that inspired *Elements I*. That was a summer spent in the creation of a single work, feeling for the essence of the millennium. That single tapestry filled me with fresh energy and ideas as I returned to the ledge over and over. I know without searching the roll and fold of Mouse.

The extraordinary message is the confluence, the coming together of sea and stone, one so enduring, where two thousand years will rub a fresh curve or declivity and the other, the sea, quixotic as the flight of birds.

A farewell to Mouse is folding the excitement and discovery of my own creative beginnings into an album of memories: a place to sit in the sun with my nibbled straw hat perched to shade me, to eat a fresh orange. This island is a calm space of air, neither bursting nor pressing my energies.

But I have moved on. It is as though I am leaving Spain or Uruguay and know instinctively that all I can do is press the learning and memories into the pages of remembrance and keep the treasure of it with me.

In the winter I turn in upon myself, constructing from memory what I can. But a shallow pool with only my own reflection will never nurture fresh ideas. Perhaps this winter I can come to know the Potomac better, and find new secrets. I have nothing to feed on unless I am free to move about in nature.

I wish to express the elegance of nature that I seldom see in manmade objects or in man-controlled use of nature. Almost anything in nature has all the qualities taught in art school, but with subtle selection, with a sense of rhythm and line and careful gradation of colors. All these things are strong in the natural world. They should be strong in art too.

As I peer closer and closer to nature and listen less and less to people and read less in books, I observe deeply and know I will have something more original to say.

~ 7 ~

Imagination Is Whimsy

Kenneth Clark wrote, "The mind celebrates a triumph every time it formulates a thought." Imaginative thought and memory tied together within the workings of the mind must in art give visual form to this mental formulation. To bring these elements together in the right juxtaposition, to generate creative flow, is inspiration. Creativity is essentially and solely the development of inspiration. We are led to develop new ideas, a painting, an intricate machine, to create a charming home, to build an Eiffel Tower because of inspiration. Those of us with the best imaginations and a dedication to work will wear the seven league boots and outdistance the others. Inspiration by itself, without the drive and the ability to work, will flower like day lilies and be gone before its beauty is recorded.

To build a finished tapestry means hours of thought, of honing the idea to its freshest meaning, and then weeks of labor. Each detail must be added with the spark still sending an electric charge from imagination to visual experience. For this I need solitude and a desire to work and work and work.

The magic of inspiration and creativity is that it holds great excitement. Nothing is so fulfilling as the completion of a tapestry that is as beautiful as I can make it. Here is a difference between what I am trying to say and what many other artists are choosing as their goal. I want my art to express beauty as I see it. I have no other aim. It is not meant to shock or surprise or test the eye by any other facet except that which glorifies the world I know. Money and the marketplace hold no interest for me. If my tapestries are good enough they will be chosen. Perhaps I will never see the day but, like Emily Dickinson, I tuck my finished work underneath beds in boxes, into every possible space because I am enthralled by the voyage I am on with my own creative expression.

Although Richard Marcus has said of my work, "Your art always has elegance," what I have captured are only fleeting passages of the inspiration of our earth. There are many areas of beauty that I seem incapable of catching and conveying even though they offer moments of extraordinary fascination.

For example, just now as I sit at my desk a palliated woodpecker has flown to the maple before my window. His powerful body and chiseled head undulate up the dark stem of tree. His red tasseled crown is bright in the morning sun. I know no way to catch that moment. I stop to watch him until with a nervous twist of his handsome crest he is gone. Perhaps the memory will be stored in my mind and surface some day to become part of a larger design. But for now I know no way.

Forest

Who clipped the pine;
Each needle pruned
Upon its slender spine?
No single finger
Longer than another?

Who put the fringe
Along the leaning birch,
And sewed in even stitch,
Symmetrical the fern?

Who wove the forest
Carpet, warped with oak
Leaf, piled with moss,
And stitched with
    alderberry?

Who brushed the leaf
With jade and lime,
And sent the sun to sift
With coins of light
The berry and the vine?

Washington, Winter 1977

As the last of my large hangings for my museum tour are completed, I begin to think ahead, to set new goals, evaluating the hills and furrows in my work. I have always worked better if I have chosen a new spot on my artistic horizon, a new focus for my future.

From my studio in the garret in Washington I watch the earth and trees heaving and bending in the coldest winter of the century.

Skaters have swarmed across the glazed Potomac; even the crust on the snow is as sharp and varied as brook ice. In Montrose Park, at the head of our hill, the sunlit surface is hard ivory with flecks of gold. I went there with my sled on Saturday, careening down the porcelain surface, skating into Rock Creek Park. I slide there often with the children. With my stocking hat and boots and the lumpy clothes of winter I feel suddenly ageless. It brings me the kind of elasticity of mind and heart that serve as a counterpoint to the hours of quiet toil in my studio.

There is no effort on my part to jump two or three stairs at once, to click my heels in the air on a sunny day, to slide on the crusted snow. The effort is to subdue my spirit to suit others. Perhaps for this reason I am happy in my studio, for there, through my art, I can still take wing.

Thinking of snow and ice brings me back to the theme of water. It is not a new subject for I have already done five tapestries for my exhibit, "Textures of Our Earth," that are inspired by water. They are *Salt Veil, Surge, Double Image, Wave* and *Borealis*. Others of course— *Mussel, Murex* and *Quahog*—are the sea's harvest.

I have come to understand the essence of the sea and ice and rain. I look ahead to distillation of these themes, using my knowledge freely without need for pictorial form, but instead something deeper inside me that catches and develops the rhythm and the essence of what I want and have come to know so well. Once years ago I painted an oil called *Sea Well* containing the sense of infinity I feel when I look down into the depths of the ocean from the bow of my sailboat. I see a great eye of ultramarine and around it an aqueous fringe of beryl and white foam.

Perhaps this same simplicity of form within the larger, more obvious patterns of the sea is the kind of inspiration that I am seeking. The tapestries that are still to be hung on the museum walls in Seattle and Richmond and Washington, D.C., are already swept astern of my rushing sloop and I am heading out to a new horizon.

Portland, Maine, Winter 1979

Today flying north to Maine in brutal cold, the sun hits the land like a sword on bright armor. Even the pilot is mesmerized by the sharp edges of the earth's patterns. He calls on his intercom for us to look about us a sky of rare clarity, spotting each jewel below.

From Boston we lift above the deep harbor, a patchwork of islands and see Mount Washington in a cloudless sky. The pilot stretches his course north to Cape Anne and Kennebunk, wings gently around the rim of Biddeford Pool, and slides quietly into Portland.

Two of my children come to meet me. How patient my family is and how loving. Of course I am laden. No immigrant ever came from Europe as baggaged. There is my leather carrying case, a huge sausage six feet long and three around. In two smaller boxes, which might be skis, are six of my smaller special collection tapestries, three for a gallery in Portland, two to show to a corporation.

We go straight from the airport to a piano recital given in the Episcopal Cathedral. It is cold and dark as we step into the silent chancel. Suddenly a Chopin étude peals forth. What a rare chance to sit peacefully with my daughter-in-law in her deep gray velour and red jumper—always so stylish—and my gentle son Rick. I enjoy the quiet Sunday moment of thankfulness. And then my imagination rises up between the Gothic arches and takes flight. I am far beyond the rushing étude, thinking of South Africa and the Wool Bureau and what I will do to honor my country in a tapestry show of four hundred works. I am to be the only U.S. representative and I ponder and reach beyond, to a state of pure being, that brings ideas and revelations.

Mysteriously the form of the Indian tipi appears. It bears no relationship to this gothic house of God, but only to the moment of calm and inspiration, and perhaps the perfection of the music. I do not know the source. I see clearly that it will be a compelling shape to stand free in the center of the exhibition area, rising eleven feet high with hardwood poles and embroidery cascading down the outside. It is surface design, swirling with my lineal veined work and I will call it *Tipi–Waterfall.* It can be a centerpiece to the South African show.

With the sudden inspiration flood in more ideas and even details of execution and design. Perhaps this will be the first of several tipis to be called *Wind, Wave* and *Waterfall.* I see them in natural tones from white and palest grey, to black and white and beige. The title has already come to me, *My Father's House.* That will say different things to different people. Those without imagination will say, "My, is she part Indian?" But the wise will see the multiple meanings. My father's house is the world of nature, the moment of quiet in a

Portland church, the vibration of a Chopin étude and the underpinnings of faith. I am always in my father's house; its roof and walls are spruce trees, tipis, cathedrals and moments of being.

The following day I drive with my son Bill west of Portland. The White Mountains and Mt. Washington crown our view. The sky is as clear as Venetian glass with the cerulean and cobalt spun together and laid along the sky in pure watercolor. In my life I have lived through so many climatic shifts in Maine, in Bolivia, and along the frozen Potomac. Sub-zero readings snap the steel of living and keep a drama of the elements whirling about me. I am aware of the impact of these phenomena on my art. Dramatic elements say so much in creating a tapestry.

In Bridgeton we meet a gentleman with the aura of a scoutmaster. He is working with high school dropouts. Deep inside he wants to talk about his origins. He is Cherokee and Scotch. Here in a small clapboard office with a blackboard I am suddenly having a private lesson on building a tipi; the smoke flap, constructed like a small free-swinging sail. The poles are laid flat on the forest floor and tied at one end, depending upon the spread wanted. They are then lifted and pulled apart to form the circumference. The layers of skins next are stretched and sewn horizontally along the frame, rising in patchwork to the apex of the poles. A door is cut and thongs lash the skins to the poles from the inside. My teacher says snow and rain fall into the tent because there is always a hole at the top for smoke. Living is around the edges, the fire is the centerpiece.

Often in my life there have been strange and remarkable circumstances to help me in the inspiration and creative development of a design. How did I happen upon this gentleman, half Cherokee and half Scotch, the day after my inspiration? I have no answers. I do seek people out and care about each one and the pattern of his or her own life. Perhaps this is part of the answer but never fully. There is a pattern to our lives if we will be alert to it. There are messages sung in the crossing branches of the birch and where people gather. I seek those messages, and they have helped me along the way like bright arrows on a trail.

My Father's House

My father's house
has no walls, no clear
definition, just sky and
    cloud
and trees that have bent
or been skinned to cover
me and my brethren.

There is no coming in or
    out,
only a place of being
always alone but never
lonely, filled by the cup
of sun of rain or salt.

His house felled or burned
can rise again to
press a flower, a leaf,
a scent upon the air,
fresh scorched.
There is no melancholy.

Only laughter on the field,
up and down the hills
where we can walk along
or hand in hand, never
beyond the doorstep
of my father's house.

Boothbay Harbor, Summer 1979

Tipi–Waterfall, my large standing tapestry going to South Africa to represent the United States in an international exhibit of wool hangings, has just been wrapped, packed and shipped. It has been hard labor: five months to embroider the lineal cascades of white wool down the radius of the tipi cover—twenty-six feet in circumference and seven and a half feet from the interlacing poles to the floor.

The first shape, nearly half a circle, was cut in paper on the floor of my Washington studio. It took the full eighteen feet of space across the length of our city house. Then the pieced wool forms were shaped to form the proper bias when wrapped on the poles. They give a sense of the dark, varied rock that plays a wonderful counterpoint to any waterfall. Although totally abstract in execution, the elements of known forms and specific natural iconography are inherent.

The sense of lyricism and lineal freedom is significant. There is no desire to retain specific memories of landscape. I do not intellectualize my tapestries, but attempt to observe and understand deeply the phenomena of nature that I have chosen. Then I try to achieve a state of exultation and freedom by linear and textural means that convey my artistic exuberance.

As clearly as the child within my womb has been nurtured by my mind and body, so each major work has a long gestation. Again, the analogy is strong for the beginning weeks and months of formulating an idea have the same urgency. Then, as the composition begins to assume a personality of its own, it becomes assertive and finally bursts forth.

Boothbay Harbor, Fall 1979

Searching for inspiration occasionally leads me to adventures beyond the coves and inlets of my home and studio. Isle au Haut, one of the most rugged islands six miles south of Deer Isle, has always intrigued me.

I call Stonington and am referred to the ferryboat captain's mother who, after more than a dozen rings, comes to the phone to tell me, "Eh-yah, my son goes out at 7 A.M. and 11 A.M. 'cept Tuesdays and Sat-a-days when he makes an extra trip at five thir-tay." The name of the boat? "The Miz Lizz-zay." All is set.

Boothbay Harbor to Stonington is only a slice more than three road hours, but we extend it to eight, savoring the September's view. Owl's Head, on the southwest shore of the Penobscot, curls out to confront the Atlantic. There is a towering lighthouse poised like a jeweled fist. Facing north I look up a wide wind-rush bay; everywhere black spruce islands fixed in passage to their granite bases.

Years of longing bring me to Isle au Haut. Once in my brother's leviathan, a glistening yacht one hundred feet long, I charged this thoroughfare, hardly able to adjust my camera before we passed. Today I sway slowly in a fresh sea out between the anchored glory of islands that are primeval, cut like silhouettes of Halloween along the soft, fall sky. There are ragged peaks, black above the granite shore. The gray stone lifts through the hide of grasses and seaweed, smooth as massive knees and elbows. Long sandbars shoot out to confound the sailor. Looming ahead, the couchant island is Isle au Haut!

For five hours I race across the island stopping to record rock formations with my camera, astounded at the force of isolation. Cliffs, cracked to their hearts, have slid past each other. Cove follows cove. To the south is sheltered Duck Harbor covered with small rocks smooth as beach glass. One cove is gray, another black stone, a third tapers to white. There is only one sand beach on Isle au Haut, on the north side. Standing above the cliffs, hair blowing, blowing like the straight-out branches of the spruce, I touch infinity and acknowledge my fragile hold. I give thanks for the strength of limb and heart that have brought me through the maze of orange-blazed trails to these headlands. Here a cliff is sheared on one face with a center of black stone crumbling like a wounded giant. The power is in no way diminished and the collapsing frame will someday be a tapestry. The contrasts and the sharp edges of the core translate into wool. I carry its impact away in my imagination, another corner for memory that will boil down and refine and some day become whole again. There is no time to stop and draw, it must all fit into my memory.

No specific process catalogues creative moments. Certain details spark imagination. The contrast of stone against sea is one for me. The shadow of early and late day light, always preferred hours for painters, are important too. Those hours accentuate the third dimension.

I see rocks as striped wools, massed weavings and also as salt-washed and grained wood. Natural elements seem to have no barriers; they merge and flow in my inner eye translating from one medium to another, wherever a third dimension is possible.

Imagination is a whimsical friend who helps me observe and duplicate what I see and even hear among the crashing sea and rock. Here at the ocean's edge, Rachel Carson writes, we see the structure of our earth. The neap tide, the hurricane, reveals the formation and dissolution of our world.

All these observations, this secret knowledge of my own discovery—even the individual stone that has cracked and separated in winter storm and ice—pounds on my imagination, cracking open creative drive.

Traveling to Isle au Haut I stop to call on Leonard Baskin. He has a wide open view to the sea beyond a stretch of bleak fishing houses. His green lawn and tall gray barn with the east face painted white is the decision of a sculptor. A room attached to his white farmhouse, all windows to the sea, is full of treasures. A raspberry tablecloth swings in the breeze.

I find him, his intense face fringed by a white goatee, just as he is heading for his barn. I catch startled sharp eyes and feel the coldness of gray stone as our hands meet. I have come hoping to buy a sculpture from him, but he cannot sell it. "Only at the Kennedy Gallery, wretched gallery," he mumbles. "They charge absurd prices. It would be nice to share work with a fellow artist but I haven't sold a work myself in twenty years." I feel he is relieved by his chains, the lament of so many of the good artists I know. Tied to an entrepreneur, unable to face the marketplace, fed by faithful salesmen, peddled but not proudly loved. I want to escape that purgatory, so far, so far. . . .

Baskin's black crow with human head that I have coveted belongs to his wife, he tells me. Artists always give their best work to their wives! He does not invite me in. I accept that. I have come without credentials. I leave the green earth with its white sculptured building and retreat down the rutted, nasty road to the causeway.

New York City, Spring 1980

I have walked miles and miles of excitement today at the Metropolitan Museum. I have seen the horse of San Marcos in the elegance of the Lehman wing, the African artist Buli, the Chinese bronzes and the Impressionists.

In a dream of fancy I see a great white tapestry of many levels hanging in the Lehman rotunda. It is *Nimbus*. Sometimes a place gives birth to an idea, but this is an idea that has circled in my imagination for several years. I can see the whole flow of wool like sea smoke floating in that round space, the circle adding to the quality of infinite light and texture. There need be no edges. The walls curve to the sky-lighted center, tall and lean, perfect for my tapestry. This time an idea has found a home. Although I do not imagine that my dream will come to live here I shall not forget it.

A special elegance comes from approaching this gallery through the high wrought iron gates of Valladolid. The dignity and hauteur reminds me of the years in Madrid. The Valladolid gates at the Metropolitan are as sharp and brilliant, as arabesque as the best of the Andalusia dancers. They are gates that welcome one with cornets and trumpets to the domain of kings.

No gates open with flourish to welcome me at the MOMA. Drenched mobs gather like tadpoles, swimming through the thunderclap. Much has been written about this Picasso; in all the critiques no one has mentioned the facets of Picasso's art that most inspire me. The very early drawings done in Spain around 1890 show such a strong decisive line and sense of volume that all that follows seems natural. The most important aspect to me is Picasso's almost total dependence on the figure. Nature never comes first, even in one small rare landscape where he has painted two figures as the roots and trunks of trees. A few still lifes obviously inspired by Cezanne and the mandolins are departures, but they are also forms. Even his musical instruments seem to have a human dimension, a sexuality.

His progression as an artist is easy to see in this large retrospective; the emaciated and socially conscious blue period, the softening pink period, and the sudden electric scarification of figures influenced by African masks. The origins are clear. I learn later that they are in many cases almost exact reproductions of artifacts that were in Picasso's own studio.

Picasso has wit and robust humor, and I am afraid to admit I feel pummeled and exhausted and emptied by the willful slap and dash of paint across canvas after canvas. I catch my breath and turn to admire his drawing of the delicate face and hands of the Fogg Museum Madonna and his portrait of Stravinsky. Here are depth and virtuosity and a measure of tranquility.

Picasso gobbled up all the art that he saw. He masticated in wolfish ways the art of Braque, Cezanne, even Matisse, always in relation to people, animals or forms.

While I want to find beauty in nature and distill it, I see that Picasso has rushed in with both fists to batter his art into shapes. I see push and overwhelming passionate momentum. There is never fragility, seldom nuance. Perhaps the harlequins of blue and Venetian pink come closest.

For me Matisse is a more magical experience—or the Monet *Years at Giverny.*

John Russell writes [*New York Times,* May 23, 1980] of Picasso that "for 40 years he worked on the theme of the seashore as the locus of some of our deepest feelings. . . . As a place where everything happened, the beach yielded only to the bullring in Picasso's estimation."

I disagree. Waves yielded to bulls. Picasso did not understand the sea. He felt and translated all the fortissimos, striking the keys harder with deadly accuracy but without nuance. Bullfighting after all is a drama with a short introductory clause, a rapid crescendo and no denouement. When the bull goes down in the bloody knife thrust it is all over.

The sea is so infinitely subtle. Even when a gale pounds in and puts its shoulder to the granite rocks the spray is fresh lace. "To measure the power of the ocean by the frailty of its foam . . ." writes Kahlil Gibran. There is a spectrum from horizon line to horizon line and a sense of its running beyond. Bullfights are visceral, predetermined and their impact is the same combers repeated over and over engulfing the audience and the artist without shading.

Picasso is above all Spanish. Those of us who have lived in Spain know what that means; a force for both strength and cruelty. The *sword,* life wrested from dry ground bring a hard edge. That hard edge, that sure delineation is Picasso. The open sexuality is an underlying leitmotif that burst forth in the explicit, French culture that Picasso adopted.

Had he stayed in Spain I believe this duality might never have occurred. By combining the Spanish and French heritage he opened up his whole being to strength and sexuality at once. A man with two heritages, two countries, he became twice the creative artist that either alone would have allowed him.

In the same way the Spanish and the New England worlds have stretched me. I have learned, expanded, hardened in the constant changes of my life. The New England woods and shore are my great source but the fabrics and wool yarns are travels. The need to survive has added strength and independence. I have learned to enjoy the art of the bullfight, the batik painters with their wax pots, to accept the beggar sleeping beyond my door. I am a survivor.

Life is more sea for me than bullfights, natural color more telling than spectrums. I think wistfully of the energy I have spent leading the traditional woman's role. I could not have been a Picasso, so demanding of others, leading the art chase at full tilt. I might have been if I had been a man. I think I would have been allowed to be more headstrong. Life has periods of work and debilitating exhaustion as I have tried to be both artist and mother at the same time. Artist and wife. Artist and friend. Always wanting to put the artist first, never quiet daring. That is my weakness.

Picasso never had that kind of duality. He has used life to serve his purposes: master entrepreneur, spoiled a little by is own success.

In his last years, he painted dollar signs in primary colors without moving on.

Just now I am shoving the dishes of life aside. Letting the clear need sweep everything else into the corners or onto the floor. I remember that what Louise Nevelson did at sixty was just the beginning of her most creative work. Even pieces done in her fifties seem juvenile and without consequence. Like Picasso she is a super salesman with her false eyelashes and closets full of costumes. She has learned to gobble up the art market in greedy bites of constructions made in her *taller* at the Lippincott forge in Connecticut and tapestries woven in Scotland. Her collage will be like Picasso's ceramics—of no real merit.

I have seen her more recent work in the park at 62nd Street. She proclaims its great importance; her first use of the lace motif in metal. It is not new or of great design. The same free cut metal is being constructed in college art schools across the country. But her original idea of the stacked viscera of wood is still imaginative and fresh. It is her contribution to art. She has said something that is sincere and strong. But after sixty. I take hope.

Bermuda, Spring 1980

I am looking for a watercolor. The hills are October now as the dry season begins. At the edge of a tiny cove returning from Castle Point, Bob and I dip into the sea to snorkel. A parrot fish, velvet blue, slides beneath me along the fluted edge of volcanic rock. I forget to breathe through my tiny air tube and my mask fills with water. Everywhere the fish flick and dance; some of the more exotic come in three sizes like bright stockings. A delicate translucent fish with threads of cadmium from snout to fantail bears a clown's name—French Grunt. Biologists are not poets.

Finally I wash over the edge of the volcanic rock to a low shelf and remove my mask. There before me float sea grape leaves, one alizarin over yellow, another the wine of Burgundy country. This is my watercolor! I will take the largest sheet, define the shape with veins like branches of beech tree and flow in the color for a moist splash. This smallest manifestation, an incredible shape, is all I can honestly grasp and reproduce. It is sculptural and utter simplicity. The pressed paper of my book will be marked by these lovely leaves as my talisman of a trip to Bermuda.

I turn the red leaf and see the wrong side is even more beautiful—softened as though placed under a delicate tissue. We always say "right side" and "wrong side." Why is right always the bright side? To me the soft, muted colors of the stain drifting through the fiber of the leaf and loom are the most beautiful. Often I see the world from the "wrong" side by squinting out the sun. It is the softness, the pale tones that blend into each other like a sunset when the globe has already submerged. Fading, a process that turns even the right side to wrong, has the beauty of age. How delightful to be as comfortable as wrongsided, as a thrush upon her nest. I see that I, myself, am a wrongsided adult, that my clothes share the same protective coloration. There are pants with worn knees and sweaters with frayed elbows in my closet. They are fifteen years old. We are comfortable shading my vivid quest for life, each day ends too soon, each cloud and sunset swirling to be remembered.

So right or wrongsided, the people I love most, the art I treasure have some of both. It is a special dough, yeasty and the rough texture of whole grain. It will rise to nurture me in large lumpy loaves like no other bread served on any table.

I have a sense of being different, of wanting to be different; sometimes I enjoy the wrong side more. In my art I search for both the mellow softening of color and the brilliance of bright days.

Lichen

Two entirely different plants, the one a fungus, the other an alga join through symbiosis to fabricate a new species.

Symbiotic poetry with Dylan Thomas, Marianne Moore and T. S. Eliot.

Down, down into the roiling stream
Lunging among the leaves
Tree rotted, pulling putrid
Soil, where viscid snakes
Welp the endless coil of coils.

A fluted shell, curled in the wind
Fringed and frosted, flung against
The scabrous rock, holding starched
And elegant its ruff and frock.

~

Unlikely bouquet;
who would have thought
so insignificant a plant
would span the continent?

Strong enough to crack
a rock with its own chemistry
working dark threads into the bark
for an eternity.

It blossoms black
in Antarctica, to catch hesitant
glances of the sun, white where
warmth is commonplace.

Almost no wooded space is complete
without this lacy fanning genius.

In perfect symbiosis, these
two friends, alga and fungi, over
rocks and trees depend indefinitely,
upon each other.

Only their congenial harmony has brought
the earth its verdant cover.

~

As she sat on the rock
Weaving her hands into
The lichen and the lock
Of hair. Her gaze was there
But I knew as the moist
Night air swirled round
Her she had forgotten
The gold and amber
At her feet, and beaten
A retreat into her enigmatic
Shell. How could I tell
Her, "Wake and see the wonder

Of this dell. Oh try
To see this simple plant,
A union so complete.
Forget your own consuming
Trance and share, oh, share
With me, this symbiotic fantasy."

Mouse Island, Fall 1980

Mouse Island is alone. Fog curls in, covering the silver day, smooth as a herring. I can wander the meadow between the tall brown house and the spotless gray, as though again it is my kingdom. I remember my first two summers and have hung on, hiding like a forest creature, waiting for September slumber and the night music of solitude. If I cross the field and head out to the southern point there is no one to break the spell of the island. Twelve cormorants startle and bend their black wings as I move past them but do not fly.

I am searching rocks with ribbons of white quartz, to see the patterns and the filigree. On the beach an oval stone I have studied all summer lies just above the receding tide. It looks like a half-knotted package—a white ribbon etched in its salt-washed surface.

The eider are turning white for winter. They are incongruous blotches like dollops of whipped cream. I don't remember this transformation so early and think, "It will be a cold winter."

Labor Day is a chasm that has nothing to do with seasons or the beauty of the coast. On that day vacations end, a sudden change leaves the harbor lonely and clean. Three sailboats have edged out into the bay today, errant yachtsmen favoring the crisp air of September. Each day the sun slides lower until by mid-month the sea is chain mail, hammered on the anvil of fall. The brilliance of moonlight lasts all day. The islands float in hard silhouettes sculptured in basalt.

Wise yachtsmen know the beauty of September. The watercolor brush of wind pulls confidently across the paper sea leaving the rough surface pebbled with contrast. I cannot pick a season. Each month of my life in Maine sweeps past, catching me tight in an embrace that crushes my body with remembrance and song. But September is a fine opal among gems.

At my studio I think of Dr. Fosdick's hymn, "God of Grace, God of Glory." I sense it was written here in the studio, where I so often sit with my feet pressed against the lichened granite and my back to unrelenting clapboard. In what other way can I explain the eider passing my ledge with their new ermine plumage or the purple aster and rock goldenrod springing from the rock for a September garland. Each year silt has pushed into a crevice below my studio. In four years a barren ledge is transformed to a bright bouquet, flowering on the same days.

Shadow and light now have greater contrast. Black and white, the strongest drama of art, come in this season. When summer and winter meet and brush past each other, they move along together melting into a world that is most beautiful.

Anne Thackeray [Ritchie] writing in 1893 about the photographer Julia [Margaret] Cameron says of her, "Many people can feel beauty and record it, she had an intuition, not only for appreciating, but for creating with the materials at hand."

"The materials at hand" are what each of us knows best. It is translating them from ordinary daily acceptance into moments of perfection: that is the difference. By limiting myself in my tapestries to two subjects, water and stone, I am searching for specific variety and strength, the simplicity and majesty that these two biblical elements contain. Water and stone we accept as basic substance of our environment but we see it only in a large way, not in detail.

There is no limit to the moods and faces of sea and ledge, the crevasse and peak of imagination mixed with this basic variety could create a million different tapestries. Perhaps after 1984 I will do an exhibition of a single rock or a drop of water. I feel that I can spin like a dervish—on and on scarcely changing the spot I stand in, but catching with my eyes the prisms of light and shadow as I whirl. And each revolution different and beautiful by itself.

My *Years at Giverny* are the quiet row to Mouse Island before the wind has chosen her path for the day, the contemplation of a single rock and the knowledge of the configuration of tide. Monet in his river-bound garden translated water lilies onto canvas, each brush stroke an inner delineation. His haystacks and poplars are my stone and water.

My feet have chilblains from the icy dew on the grass as I scurry laden with oars, my camera, and a leather bag full of wools to my morning row. The sea, a bright filigree of Moorish windows, pierces the spruce trees around the cove. I pull out at half tide, the rocks draped in seaweed rinsed by the fall of water. Silent island, serene island. Without hesitation I push open the door of my studio, clasp the red *tabis* to my feet and stretch out on my folding cot. No one is near. I think of the rock shelf at the south end of Mouse, asking myself if I have it securely in my mind for the winter, then of the patch of flat rock with its gray riband west of the beach and the Roman strips of rust and iron that I see in my mind as a great horizontal tapestry. I know ahead the days and months of work each of these ideas claims but I am exhilarated. It is a journey I lay out for myself with anticipation. If only I can keep fresh and clear the stored memories of my inspiration. Even the fading reality sometimes gives my final tapestry a greater strength as impressions blend and ripple like distorted reflections in the sea. These last days of summer are for storing.

Although I have only my sketches and my remembrance as I stare at the long white tables in my city garret, I know I will work with passion. The loss of Maine is like a collapsed lung, the pain of departure and separation is so intense. I lightly close the door each year and return to the city with inner agony. I hold it close. My arms are full of wool; I pour out my need and the beauty I have lost. Perhaps the change makes each tapestry stronger. *Flow of Inner Seeing* is a product of this expiation.

Mouse Island, Summer 1981

The air is still, boats float like models in corked bottles as I row to Mouse. With all the blueness and calm I feel bereft. A participant in the wake of my own creativity.

Thinking back five years I remember the magic of the pine path across the northeast face of the island. The fields of wild flowers are gone, the monumental flag staff that waved at every sail has disappeared. Mouse has become a suburban enclave. The rocks are the same. No one walks the beach or knows the hiding place of the sand dollar. The inhabitants are water skiers, keen for tennis and I am slipping slowly on wet seaweed into the sea and back to my shelter on Juniper Point.

The Loft is a shining star. The final polish came last week. With cabinets for yarns, drawers that move like feathers, even flower boxes of zinnias and petunias to remind me that my studio is earthbound.

Sailboats coursing the channel flaunt and disappear between the layers of spruce below my tall windows. A mysterious and beautiful place.

Florence Eldridge March has visited us this week and we have lifted our spiritual champagne to celebrate the Loft. Her wit and intelligence and acceptance of life I want as talismans for my studio.

In the Loft walls and cupboards are white. Birch and maple and the sculpture of the pine circular staircase to my balcony are golden tones. The textures are tapestries hung on the dominant east wall between the large windows and hung southeast and west on every space. I am already out of wall areas!

Rock Blooms, fourteen feet high, clings and curves on the major east surface. I designed it for that space, its looped gray form, cleavered by white wool and brushed with color. It is felicitous.

South is *Ascent* inspired by my winter on the Potomac River where I watched each day the turning back of the river craving its source. It is acceptable here but instinctively suggests it does not belong in Maine. Texture and curved surface are right, but it is softer somehow, a Dulcinea among giants.

The Loft is my measuring rod. I seek sweep and strength because that is the essence of coastal Maine. *Ascent* is another phase of *Aqua Lapis,* a more docile, less startling presence for all the grandeur of the Potomac.

But I am weighing the need for Mouse Island and I am loath to leave. How hard it is to make decisions that depend only on me. Because of the opulence of my new studio, this tiny room, twelve by ten, seems confining. I wonder how I contrived huge tapestries here or is it the rocks and the out of doors that have always mattered. I think that is it. The house means very little now that I have the Loft and can pull and unwind twenty feet of yardage like a great sail lifting it to the ceiling.

As I write this I am deciding. The rocks are here for inspiration; in May and September I can return to search every corner without hesitation. I was already here when the island awakened and no one notices as I slip past in my straw hat and shorts.

I will take my possessions ashore. This week I will write a check and call it quits—move on. There are other places I need to know better, rocks further out to sea at Newagen and the outer islands.

Muscongus Bay beckons. The granite with veins of quartz like cream and house paint are miracles of sculpture. That is the country my Loft demands.

Yes, I am going. I have walked the beach just now, past some granite rocks of rose and copper that will embroider into a tapestry full of pain at departure. My Loft is a citadel for work but here the chanterelle blooms, pure gold, and I am saying good-bye. I have done it and it hurts like dying must hurt. I cannot embrace so much and so leaving is a need too. I have told my island friends thank you, that I am going ashore.

I rowed out today on a north wind, drifting out to Mouse Island. Now the wind has turned scurrying between the islands, hard from the south. I will drift back to shore and set a new course.

Boothbay Harbor, Fall 1981

There is salt remembrance flowing the ridges and hollows of my face for the sheer wonder of the earth. Where rock and water meet, where fragility and strength test each other, sea pounding the granite ledge, changing while I watch, that is a fair time for tears of wonder and bereavement. And then as I watch the partners change. The quartz, tough as a knuckled fist, withstands the wave and the sea spreads about it like a carpet.

Almost every hour of these summer days I ask myself, "What is the most beautiful?" Always there is a cluster of answers, the pearly everlasting, robed like a bride, standing on bare rock to bloom, or the osprey cheeping above the harbor scolding the fishermen. He is brave these days and I hear his presence as I work. I find myself saying, if I have not been in a boat or run along the rock, "I have not been on the water today." It means my mind and heart have not been nourished. I am famished. I will dream about my sailboat when I leave and wish for water and stone. Long ago, when I lived the hot days of the Dominican Republic, and the dry spring of western Mexico, I had this same dream. My sloop, teasing her mooring, pulled and twisted in the wind, but I could not reach her. I would struggle to swim or row, to wrench myself out of the water onto her narrow deck. It was an endless dream, gnawing at the corners of my subconscious.

There are so many choices here by the sea and I choose all of them:—the long reflective mornings in my studio or on the rock with my sketch pad, and then sailing, swimming, and tennis with my family or a book to read in the sloping curve of the hammock slung beneath the spruces.

This is Rachel Carson country. She lived just a few miles along the shore of the Sheepscot River, a quiet reclusive woman with a pen full of poetry and truth. She seemed so vulnerable, speaking softly into an east wind—unheard. Now in tribute, the Coast Guard comes in a massive buoy boat to set protective buoys outside the osprey's nest. We begin to understand the levels of sea life at the ocean edge. We garden organically, carrying the rich minerals of seaweed to nourish our vegetable patch. More than any other single person of our century, Rachel Carson taught the protection of nature.

We share the strength and meaning of the earth and sea in this extraordinary place. It is eternal and we are the privileged. Here I feel not only continuity but regeneration and levity. I am not house conscious or dependent on people, but reach up instead to brush the shadow of a seagull, touch the pulled air of fog, and watch the unplowed fields melt from lupine to daisy to aster. My five months still seem so short. Leaving is an amputation.

～ 8 ～

Start Somewhere and Progress

*M*y eagerness to know creative people leads me here to a small colony, held together by a thread of thin silk considerably frayed. The day is autumn blue and gold, the red maples have shed their glory but the noon warmth lingers on as I drive into the yard past a stark white house called Frazier. There is no one anywhere. I walk from one small outbuilding to another finding shabby, dilapidated quarters, a chicken house, a garage with curtains, a music studio full of broken furniture and naked, suspended light bulbs. I feel suddenly that I am part of a colony of monkeys that have fouled their old nests and moved on just ahead of me.

I came without great expectations for amenities, to have solitude and to share with others the moments of creative conversation. The disorder is troubling to me and I question my own priorities. I think no wonder museum directors are astonished that I have planned five years ahead, chosen *Aqua Lapis* as the theme and set out to make a fine garment of imagination. If I lived like this in a house without beauty or the narrowest caring how could I create beauty? Am I right or wrong to value ambiance? At the Loft the precision of the work area is there and yet it is the long view that inspires.

In creativity the same unconscious selection leads me to choose the beautiful, innovative, imaginative facets of the world that is mine, the coast of Maine, the years of foreign travel and the steep hills beside the Potomac.

Cummington, Massachusetts, Fall 1981

For two hours I wander and wait, finally finding where I am to live. No one seems sure when I was coming. My new quarters, posted on the bulletin board, are "The Den" and "Skylight Studio." I find someone living there who is ill and has not moved. The room looks as it might if squirrels had been trapped in there all winter. Bits of paper, knots of dust and dog hairs from a forlorn gold setter are scattered about. I have chosen to come and will see it through. I am sure I shall learn and grow and perhaps see new meaning in a simpler life style. Perhaps, even cleanliness isn't godly at all but just another sinister device to keep women's hands busy at endless toil.

The young girl who is ill empties her loving rags and papers into boxes in the hall and shows me how I can start the wood stove. The sun is nearly down and the harvest moon is just rising. The warmth of the iron stove, grate open, flue full of flame, gives me courage. I look about.

I have a mattress balanced on boards with agate stains on both sides. No blankets, sheets or pillows. No pictures, no curtains; one straight back and one molting turtle of a chair sulking in a corner as dusty as a country road.

At the main house they have given me a rag and lemon oil to clean with. I laugh out loud as I examine the bare bones of my new home, thinking of lemon oil and the fine mahogany Pembroke table that my grandfather made.

I balance my sleeping bag at the edge of the bed, place newspaper over the dark stains, and prop up the small pillow I fortuitously brought with me. I lie down to look at the white oak umbrellaed above the skylight. There is a moment of beauty almost everywhere and this one I have found just in time. This is the spot I can return to when my spirit lags.

There is a front room with two narrow tables and a broken chair. I have mended it with string and laid out my tablets. A narrow drawer is lined with clean paper and here I put in order my pens and paper like tin soldiers ready to do battle.

The departing tenant, who is moving on to scatter a fresh nest, comes to join me and we walk together down the hill through a deep wooded bower to dinner. She carries a bright yellow lantern.

Swinging along in an easy gait I see the orange disk of the moon and anticipate the evening. These are people to whom earthly things are not important. I chide myself and march behind my guide through the open door into a large kitchen with huge pots and an enormous butcher block table. Beyond is the main meeting room. There are no ceremonies of living. We do not eat by candlelight but grasp our oval cafeteria plates and fill them with food. Adults hedge and circle like children asking a question here and there, and poking the hot coals, seeking warmth and color.

My plate full of hot rice from a great bowl, a chicken drumstick and salad precludes conversation for now. There is advantage in silence and tranquility. We are ten women and two men, about half are writers. I fit the conversation together like parts of a garment, sewing the easy seams first.

It is Monday and the weekly chores are handed out. Each of us will work a few hours at cleaning and once a week we must cook dinner. I am assigned to dinner on Thursday, with the poet. He wants to read his work but his message is temporarily lost behind a request for someone to drive the trash to the dump and the need for new shower curtains.

The poet surfaces again and agrees to read his poems tomorrow. The playwright on Thursday. Their willingness suggests we are a captive audience. I am eager to hear them. Two young women volunteer to show slides. No one is urged; it is only by choice.

After dinner the playwright engages me in conversation about my life of travel. I had mentioned that I had lived in many countries. He is just back from nine years in Greece. The Greek play is the vertebra of his writing. He sees it as the cry of a dying society. We sit and talk with pleasure while the others drift off. We ourselves drift to the idea of form in art. He calls it the essential, the core of beauty; form as in Brancusi and Arp. Sometimes I have called it rhythm or the world of the spirit. Form is equally acceptable. It is a certain inner order or shaping of thought that is creativity in essence. The playwright is a man without metaphysical involvement. He finds much of his world filled with agonies and form is his savior.

I have two elements. I have the belief, the deep hope and trust in a power beyond myself that is the buoyancy, and then the creative will; perhaps one comes from the other innately, but not as a form, not as a structure I have created to save myself.

The poet speaks of women and how they do not have the agony or creativity because "they are 'earth,' the bearers of children and all that." I ask him how he places the southern women writers in that

185

category. I remind him of Eudora Welty and Carson McCullers. The southern women have been twisted and tortured the most in our cultures, held to tradition and magnolia purity. They have need for expression of inner self. The great strength of the women who saved the South after the Civil War is heard in their literature.

The girl with the bright flashlight is gone. The playwright and I walk up the pebbled road together, still talking. This is what I want these weeks to be, an easy exchange. I walk alone down across the plowed field by moonlight and into my warm cottage with the bubbling stove.

Already it is my space, the rudiments of living, a pallet, a table and a chair. Moonlight fills the room as though the walls are transparent, flowing through the skylight and joining the glow of each window. I feel peace and simplicity. How quickly the pace of living here is teaching me its measure. I curl into my down bag and sleep.

This evening the poet reads to us from his memoirs of a year in Greece. His prose is heavy. I remember passing him by the barn this afternoon as he smote huge logs with a maul. I think of the analogy now as I sit on a sagging velour couch, all of us misshapen and formless while the poet reads on, savoring the words he has chosen.

Somewhere the reading softens as though the Greek air has melted him like wax into its own design. He read about a suicide and there is tenderness. The colors of words are no longer primary but mauve and soft, gray and rust. I no longer know the wood-cutter poet but see a new face and a hand that holds a pen gently. I then think that each of us has the capacity for poetry, but it involves work and much seeking and pain and caring. The wood-cutter poet may have all of these and if he does he will succeed.

He asks for comments. The room is silent. No one wishes to speak dishonestly. Someone says, "Thank you." I remember Jane Livingston coming to see my tapestries in 1975. She sat on the edge of the pink Victorian couch in my attic studio and never said a word. Silence can be a branding iron when your soul is gagged and cannot scream. It is the face of a dying man amid spring flowers.

I thank the poet too, tell him I am moved by the lines of "The Suicide," and suggest that the end is too long. Each of us speaks his or her heart then. Silence is a selfish thing. We say we do not want to hurt but in truth we do not want to expose ourselves. I am thankful for the wise people who have cared enough to be truthful. They are so few I remember each one.

The quiet and cadmium light of the hilltop of Cummington is already burnishing me. How lucky that I have come here where I can sit on a birch log and savor yogurt or walk the hills at my own pace. I had chosen to go to the MacDowell Colony—perhaps for its prestige—but now I think the total casting away of schedule and orderliness, the removal of curtains about my eyes and rugs giving way to leaves and fresh fern is the finest of all experiences.

I am back again to my days on a farm as I leave the circle of light and walk the stubbled field to my cottage.

The sun raced ahead of me this morning as I walked the hill before breakfast. I stopped to marvel at the stone corral built in 1783 "to contain beasties"; dark, flat rocks stacked five or more feet high in the shape of a thrown lariat. Beneath the painted maples the circle seems an enchanted ring, soft with fern turning to umber. Just beyond is a modest green with a plaque announcing the first church of this area in 1781. The road to the left swings easily along the ridge of hills. The sun warms my hair, the stone walls I pass are dark and flat, wide as a table, regal. They have stood two hundred years, built by strong hands and hearts. The energy of their presence bordering my pathway excites me. I was not looking for images here, only solitude and peace.

Being at Cummington is that way. No one here knows who I am and I learn that I don't know either. I expected to feel unimportant and it is a good feeling. I knew I would find other souls keener and more gifted than I am. I learn from their writing and slides where I fit in the group of twelve. It is not the fitting in so much as a sense of learning from each one, from what he or she does exceptionally well.

Walking over the fields at night and down to the wooded fringe to my house I am accompanied each night by the harvest moon. There still lingers in my mind the strange man outside my bedroom door in Washington who came to rob our Christmas peace; the sharp steel point of a few seconds of cold terror. I recall his escape and capture. The knowledge that I have been inwardly maimed for life and cannot shake it totally off repels me. In Maine I am at peace because I know the people and place so deeply. Reason tells me that no one is lurking in the woods by my cottage with its two lonely chairs, a stained mattress and four hard-boiled eggs. Fear is just there and has to be tilted with each night.

Frazier, the salon of Cummington, has sagging chairs and no rugs or curtains. It is like the living quarters in a mental institution where no one cares. The fireplace has been destroyed by an old wood stove with feet planted sideways across what once was the focal point of a gracious room.

Tonight the writers of laughter have placed a reading stand, and first the tall, friendly girl from a Boston tradition reads three chapters of her novel. She explains that much of it is autobiographical. Some of it would scandalize her proper past but all of it is imaginative, clear and pithy—straight out talent which is so hard to find. The need to express herself and even a sense of vindication not only as a writer, but as a woman is wrapped up in her rollicking, laughter-and-tears prose.

The second novelist is plump with a marcel that runs around her head in a single wave. She loves to eat and her jolly body vibrates as she stands in front of the buffet table choosing seconds. She is pleasant and easy and likeable, a real candy bar, neither expensive nor memorable but with a self-indulgent simplicity. Instinctively, I knew her short stories would be light and as revealing as a glass-bottomed boat and that there would be talk about food. She read two situation stories, the husband and wife conflict, and gratification of the senses was the message; marvelous sandwiches concocted to add humor and as love offerings, neat little dresses described that she herself would choose to wear. It was fun but so superficial as to dry on the paper in invisible ink before I could lift my eyes.

At almost eleven I slip out of Frazier and walk the long meadow to my cottage. Each night the moon rises later and later like a sleepy truant, but always in time to fill me with warmth and companionship as I follow the furrowed path to the hollow where my falling-down home leans upon itself. Strangely, it already seems like home to me as though its sparse chairs and sunlight, the deep woods on two sides and the coins of light on the lane that separates the two meadows are a permanent part of me. No one has come to this house except the plumber to turn off the water. I still have electricity, and my mighty cauldron.

In the night I walk out into the stars with the same sense of passion and fulfillment that a singer steps forth to sing a lyrical aria. There are no sounds. Not even the copper leaves hanging dry on maple limbs move or sail forth. The stars are as bright as I have ever seen them and from my hilltop close to my sky-lit studio I can see the whole circle, the Pleiades, the Dipper and a thousand stars I wish I knew.

For the first time I understand what it is like to be a "hillbilly." The tar paper thin on the roof, the front door does not quite close unless I lift the lame hinge and place it in position like a broken limb. The water has been turned off so that I use a teakettle to hold water for my hot tea, but I also boil eggs at the same time and slosh out my bowl and cup with the same water, leaning out of my doorway when it is cold. A small plastic container makes an adequate potty and that, too, goes out on the dried leaves beyond my house. The floors and the walls are totally bare, the windows black spaces at night and full of fall glory with the first rays of light. I am finding this is not a bad life at all.

My lunch is a hard-boiled egg, a slice of brown bread, a cup of milk or a dish of yogurt and a yellow tomato from the garden that has not yet frosted. I have not had a teaspoon of sugar since I came and feel no need. Every two or three days I replenish my jar of milk from the main house. It comes from a local dairy with a swirl of cream on the top and a taste I had long ago forgotten. There are no interruptions.

Today I have finished the rewriting and tightened the script of my journals. This is the fourth revision and I begin to see a possible shape of observations and song emerging. There are about three hundred and thirty pages typewritten now. A bit more than we expect to use but as we polish, some of these choices will be removed and new works will take their place. The book will continue until press time in order to be complete.

No one has come in ten days to my studio to talk to me or interrupt in any way. It is a luxury I have eagerly sought and I am comfortable with it. I will always have more to do than there is time to achieve and here in this quiet I can take time to rest, to close my eyelids and feel the sun, to walk the fields and woods. I stop to listen as I work and hear the stamp of deer shaking the flies at the forest edge or see the red-shouldered hawk above. The country is strangely silent, not like my youth. Now the songbirds are so few. It is quiet night and day. Where are the bobwhite and the whip-poor-will and even the blue jay scolding? Only quiet, the gentle rattle of leaves in the wind and the humming of larger circles of wind that slide up and down the hills and through the branches of hemlock and pine.

I have taken my sleeping bag out onto the field and lie there as still as the earth savoring the quiet.

This was to be two weeks to work on my book but already I have a tapestry in my imagination, a rare surprise in a place so new. I will call it *Field Stone and Fire*. It will be about the fieldstone walls, their black, flat shapes, the schist from the bottom of an ancient ocean lifted up and layered above black stones.

In the last week I have drawn closer to the group and especially the novelist. I not only discover that I know her mother but that our backgrounds are very similar. She is full of uncertainty about her course even though from her youngest years she has been singled out as a brilliant student, winning prizes for writing in high school and at Wellesley. She has read aloud here twice and each time to unanimous approval. She is very gifted and also dedicated to writing. She sees stories everywhere and while I have been here these two short weeks I have shown her some of the threads of history of this beautiful area. She has almost finished a story about our visit to the Bryant and Melville houses. She has put her novel down for that moment and sent out her first story to *The New Yorker*. That would be like my taking my first tapestry to the Modern Art Museum.

It occurs to me that the Whitney and the Modern may never show my work until after I am gone and then only *perhaps*. New York is supercharged with people shoving to have their work shown and with skillful public relations people selling. The same is true for literature I am sure.

Prophesy

Autumn has folded in her wings
The eleven nights I slept
In the Berkshire hills. I watched
Her settle in her nest, tinged
Rust with frost and then

Her limbs laid bare waiting
To mate again and fill
Her nest with lilacs and fresh rue.
Snow will lay a carpet
On her life while patiently
She crouches to the suffocating
Burden, bends in her frozen
Wings to fill the hollow nest.
Her own resignation taught to
Feathered children who
Will warm new generations.
The cock's comb needs
No help against the ice.

This autumn of eleven days
Tells me the bird will not
Be there next spring, but has
Flown out straight at Alderbaran
Leaving the frosted hollow to her mate.

With my new friends we talk on many subjects. I listen to a discussion of lesbianism, a solace that has replaced the failed marriage of a gifted woman. It fills her need and I understand again the torments that face young women. Almost none of the bright ones are waiting for the perfect man. They feel he does not exist and instead are veering in directions that test their heritage. We talk about the women writers who profess their sexual needs, of Virginia Woolf, Gertrude Stein and May Sarton. That personal aspect of their lives has shadowed all their writing, not because it is important I think, so much as for its affront to the male mystique. Many of the homosexual writers we do not even know and those we do are generally accepted for their skill as writers. Their private lives are of no consequence.

I realize that in my own life I have contained my rebellion at the role I often was called to play. My deafness is a testimony to that withholding. I have cared so much. I am driven to reach up and say "Follow me" even when I am not allowed a choice.

Here at Cummington I have made friends. All the conversations start somewhere and progress. I do not have to go back to the beginning and explain. We understand. There is talk of creativity on every level and sharing of hopes and need for counsel. Tonight I help the child painter with the pink face and curly hair to fill out a Fulbright application for Spain. I test her Spanish, X the proper boxes and suggest she get some Spanish books from Smith to read to widen her knowledge. She is full of dimples, disarming and eager. She has written that she wants to go to Spain to turn her art into that of a woman. Open and simple; perhaps it will touch a critic. Probably not. They will prefer an erudite intellectualized painter who wants to paint the separation of church and state or the Spanish olive in ten ways. Those ideas get prizes, not the flowering of talent.

Tomorrow I leave reluctantly. The company of friends at Cummington says they will all come see me at Thanksgiving time. I beg them to. It would be reliving a wonderful adventure.

Washington, Winter 1981

For Christmas I receive from the poet two delicate volumes of poems inscribed to me. Surely by now they should have forgotten who I am. I am deeply moved.

~ 9 ~

Art Is My Passport

I am at Dulles Airport. They call it preparation for the first leg of a voyage. It is more like the outer room of a surgical ward. Not just one leg, but my whole being is caught and pulled into a huge machine, shuttling me to the wide aisles and rows of seats like giant teeth on a hungry monster. There is the same sense of inevitability.

I have been lured to my narrow leather seat on the elevated space cars that Eero Saarinen, the wizard of architecture, designed to carry passengers to the great sharks—the 727s lurking at the edge of the landing field.

A trip to Africa, to six countries via twelve airports, is a prize to be sought. It has happened in surprise and was unsought. I am tempted by adventure always, since I first learned to read the bright paper and childlike prose of the *National Geographic*. A grant from the National Endowment for the Arts coming at the age of sixty is surprising. It must have a reason and a meaning in my creative life. I remember the mohair and karakul discoveries of my trip to South Africa five years ago and hope other discoveries await me.

There are long stairs we climb in every life. There are choices and resting places and we can stop on any landing, for breath, for good, or to turn back. I suffer from the compulsion to press on, scarcely touching the treads, looking back only with warm remembrance and ahead with anticipation.

Last night at a farewell dinner around our oval table I saw the reflection of my children in the polished wood and remembered the laughter and loving of so many years. To have a son already thirty-five and still be invited to tour a strange land is thrilling.

We are airborne, lifting sharply with almost the surge of an osprey. The wings of the wide earth open to let us escape and we bend toward Paris. In the night the stars from my starboard window float above and below me. I think of space travel. Perhaps John Glenn had this same transitory view before he lifted away to see the curve of our world. People hang in sleepy shapes over the seats, like figures fallen in a battle. Humanity unconscious is so vulnerable and transitory. Only children are beautiful in sleep; every curve rounding gently into the next. I will always cherish the movement of a sleeping child, a beauty as rare as the May blooming of the tree peony.

The first lines of pink and orange appear as we drift down through clouds to Charles de Gaulle Airport. The layers are like rowing to Mouse Island on a foggy day. There is a suspension of time, a feeling that I am nowhere and everywhere. I am conscious of a deep belief in the beauty of life and in the eventuality of death. At the end a gentle fog sustains me. I think of Mother and how she wrote on her travel form under "Religious Belief" first, "Protestant," and then, dissatisfied, "Christian." Still not saying what she wished, she crossed that out and wrote "Believer." I share that feeling here in the clouds above Paris. Here in the sky where I have had a vegetarian dinner, gentle music, a cup of fresh milk, I find it easy to believe, especially in the clouds that cannot be captured and measured. I know that in Benin or Lesotho or Madagascar I will share with those I meet not only our love of art but our believing. I can be happy wherever there is warmth and trust. It is my baggage we will share.

Charles de Gaulle was quite as forbidding as his airport; the long electrified corridors carrying us relentlessly up and down hill at good speed. Even graffiti would add cheer. Delays are exaggerated by our high school French, although these weeks when I have been practicing my speech have been helpful. The temptation is to bolt a croissant and coffee and race to Paris for a day. How I would like to see the new Pompidou Museum with its painted viscera and limitless space.

Weariness overcomes us. We cast aside the notion. The capsule of isolation for a day catches and holds us. It is a dichotomy, an isolation of sharing. Fitting for France that we choose to curl within each other, share a warm bath. I am reading the last *Diary of Anaïs Nin*. Nowhere better to comprehend her sensuality. I look at my naked shape in a bathroom of mirrors. I am surprised to see I still have breasts that tilt up and a small half melon between my hip bones. It is smooth and fits together not on a long stem of beauty, but the curves are agreeable. Perhaps a Puritan ethic pushes this acquaintance back in my mind. This was part of my education, a once-a-day look in the glass to test cleanliness—no more. Also a forgetting of self. A compulsion. It makes the occasional discovery of my own physical presence a revelation. I remember last summer a new wine-colored swim suit, stretched from breasts to hips in one splash of color. And that Bill called out "What a bod," as I ran to swim. I liked that.

Paris is behind in fog and cold north wind, and we are swaying, swaying gently as sweet dawn reveals the Mediterranean. Across the aisle a passenger lifts the *Ne Pas Avoir* sign to reveal an empty space where a life raft should be. Air Afrique is a bundle of compromises. Half the bulbs overhead are burned out; there are no pillows; baggage is piled everywhere. The aisles look like a public laundry. There is humor and good-natured laughter as a snore explodes from a weary passenger.

Over Rome we lurch and race through the clouds like a drunken osprey. The air beneath us parts and suddenly we plunge, barely regaining our wings—back to Marseille to sit out a storm in Rome. Babies scream, putting their voices along the highest chord of the violin string of their being. It is one-thirty in the morning. We are closeted in our plane while we wait for word from Paris and from the storm in Rome.

On most European flights there are one or two children. They usually make a sound either of laughter or need. Tonight at the edge of the Mediterranean this is a different world. Babies with their penises and harp-shaped organs lie about us in wilted diapers. They are eager and hungry to fill our world, yet their land is one of growing poverty. Will they come to adjust to the ice age countries, or devour each other? It is a terrifying question. I am calculating how many hours of cultural exchange there will be during the days of this journey.

To the moment of departure, time has slipped away in air schedule changes—the final itinerary, if all goes well—four days in Benin, two each in Lesotho, Botswana and Swaziland, and four in Madagascar—if the Tanzanians will give my bundles of baggage passage (I left without the necessary visa!). I shall be traveling for more than thirty days in all. More than half my time is taken with work and I rue the tapestries I will not be able to work on for these five weeks. This is a lesson in patience. To learn again the drudgery as well as the triumph of travel. The hours of paperwork, packing and unpacking—of counting luggage and hauling the great beasts from one rack to another. I have ten pieces of luggage, two cameras, eight tapestries—all but one of them larger than four feet by ten feet tall. And a bundle of poles. Clothes are the least of it. I have three long bright costumes for my lectures, a pair of black tapered silk pants with a silk jacket as vivid as a jungle bloom, and a soft lavender and orange floating gown with a beautiful orange manila shawl that Marion Scott gave me. I will wear my copper necklace with the turquoise as big as a silver dollar that I designed in Mexico. I chose the copper to complement the cool color of the green-blue stone. We reach Abidjan four hours late but our next flight is still waiting—on to Togo and Cotonou.

We dash from one plane to another, short-cutting the low shed and the endless official paper shuffling at Ivory Coast. Our plane arrives without food or water. We have not eaten since our meal at midnight.

A tiny girl in a yellow pinafore comes aboard with her father and climbs onto the seat next to me. She balances in one hand two small silvery cartons of jelly from a breakfast tray. In the heat and long wait they ooze like honey onto her tiny black fingers. Immediately she wipes her gooeyness on the seat and on my long-suffering travel suit, already on its third day of continuous wear. Softly I wipe up the sugary leavings and offer her a magazine. I am so touched by her tiny presence. Her hair is parted like a vegetable patch and each section twisted and separated to sweep back in a spiraled line to the nape of her neck. The "Afro" of ten years ago, the close-cropped cut I find so handsome, is no longer popular. Now every stylish black woman has a headful of tiny braids and twirls, caught like a bouffant headdress of Medusa. The ancient Bernini bronzes show this same kind of scarification of women's hair. Ancient wood and metal masks worn by men in rituals also have the same looped and braided art.

A brief stop in Togo is perhaps the most picturesque moment so far in my two trips to Africa. Men and women dressed in flamboyant prints of orange and white, great motifs of the universe or of a neighboring Saturn have been printed against an apricot background and made into two-piece suits for men and long dresses for women. All of them have the same print for hats and semi-turbans. Outside the shed, twenty or thirty people are dressed in an orange print of a similar cloth. Their costumes are more exciting than those of a beautiful Broadway musical. The dark faces and the undulating bodies with their cadmium plumage seem from another planet.

Benin

By comparison our arrival at Cotonou is quiet and dignified, and of no particular consequence. Mr. Rivera, our public affairs officer, waits patiently. No one tells him why we are late or even that we would be. This is a holiday but he has been here since 11 A.M. assuming we would come. Benin is a country ideologically at odds with what they suppose us to be. The stereotype is so wearisome. Our representative must channel all programs through a government committee. I am the first visitor the government has allowed and will go one hundred miles northeast to Abomey to talk about art with the appliqué makers, men who in previous times worked on banners and umbrellas and clothing in primary colors to the order of their king. That adventure comes tomorrow.

Abomey was also the home of the legendary Amazons. They were the fierce women guards of the royal palace at Abomey, given their name when the British came to Dahomey a hundred years ago. I am the first Amazon to come here with needle and thread. Will they be mightier than the sword?

The real Abomey is a surprise. There are no signs of the Amazons or of their heirs. Women shuffle through the streets bearing all the burdens of constant childbirth, ignominy, and disease. The town or city has two paved streets teeming with *les peuples*. A large red clay enclosure in the town's center is in disarray. If I had come here from Manhattan or from the great museums of Chicago and Washington without the detours to the Puerta del Sol on the altiplano of Bolivia, or the central plaza of San Sebastian in Mexico, the shock would have been unbearable. I take a long breath as I view desolation, decay. Low, decrepit buildings lie about like wounded animals, edging the wide enclosure. Walls are collapsing, leaving red earth and weeds panting up above the grass. One handsome baobab tree is the only grace note and shade. Here I will work out of doors. There are no facilities, no water, no shield against the dust. The men have only their mats in this so-called palace where the famous appliqué makers of Abomey cut deft figures for the ancient kings of Dahomey.

All my "students" are men; the descendants of the earliest tapestry makers, the designers! They greet us with a tribal party—with drums and dancing. Chairs in a prim row for us; a semi-circle of figures in bright batiks for them. They all wear hats over their stiff black hair—a wool stocking cap, a turban, a flash of orange baseball visor. Each dancer solos, kneading his legs and arms, down, down in muscular thrusts almost to the dust of the red dirt.

The cadmium baseball hat is the humorist, a vivid tropical bird among the dancers. Dignity and deep feeling pouring from these men who will sit quietly over the next three days, scarcely moving as they cut delicate figures with huge shears from cotton cloth. I can imagine that I see in the shadow, under a long shed, the lions and giraffes, the wading birds and peacocks that they have fashioned. My own plumage is white shirt and pants and a red straw hat. I am happy to have chosen the red hat as my symbol. Each one of them will find me instantly. It is my badge as their hats are for them.

The dancing subsides and we start together to see the handwork made in this patio, springing from dry earth like rare flowers. There are tables of bronze herons, of native figures and a wonderful fat snail with his antennae stretched in elegant length. And there is the shed of the tapestries where King Ghezo chose the form of the buffalo in 1818. King Glele, his successor, chose the elephant; and the last of the kings, Behanzin, the shark. In ancient times these wizards of appliqué sewed not only banners but also pillows, ceremonial clothing and umbrellas. Now they only make wall hangings.

Ernest Fiogbe and his brother Richard walk with me, eager and generous, all talking at once in French. Reaching into my newly nurtured vocabulary from forty-five years ago, I find a few adjectives to show my pleasure. I shake every hand. They seemed tortured, agonized men in their dancing, utterly remote. Now they are like puppies; we move closer. We all smile easily and laugh together with the naiveté and excitement of their art.

From there to the only solid structure—a long narrow adobe building—with a dirt floor, where the weavers have their looms. The long threads of cotton woven in twenty-inch (half-meter) widths stretch fifteen and twenty feet, crisscrossed above the red dust. They use white with bright accent notes of classic shapes they have repeated for generations.

Each day I travel eighty-five miles from Cotonou to Abomey and back, the narrow road nibbled on both edges by carts and rain and the constant shuffle of motorbikes and country passage. It is flat country, with one verdant valley where the road is as ridged as a tin roof. Our large, heavy sedan moves in the slow pattern of jolts like an ancient prairie wagon. Leaving Cotonou at eight, stopping for Dennis, our escort from the Ministry of Popular Culture, we will reach Abomey with luck by ten-thirty or quarter to eleven. They are long, hot, exhausting days working under the tin-roofed shed.

They are also exhilarating days when I use every facet of my mind and heart to reach these people and share with them a memorable experience. The workers are magnificent. Ernest, the leader of the appliqué artists, is all muscle and bravado. He smiles warmly, with a flash of white teeth more beautiful than carved ivory. I show him a quick sketch of a little boy dancing from the ceremony of yesterday. I cut a figure in sheets of paper, old maps of the U.S.A. that I have brought from Cotonou. He lifts his own shears and cuts an African dancer that writhes and twists before my eyes—the hands are so expressive. I am excited by his skill. He has cut the African message—the undulation of life—as I never will.

But the face of the delicate child is a man's face. A small boy has brought his drum and sits near us. I call him to show Ernest the pear-shaped face of the child—that nose and eyes are not important—only the oval and the pointed chin. He takes his scissors again, sits thoughtfully, and cuts a gentle shape, stops again, and cuts the cheek and the chin out of white batiste. I am touched by his sensitivity. How fascinating that he should choose white to say innocence and purity.

Here in Abomey where everyone is black I am completely at ease. I have no sense of color, of mine or theirs. I see their beauty of body and spirit, and a warm current flows between us. At the end of my visit when they present me with a tapestry, and cheer me, and shake my hand over and over I can say with a voice that wavers with emotion (and even as I write a few drops race down my cheeks) *"Vous etes mis amis pour toute mi vie."* I will never forget them.

What have I left behind of myself? Will there be something that lingers on to add to the culture of the kings of Abomey? The idea is preposterous. And yet I hope I have opened in their creative hands some new vista, some new knowledge that will expand their world as they have enlarged mine.

I have taught them to look at nature, to see the shape of the baobab tree as different from the palm and the banana. Somewhere near the turn of the century they stopped depicting the human figure. Together we do a large tapestry with a cluster of dancers, all cut by them, with a tom-tom and under the shade of a great tree. Their figures are isolated shapes unrelated to each other. Together we group them into a story of my welcome. They cut a hat (my red straw) for the tom-tom player.

Isn't this how art evolves? My hat, their scissors, their rhythmic scissors, my sense of story. The director of the museum, an overbearing political puppet, believes that only the past is important and nothing in the art of Abomey should change. He sprawls in his chair, picking his nose while I stand. "This will be the only tapestry of its kind—no copies." We are presenting it to the Committee of Popular Culture. Undoubtedly he will burn it before I am airborne, but he cannot obliterate the current of learning and sharing, the hours I sat cross-legged on the mat under the tin roof, laughing and working with the appliqué artists of Abomey.

What are other women of sixty doing in Abomey? I suspect they are all in heaven. Only one derelict, propped between two posts with her worldly misery about her may have been my age. What a rare gift to be vital and caring and chosen to share these hot, intense and extraordinary days with scissors and needle among friends who speak my artistic language.

Will I change my style because of them? It is too soon to evaluate the meaning but it was meant to happen that I should have traveled here, the first woman ever to enter their professional ranks, the first American invited by a hostile government, to be warmed finally by their artists' generosity and comprehension. A rhythmic impact will be added, of that I am sure. They bend their bodies and scissors with more abandon and I will follow their lead.

For our country it signaled a new understanding in a totally apolitical way. At the closing ceremony, with speeches, a band, the typical dishes of corn cakes, spinach and liver, Cokes and spirits, they shook my hand hard over and over to speak of *plus cooperacion*. The future may diminish or grow. I cannot decide that.

I have left my Georgetown house, with the vaulted ceilings and the green garden, to travel three long days and nights through a teak forest to their workshop. It has been a transition from velvet couch to straw mat that I could not have imagined. Art is my passport. It transcends and contains those of us who follow it. Art is as universal as moonlight, as sure as the North Star.

Benin teems with activity. I am reminded of Indonesia by the poverty and the omnipresence of crowds of people as well as their grace and carriage. Nearly every woman carries a baby swaying from her hips. And most are counterbalanced by a blossoming pelvis, announcing the imminent arrival of the next cherub. Goats and occasional stray dogs are the four-legged life. The goats are rickety and cadaverous with a humped back like miniature Brahmin cattle. Children and adults alike have learned to jump into the bushes quickly as horns blow and jeeps and small European carts rocket down the narrow roads. Drivers are supreme and humanity is wary. Benin traffic lights are infrequent and everyone tries to be first. It is an African disease of epidemic proportions. (Later in Lagos, Nigeria, we saw four major accidents in less than two days. Two of them took place before our eyes.)

For our last afternoon in Benin, we hired a small boat to visit the floating village of Ganvié just 18 miles from Cotonou. The trip is instant wonder, from the first narrow cypress boat paddled by a long oar with a round blade, to the brightly painted houses on stilts, just inches above the lake. Sails are squares of batik or discarded cotton print flung up on forked sticks to pull the fragile shells across the bay to Ganvié.

This is a truly stilted village. Its houses are two feet or more thick with thatched roofs and are propped one against the other. Our bateau drifts past open doors and papier mâché walls, on narrow porches pigs snort, and little boys jump from them into the water and jostle. The market is a collection of boats, each one peddling new straw hats, tomatoes, or even a bucket of fresh water. The marketers are all women, most of them sitting firmly on the rear thwart with a brown babe tied to their waists. One mother holds her infant between her knees while he suckles and she serenely paddles. We stop at a small curio shop—a large thatch house of two rooms, the front one open to the water just inches below. A fire burns in a round hearth and a gibbon is tied to the front post. Their handicraft is mostly voodoo carvings—family pieces they do not sell. I find a wood box of *mancala*, the arithmetic game of stones placed in twelve cups, six to a player. We intend to learn.

The delicate beauty of the butterfly sails, the bell-shaped nets and thatched roofs drift past as I fill my sketchbook. I see it is a civilization of mayflies—a people who are born today and will live their short span on this watery curio, floating in a lake. Their nourishment is tiny fish and occasional scraps from the mainland. It is a civilization I cannot fathom. I am without judgment. Their happiness does not seem resignation, nor is mine. Our worlds touch only lightly as two migrating birds headed for different shores. They scarcely acknowledge my presence. On their canals, passing their nets, I move as a phantom, scarcely believing my own racing pulse.

It has taken all these years to feel neither pity nor scorn. My work-for-the-night-is-coming ancestry has filled my life in a cheerful, sleeves-up, head-held-high kind of way that I am comfortable with. But now I see that the girl stretched on a bench on her watery porch is just as happy. If her fleeting moment is shorter, she has no comparison to make, and would not trade ice and snow for sun and water or starch and wash-and-wear for her vivid gown. My pleasure is that in Abomey I reached an understanding through my art, and here I need only drift by as in a picture gallery.

Nigeria (A Stopover)

Nigeria is quite another matter. Red wine flows through the energy, the pulse, the tempo of this country. Oil has brought affluence and with it a throw-away society. From the airport the scene is festooned with piles of trash. Cluttered scrap and garbage and demolished cars litter the freeways. Men dress in white eyelet cotton with woven hats (fez). The "best" hotel, the Ikoyi, has one intermittent elevator for fourteen stories, a dining room of dirty table clothes, bad service, surly receptionists. The driver explains to me that many Nigerians are brutish, especially to women. Some, particularly the porters and the less important economically, are charming.

The National Museum in Nigeria is an oasis. Everything is carefully explained, the costumes of the Yoruba, especially their love of masquerade. To fit oneself into another skin of knitted body suit with ruffs and cuffs or into a great headdress that transforms one into a spirit is to be two distinct persons. The heritage of Nigeria's province of Benin is arresting. Here are the serene heads in bronze, with their native necklaces of coral curled from shoulder to chin. There seems a clear link between the oriental bronzes of China and what we see. In ancient times the kings dressed from head to foot in coral. The interlude of art is nourishment. Art shines forth bringing inner intelligence and peace.

Returning to our hotel, great plates full of rice and chicken await; huge chunks of meat are shoveled down with intense animalistic concentration in the shabby dining room. Gratification of the flesh overwhelms me perhaps because this is a jazzy hotel for the pretentious *nouveau riche*. In Miami we find much the same. It is not color or country but circumstance that sets the stage. Isolated families come to dine with lively young children and a glow of happiness that is infectious. We dance and chat with a Brazilian engineer and his bride, walk the sidewalk at evening to the edge of the sea and look across the island of Ikoyi to Lagos Island and the mainland. The port full of ships will work even through the Muslim festival of Eid el-Kabir.

I never knew that Lagos, the city, was three islands, rimmed by a magnificent beach and with a wide and beautiful series of harbors. The air is cooler than farther west on the coast and one feels that early ships floated here on wind currents bringing them from the Cape of Good Hope. But now I have the feeling as I search for even a blossoming weed between the cracked pavement, the broken glass and the twisted automobiles flung up on the roadside that no one thinks of trees, or birds or notices the small rind of moon I can see from my narrow balcony. Crowds are out on their thin ledges to view the accident below where two cars careened into each other at 5 P.M. Now, at ten they are listening to jazz in the patio, but the rising moon and I are alone, watching each other shyly.

This morning as I leave this wastebasket of man's greed and carelessness I hear a bird. It sounds like the Carolina wren from the Virginia forest. It cannot be, because I know from my trip in 1975 that the birds of Africa are really different. I try to see his wings on the still air but even the direction of his song is impossible because of my deaf ear. I have no triangulation of sound but I can listen to the clean notes as they drop like dew on my parched ears. It is a clear call of hope in a frantic world. I think back to my first weeks in Bronxville and to the wood thrush that came to my suburban lawn like a robin and sang to me so often. I hope to see that side of Africa too, not just the lusting and the abuse.

The papers are full of African famine—it has spread from the desert countries of the Sahel, of Mali and Chad and east to Ethiopia and into Somaliland. It is pressing south into Kenya, but the famine is not the wrath of nature; it is the work of man. They give three reasons—war, greed and mismanagement. It is a pitiful time for a continent eager for independence, unwilling to show restraint. Nigeria shows this lack of self-control most clearly.

Nigeria is a masculine country. While I wait for my ticket at the Nigerian Air terminal I face a girl in jade green uniform, enigmatic and hostile. I need her friendship because there are problems with my ticket. Our tickets carry the wrong letters although the flight number is correct. They refuse to take us. When the men withdraw seeking a correction, I step close and ask softly, "Is it hard for a woman to get a job like yours here in Nigeria?" I have pressed the panic button, and she says quickly, "It is very hard for women here. I cannot get into the university to study. I want to go away. I have all my papers, but you must know someone important to get in." I slip her my card and give her an address where there may be help here in Nigeria. When our flight is finally approved, she races to the plane with me, carrying my heaviest bag. At the last moment she slips our passports into my hand as the door of our plane closes. Inside is her name and address.

But I leave with no regret, unable to accept the hot breath of tribal heritage upon my centuries of Yankee culture. I do not belong. I want to live in gentler places. Perhaps it is not the tribal so much, or even the voodoo—as the Muslim. He seems a pompous unsmiling sphinx in this part of the world. In my red straw hat, pants and independence, I am as much of an enigma to him.

Again it is like the floating houses of Ganvié. I will float away in my airplane to another culture and each of us will be complete. I am too far removed. Only art has opened a window for me with the scent of a simple flower of an ancient time.

There are so many I want to help and my strength fails me. By the time we are airborne after two hours of tension and blunt refusal,

I am drained. The flight east is clean and level on an empty plane where I can stretch across three seats and sleep.

Air travel is for me a needed vacuum. It offers a solitude that sustains me between periods of deep giving as I seek to share all of myself with each place we visit. In Abomey I slept perhaps five hours each night, practicing my French, planning designs, anticipating directions and needs of my pupils in a village living a century behind me. Nigeria was visual conflict and the sense of being on ice in a hot country. But the long undulating ride has restored me.

We fly past Lake Victoria seeing her northern end, the islands and shores, the gilded edges of beach. Then I move to the starboard side, looking south, and the lake disappears over the curve of the world. What an amazing woman Queen Victoria was, with or without Disraeli. This is a tribute to her and the men of her time; the exploits of the Stanleys and Livingstons, the Richard Burtons—an extraordinary parade of men. And the men and women who were given wings to see lightly and easily all they uncovered.

Kenya (Another Stopover)

We swoop down to Kenya. The spring rains have not started but the jacarandas are blue violet lace. There are parks and flowers everywhere. Best of all the black faces are beautiful; everywhere elegant people with polished dark skin and blazing smiles. The contrast to Nigeria is as lead to opal. English in their throats is a beautiful language. They give it new grace. Our brief overnight is one of delight. We are ecstatic to be returning after five years.

Somehow in Nairobi I am unprepared now for the flow of black and white together. We share the same dance floor, chat easily, laugh a lot over Cokes and beer. Where I have been before, one color or the other dominated. Benin and Nigeria are black and I am an intruder. There is no escape. Here in Kenya I feel for the first time since I left home that we all belong. That is what I want. To be able to grasp softly the hand of a small black child and say with the same humility I do to my own grandson, "I love you," and to know he loves me too. It is possible, and the liberals so often cannot see it. I believe the most liberal minds want a world we all can share, but they write and talk as though all that is white is wrong and oppressive and do not see the dignity and learning the white man has shared. There is the tribal dignity too, but the history of tribes alone is not reassuring. Nairobi is. Perhaps Zimbabwe will be too. I know that neither white nor black is more beautiful, that only the two colors side by side have the greatest impact. This is an artist's knowledge. Look at the slashes of black paint on white of Motherwell and Franz Kline. Or study black and white embroidery. The contrasts come together to make a beautiful whole. As an artist I see the visual impact as a deeper message. I believe we can share.

The Republic of South Africa (A Stopover)

Our arrival at Johannesburg is cold and efficient. The Afrikaners seem solid and unmovable. Efficiency and cleanliness are accepted without question. They seem a race unto themselves, a Germanic-Flemish strain that for 200 years has doubled back upon itself producing large lusty people, porcelain blond babies, muscle, a strong jaw and determination. In no sense do they think of South Africa except as "their" land.

A few subservient blacks slip noiselessly about at the airport. It is an intolerable situation; the more so because the unavoidable collision lies somewhere down the road ahead. I do not believe they will find an accommodation. Each is determined to crush the other totally, and as time progresses the anger mounts. The Afrikaners will defend to the death. They are still the Boers. The blacks will perish in shocking hordes, mowed as mercilessly by automatic fire as partridge before sweepers. But they have more to lose. They will fight ceaselessly and will survive because of their numbers.

In the midst of my own dire litany we visit with an Afrikaner family in Pretoria. Anna has come to pick us up at the airport—a renewed friendship established five years ago when I lectured at the Pretoria museum. She is graying now, shy yet warm. I hug her spontaneously, drawn to her by the years of letters we have exchanged and our mutual love of art. Art is a castle that shines across the darkest plain. It beguiles both of us. Anna and I become reacquainted as we roll north across her verdant country thirty miles to Pretoria.

Our bedroom in her white-washed house is full of dark Victoriana. It has the feel of the estancias of Argentina. Anna is from a farm in the Free State. She tends to six sons, one daughter and her husband. She and I pull wools from a high closet and laugh and joke as

I collect bundles of her homespun mohair to take with me in a duffle bag back to my workshop in the States.

We visit the Wool Board in Pretoria. I have a chance to see the lovely tapestry that Anna wove for the International Wool Show of 1979–80, the same exhibit where my *Tipi–Waterfall* was shown. In a large collection of handsome tapestries hers shines. She has managed, even with seven children, to spin, dye and weave a subtle composition three by four meters with a suggestion of a great bird and doves. The colors are so soft, and even the white areas have a range of texture that is breathtaking. Her looms are on a side porch beyond our bedroom, and beyond that lies a garden with bird of paradise, hibiscus and bougainvillea in full bloom. It seems an idyllic life of art, children and comfort. But the lengthening shadow is always there, the extra locks on the gates, sons doing their "military." It all seems so foreboding. Now, more than ever, I am deeply moved and made whole by caring.

Tonight, in a narrow bed, I think of three births and the beginning of life. It is two in the morning. The purple jacarandas are pink in the euphoric glow of the city, lining the streets with dark stems of natural beauty. This evening we walked through Burgers Park and saw the bougainvillea high in the fir trees, spilling over the crests and dropping like great umbilicals, overwhelming the trunks. There are many parallels of beauty and pain, and they run together like watercolor, partly from intention or because the rain of sorrow and joy brings thoughts together.

Trilogy for Sons

I lie on my spine
balancing the unborn
weight on my backbone.
My ribs curl
gently up like thin leaves
to shade the corolla
blood like a rose quartz.

Sunset flows along
the horizon of time.
The ninth hour ticks
hard in my heart clock
and the swelling, pitching
and tossing, send
me to the agony,
the rapture of new bloom.

Death and life sing
a fugue over my leaping
body, but the end is
a consonant chord of love.

Flat on the snow sheet,
flat, dancing the dance
of pain, naked before strange eyes.
Costume of pilgrims,
The grey and white of my innocence
peeled away. Nine
pairs of eyes
devour me. Keep me
there on my white ledge
of pain.

I write now at the window
ledge. It is two A.M. Not
even the half eaten moon
or the bending light of the city
are comfort.
Only the verse torn
from my memory like
a wave against granite
tells my remembered despair.
and the gift of my agony.

Blue velvet quiet,
cream cheese softness.
time flowing. The last
vibrations of opera
gilding the morning
here in the Little Company of Mary
where boys wear blue and
girls the reflection of roses.
Time is endless and gentle
under the warm hands of
the midwife and a
nameless doctor.
Not slipping into a void but
floating, one small
cloud separates from another.
We are two.

Lesotho

Lesotho, an independent kingdom surrounded by South Africa, is a country friendly to the United States and in every way, welcoming and receptive to the visit of an artist.

Arriving at noon in Maseru, the capital, we drove almost immediately thirty miles into the country to visit a major weaving workshop. I was impressed by the quality of the work and the excellent rapport between the women weavers and the director. It is an outstanding workshop with the most developed sense of design and production. The director brought three of her top artists and weavers to my lecture. At this workshop I had my first chance to evaluate the tapestry industry of Lesotho. The first evening in Lesotho, the PAO and his wife gave an outstanding reception for me to meet government officials, artists and writers, and representatives from all the tapestry industries that cluster the countryside around Maseru. I carried two tapestries with me to show briefly. I congratulate the PAO and his wife on this first meeting as it made my short stay in Maseru much more effective.

In each country, although I have studied carefully the art and culture before I left home, I still had much to learn about their tapestry-making and crafts. I have to make an evaluation as to where my time can best be spent. A two-day seminar at the U.S. Cultural Center brought weavers and artists together in a spontaneous exchange. I showed my slides and explained my techniques three times to different groups over the next two days. We also viewed an excellent film of weaving and art in Lesotho.

Some high spots; we held the first art class ever held in the out-of-doors in a small park near the cultural center. None of the tapestry makers and designers had ever done this before. Again perspective was of great interest to them. We looked at leaves and tree forms, discussed composition. We also held at the cultural center a session dealing with figure drawing.

The second day, artists came and drew us as we worked at long tables learning a series of basic embroidery stitches. All my students were eager and clever. By the second day we had established a warm rapport and the cultural center became an art celebration in many forms. Our outdoor drawings were pasted to the walls. Six of my hangings were displayed and several artists kept busy as we sewed. More people heard of our activity and came in curiously hour after hour.

The afternoon of my last day the Queen of Lesotho came to the center to witness our art festival and stayed to take tea with us. I talked with her about the various colors of mohair and such things. We closed up the workshop after quite a time together. Each person gave his or her own response to what had most interested him. Several spoke of drawing in the open air as innovative and exciting. Some spoke of learning new techniques to incorporate in their work. They seemed especially interested in the concept of subject matter and the idea that they should be selective. They ended by singing me a song that ended, "Alleluia, Nancy." I am gratified.

Swaziland

The Kingdom of Swaziland offers a kind of enchantment. An island, surrounded by South Africa, it exudes a regal dignity. The first key fitted to the lock of this hilly green country suggests that the door will open easily and there will be no dark corners. Crossing the miles of plowed earth between Pretoria and the Swazi border we stop briefly to see water birds, cattle heron, a white spoonbill, stilts—or their African cousins—wading in small water holes. A low fog and rain surround us as we drive east up into the mountains. We are engulfed, rising slowly on a perfect road with only the narrow white ribbon pulling us around each curve. All voyages go this way to Shangri-la. There is no easy transition from one world to the other, and a veil is right there to shield and surprise us.

The Swazis are sturdy and short, built to climb the hills easily, their bones cushioned, their legs strong. They are well fed and exuberant. I think of the sun-dried Bolivians whose land gives them beauty of mountains but poverty of soil. Here both come together to nourish a culture. The hills are planted with loblolly and slash pine.

We entered Swaziland by auto at noon and were met at the border by PAO Conrad Stolzenbach. We drove immediately to the Theater Club to hang my tapestries for a 2 P.M. opening. As always, great ingenuity was necessary. Though it is the best hall in town, the walls are dark crimson and adorned with narrow peg boards in two shades of blue. We brought with us nails, tape, and a slide projector. No one seemed to mind. By 2:30 we were finished and everyone who came was enthusiastic.

At 6 P.M. the exhibit closed, only to open again at 7 for a by-invitation-only reception with my lecture scheduled for 8. Both Bob and I greeted each guest warmly. Our years of diplomatic experience are a great asset. A large group of art lovers, educators, artists, and some outstanding weavers were present. I enjoyed explaining my art to all of them. A good Q&A period followed. We all returned to the exhibit room afterwards for a further chance to talk.

The following day I left the hotel at 7 A.M. to visit Mantega, a craft workshop in the valley below Mbabane. Several gifted tapestry makers who had been at my lecture were there to talk with me about their work. I purchased two tapestries which I plan to loan to the new African Museum in Washington as they are of outstanding quality. After a much too short hour at Mantega, where I also talked with Pauline Woodhall, the director, I drove with Conrad and his assistant, Susan Eagle, to a nearby training project for women.

We arrived to find a small room crowded with more than fifty women who had come in from various parts of the country. They opened with a welcome dance reminding me of conga-chain dances at U.S. colleges in the '40s. I joined them with pleasure. I found the women responsive and eager to share. Their training so far has been rudimentary; mostly the sewing of uniforms and some basic dresses which, however, were nicely done. The director Linda preferred that I not show my slides, and so I began with a class of the simplest embroidery stitches, having brought needles and yarn with me. Linda provided white yardage for samplers. We separated at 12:30 for lunch.

In the afternoon I examined their work in more detail, talked about uses of embroidery and with paper that I provided took them into the garden for the first outdoor training class they had ever had. We looked together at the green hills of Swaziland and many admitted that although they had lived there all their lives they had never really seen their surroundings as they did now. I showed them how to draw a round house and the trees we could see, and tried in every way to make them aware of the shapes and forms of simple composition.

Conrad's plan was to have me return the following day to continue the workshop, but Linda, the director, was informed at 4 P.M. that only two people could return as the next day was Saturday and she would not be there herself as she was going to meet a friend at the airport. This was most unfortunate. I never had a chance to show the women my slides or follow up on what we had started. This was the only time I was not able to complete a workshop or show my work and explain it to them. It is a disappointment.

So on Friday night we stayed in a mountain inn near Piggs Peak. With Saturday open, I made arrangements with the help of Susan Eagle to visit the workshop of Coral Stephens, a distinguished weaver of international reputation who employs close to one hundred women from the countryside around her home. Many of them have worked with her for thirty years. We spent three memorable hours with Mrs. Stephens and her husband. Coral's workshop is the finest I have seen on this trip for quality of work.

A remarkable man, Robert Stephens, and his extraordinary family will enter my life, I pray forever. He came here in 1948 to plant trees and made his home in the mountains at Piggs Peak. His beautiful wife, still with an aura of white hair and fair skin, began to weave curtains for her new home. Near her courtyards cloaked with native flowers, she has fashioned an incredible workshop of mohair that is clouds, a mist on the mountains, a pink blush of sunset columbine, all woven and spun by jet black Swazi ladies who live up and down the jade mountains.

Today I have spent four of the most glorious hours of my life at Coral Stephens's home and workshop. First there was Jane in blue pants and a soft striped sweater who came from nowhere laughing and saying easily, "The front door is over here. I am Jane." She has soft brown hair and clear eyes that see colors as close and as separate as shades of the red earth outside the long room with looms. A pale pink and rose mohair rug lies with a ridgeback dog atop, lazily asleep— and outside the window the earth repeats the same soft shades. The tapestries I have fashioned to share with them are opened. In their long windows framing a view of blue hills we hang *Chrysanthemum Shell,* one of my organdy hangings. It floats lightly in the clear mountain air. I am moved by their delight. Then together we unroll *Rock Lichen, Wood Lichen,* and *Aqua Lapis.* Jane tells me excitedly that they are just like lichen she has seen at a mountain waterfall five minutes from their house. She promises to take pictures and send them to me. I promise in return a copy of my catalogue.

For five years the idea of a great tapestry full of mood and many facets has been turning softly in my head. It will be called *Nimbus* and I suddenly realize that on this faraway mountaintop I have found my weaver. I am so thrilled for a moment I think I will weep in joy. I grab Jane's hand and we slip to a corner of the dining room to talk. Instinctively we understand what I want. I have seen a gossamer curtain she has fashioned, and that is our beginning. Jane has caught her mother's gift of color and texture. There is a unity between these women—a bonding where one relinquishes into the hands of the other through eyes and heart the great gift of perception.

I am moved by this because I do not have a daughter to touch my fingertips and spin the thread of my life and creativity for the next generation. I suddenly think of my three beautiful granddaughters in Texas and Darien and know they are my messengers. Already this summer when they bubbled around me as I sewed, I have offered them a chance to work with me when they are fourteen. And each of them has given me a small innocent gift of her own making which I shall treasure forever. I have come all the way to Swaziland to fulfill my need. "All things bright and beautiful" suddenly arises as a chorus in my head.

Gigi, Coral Stephens's French daughter-in-law, answers another question when I ask her how she manages with such a gifted mother-in-law. Her reaction is one I anticipate but in a sense it cleanses me and expiates my own agony. "It sometimes is terrible," she says. "My mother can do anything. But we share ourselves; we are friends." And I look at Coral with her serenity and strength and know she has continued to love and encourage as I try to do. Each of us has the demon of perfection and equally the desire to be close to those who join our family. It is like a soft recapitulation of a theme to know that all of us fail in some ways no matter how we try. I can't help caring about my daughters-in-law, but I can understand their conflict.

Gigi also told me about her youngest child who is brain-damaged, and showed me a little tapestry she had fashioned with an awkward bird that could never fly. I put my arm about her and knew that because I was a stranger she could share her sorrow. In some way my tapestries spoke to her and gave her happiness, and she had come all the way from Mbabane to see me. This is what makes the long solitary hours of drawing and sewing fruitful.

Down the mountain in the deep valley below Mbabane is another artist. She is Thoko Zile, a country woman with grown children and a family which has no knowledge of her gift. I first saw her in her red cotton scarves and fur skins at my lecture. Her strong face is crowned by a globe of black hair in the Swazi manner. Given the idea of developing an art form from the African hair mode, she has carried that theme to a highly developed weaving style. She sews narrow rows of black or white thread into a heavy wool base and proceeds to knot and wrap each tapestry with beauty and skill. Cinnamon, ochre and yellow are often colors in the background. White on white is less frequently used. She is the finest native artist I have met on this trip, devoted to her work and creating innately beautiful design. Her "tree" is one of the most popular.

I bought a huge piece to show to the African Museum in Washington with the hope that they will offer her a one-artist show perhaps in two or three years when she is able to get a collection together. Each canvas is a painstaking process, and although Thoko works constantly, production is necessarily limited, as she must do everything herself. To see this imaginative unschooled artist at work is a thrill. She instinctively understood my own art form and a current of comprehension and art communication flowed between us, a warming of our hands in front of the fire of art. Thoko represents the rarest of people, an untrained artist of humble home whose creativity finds expression in its most sophisticated form. I feel that her tapestries are equal to the best being made, and said so. Imagine my surprise to learn that one of her works had been chosen for the *biennale* of tapestries at Lausanne (although unfortunately under another artist's name). That makes me even more positive that she should have her own show, although I am more and more dubious about fame. It can be so destructive.

Fame is necessarily one facet of ambition, perhaps its purest, and at the same time its most destructive aspect. On this journey I have read in airports and high in the clouds, the last of the *Diaries of Anaïs Nin.* She thirsted for reassurance in the world of letters, for recognition. It came in a burst of lightning, and destroyed her. Everyone wanted her to speak, to comfort, to reassure. Her diary is of exhaustion, and no time for writing. Only the eloquent letters to people in despair, wringing her blood from her body until there is no breath.

It is a terrifying lesson, and I think of it often on this trip because recognition has brought me to Africa on a long exhausting odyssey. My body is being used, pushed and pulled in a Land Rover to Abomey to make friends with a turbulent country. I have flown two days and two nights without rest, through a storm over Rome, and finally into the hot jungle. It is impossible for me to give less than all of myself, and I see my face each day more drained and more the color of clay as I reach out to help the women in Swaziland see their velvet mountains for the first time. I want to help these women who had come in from various parts of the country just to see me.

On our return to Mbabane we stopped to view a new hand-blown-glass factory which is producing work of excellent design. Altogether it has been another full and delightful day. The seven o'clock news carried a brief report and picture of my visit to Swaziland.

Sunday morning before leaving for the airport I drove out to visit Pauline Woodhall at Mantega again and discussed the possibility of a show at the African Museum for Thoko, her most gifted artist. She also told me that the weavers who had come to my lecture were noticing for the first time lichen on rocks and tree forms which they said they had never seen before. I have tried first in each country to make the artists and artisans aware of their beautiful surroundings and it is gratifying to see their delight.

Botswana

Botswana social life seems to center around the Holiday Inn. You enter to the sound of slot machines and the crush of people playing the odds. Even on Sunday afternoon there are crowds everywhere. The garden off our bedroom has a pool with waves as children of every shade and color jump joyously in, surfacing like porpoises. Tea and sandwiches around the flower beds, tennis, even in the heat, goes on.

When dusk closes over the distant cerulean hills, I take my bird glasses and wander into the garden. There vigorous groups of young people chatter, but the birds are pursuing their own patterns untouched. I find the red bishop bird, his rufous head as pompous as his name. It is spring but he is not of God's calling, only of his own making. He is fluffed up with courting. The weaver birds, yellow with black faces, cluster on a tree by our garden door. They are weaving their basket nests with a hole in the bottom and a side pocket for babies. A single swaying twig deflects rain like the round thatched houses of the Botswana countryside.

Gaborone is new with a central mall and an ambitious museum. The people believe in themselves in a natural way. There is no boasting. It is a multiracial and democratic society. There is little or no talk of tribes. Instead they are eager to find suitable crops, to build self-sustaining industry, and to welcome assistance from all over the world. They are open, wanting to learn. Women play an active part at every level, except at the very top. I met a woman in sleek aquamarine, tall and comely, ageless. She has nine children and works all day as an accountant for the city government. Her youngest is six. The matriarchal system prevails; aunts and grandmothers fill the void lovingly.

The earth is powder in October, thirsting for rain which is late in coming. Wherever water touches the red clay, flowers and trees flourish. The city is so new that pavers push out into the flat dust of the open country just ahead of the builders. The water table is deep below the crust of earth and there is always a scarcity with only the summer rainy season and a short period in the fall to replace the supply.

As we drive to Lobatsi at four in the afternoon, the strong sunlight slants across the hills in patterns of blue and purple. Tall hills point red pinnacles into the sky. At Lobatsi I met Ingebro and knew at once we would become friends. She is a tall Norwegian woman, a dedicated weaver, and a warm and intelligent spirit who has brought her knowledge and enthusiasm to Botswana to start a karakul rug factory. She has visited the arid terrain of southwest Botswana many times and now intends to clean and spin the entire yearly production of sixty thousand kilos. She has cajoled her country into giving her funds for a factory. Our mutual professions are a bond. I remember karakul weavers in Omitara, South Africa, and suggest she seek the seal of approval from the Wool Board.

We eat lunch at her modest house, scrubbed like a doctor in surgery, trimmed blue and ornamented by artifacts from Botswana. She still gives me her Norwegian address; it is obviously home, although no regret mars her strong face full of joy and expectation. She is giving of herself to all these young Botswanan women who work in her studio; they are her family, not her children. They are also a repository of need and achievement that are as allied as rain and green earth.

The karakul rugs still have a long road of design and texture to follow to achieve first-rate quality. I hope she will visit Coral Stephens's studio in Swaziland. She will be amazed at the refinement of wool with color and design found there. It will give her a new perspective. Still, if it seems too much, at least she has the factory and wool spinning to carry on.

I feel more than ever that this trip has many meanings. I am surprised that people think of me as a famous artist, but that slips past because it is not true. In Africa, anyone who comes so far must do so with a sense of discovery and satisfaction. So we look at each other; I at them, not by color but by warm hands—often very moist—and easy smiles. What do they see? I find myself looking fleetingly in the mirror—so many photos are being taken. I hide under my red straw hat to dissimulate—the wrinkles at my eyes—the patches of stained skin. There is so little of my freshness left, and I care only because I do not want the skin of my spirit to suggest that the fruit is dried within. I am exhilarated that so many people can respond to my art and to our sharing. I stop for a quick breath. I am so carried away by the events of each day.

I did not come to Africa to teach chain stitch or to talk much about myself. I am not sure if I knew why I was coming except that a small voice convinced me to accept the challenge, and watch for signs along every road. It began as an uncertain journey full of surprise. The appliqué weavers of Abomey challenged me to decide what I could share with them in three days together. The challenge has been to open their eyes in Abomey, Maseru, Gaborone and Swaziland to the beauty about them. To help artisans who have never held a pencil to draw; to see the shapes of baobab and palm, to see the green hills of Entojeni as great pillows of color, strong and reassuring. The spirit of my beautiful mother has never been closer. She taught me to "lift mine eyes up unto the hills." With these simple women, burdened with suckling babes dressed in red cotton wraps and deerskin, I have a biblical message that is the great secret of art: "Seek and ye shall find"—for in this simplest of ways my class of forty stand outside the small stucco office, and together we see the blue-green hills, all of us for the first time, although they have lived here forever.

Madagascar

Madagascar—a lumpy island full of rare geological surprises. As we wing in from Tanzania, the terrain looks like the surface of a dusty brain. The convolutions and crevices of the earth furrowing the bulging surfaces. The sea between the continent and this strange island has cleansed me. Here rice paddies flourish and green terraces float like emerald flakes flat along the earth.

I think of the map of Africa as a buxom woman heavy corseted from waist to thigh, contained in a tight skirt. Her bulging bosom is the north portion spreading west to the Atlantic and east to the Indian Ocean.

We have traveled the width of her ample shape. Without question Nigeria and Tanzania are the armpits. Whether the wealth of oil or of wild animals, they are now moist dens of corruption and filth. Nigeria, a country of strutting brigands lounging in their white lace and misshapen suits, representing the bloated corruption they spawn. Tanzania, brigands again. The houseboy has stolen our small alarm clock, a calculator, and other minor treasures while we ate our breakfast. We are advised not to cross the street alone or they will rip away your bag and camera. Our entrance into the airport might even have surprised Ali Baba; wiry black hands itching for our pockets. I felt as though we were dumped into a nest of spiders. Our plane careened around Mt. Kilimanjaro, while for us it meant a five-hour wait in the dust and degradation of a lounge that is never cleaned.

The slender Indian-Tanzanian, who met us on arrival in Madagascar is a contrast to this scene like a piece of carved ivory. He is refined, intelligent and eager to escape beyond the boundaries of his birthplace, but not a penny can leave the escalating economy except for the pompous trips of the Communist comrades. We will leave to see these falsehoods of government exposed but not until the whole face of Africa is in ruins.

It has nothing to do with race or color, but only the same greed for world domination that flogged the tribes from the jungles and veldt a hundred years ago. The Russians and the Chinese do not think of the blacks as brothers but only as ciphers in their political games. Each one is grabbing to himself tribes and cinder land, overgrazed and pockmarked with thorn that will eventually impale him. And somehow one feels the African will survive it all, with a patience like bittersweet and by seeing through us with bright eyes marked with a veil of resignation. I may never live to see them get rid of us, all of us. They will conquer. The foreign cultures beat on their sun-burned skins like hard spring rain, only washing away the dusty patina of one society to leave the ebony surface lush for the next assault. Eventually, nothing will penetrate. The Africans will own their land.

Where the black men and women of great tribes like the Kaman and the roaming Masai of Kenya predominate, the white man can live in perfect harmony. As a minority, he carries with him his inner confidence and self-worth, and if he or she is only one among hundreds either feels at peace. That is why Kenya survives as an integrated society. It is a place where the white smiles on their jet faces are more arresting than the same ivory smile on a pale face. But both are found everywhere. The Kenyans are offended by the U.S. export of black artists and black dance groups to their cultural centers. They ask, "Are we a segregated society? Don't we have theater and dances where black and white bend to the rhythm together?"

And somehow although we have such unity in the arts at home, we do not have it in our lives. The blacks in my country are still apart from us even though many of us wish it otherwise. There is self-consciousness between us—like children in a new house thirsting for friends and boasting a bit, eager to join the game of life together.

Those of us with pale skins know the affirmation of our birth but in my country the black does not. I see the beauty and grace of the tall slender girl with skin of malachite. I watch with a ripple of joy as she moves along the path of my eyes, whether in Kenya or on a George-town sidewalk.

I see the heavy bodies of black women who have labored for years in the homes I frequent. I see their roundness of spirit under the slumped flesh and marvel at their faith. When I greet them on the street with caring, their melodic answers move me. But they will never outnumber us and must come to terms with that fact. Of course color is not all. Whatever our hue many of us never anchor in the harbor of tranquility. We do not know our good fortune. Perhaps the most beautiful facet of my African adventure is the purity of feeling that I experience here. My relationship to the appliqué makers of Abomey, strong men from a kingdom as old as America, to the reclusive Masai, wandering their savannahs in their red banners of courage, is a sense of oneness with them. A unity that is beauty of movement and style in an artist's eye, but also an understanding and respect.

This may also be age. For now that I am wrinkled and my eyes are pale, they perhaps accept me with the benevolence one feels for a small child. They know that my time is running out and that the lines are the results of my travels. There is a reverence for age here and in Asia that we have failed to comprehend in America. I shall miss it when I return home. Sixty is a venerable adventure where life is harsh and the sun has withered the land. My travel to this end of the earth fills me with ideas and contemplations pouring out like a trunk that holds all my belongings and will not close. There is no need for a key or a special combination. Only which scrap of bright cloth to examine first, and in what order? And each piece, whether an object of meticulous needlework or a torn scrap, as transient as a floating feather, has its place and value. Such is my safari to the countries of Africa.

A Kenyan Rest Stop (Reflecting on Madagascar)

Ketchua Tembo (Elephant Head) is the name of a safari camp on the Kenyan savannahs of the Masai Mara tribe. The gazelle and zebra, with their sophisticated beige and grey hides prance alone in the pale

November rain below my lean-to porch. I am retracing steps back to Abomey and on to Madagascar in a watercolor book. For each major journey I have recorded our adventures in Japanese accordion-paged temple books. Long folded pages stretch out to blend the sweep of my eyes from the round huts of Lesotho to the waterfalls of Swaziland. I tuck in the embracing arms of both the baobab tree and the Swazi women in their costumes of red cotton and deerskin. Then I move on to the markets of Madagascar. These picture diaries are a secret journey that Bob and I return to savor, not a public endeavor—and of no particular consequence. The clear tones of watercolor clearly say it is rapid and transitory and done with a flick of the brush as whimsical as the flashing tail of a Thompson's gazelle. On this trip my brush is less lucid and merry because I am weighted with schedules. There have been lectures, three to each country, tiring workshops for as many as sixty at one time, and often without materials, so that the spontaneity of a traveler's eye has been diminished by exhaustion and lack of time.

On Sunday, after my last day of work in Antananarivo, I sat before the open French doors of my hotel room, the clear wet palette shining on the table before me. I was looking up to the palace of the kings and queens of Madagascar. The steep slope of the city falls away before me like a beaded curtain, catching the red and green roofs, the jade trees and the amethyst of the flowering jacaranda. For three hours I dipped my brushes into wells of color, floating the vision that holds me speechless onto the small white paper. I paint first from memory the diamond scarves of umbrellas of the Zoma market of last Friday, and then on into the hills and palace. Antananarivo is really a simple French village. Now that house paint is no longer available, the sun is blending it like a quaint pre-Columbian tapestry into the softest of pinks, blues and lavender—always touched by the Venetian red of earth and brick.

Here in Madagascar the marriage ceremony is crowned by the wish that each slender bride become the fortunate mother of seven sons and seven daughters. I think as I paint the fluted chimneys and drop cerulean into the areas of sky, what all these children will mean to Madagascar. A rice-eating country that is already importing rice to feed its people, there is no indication that the birth rate will slacken. I see their gestures and accommodation and know that one day like the Bolivians they will erupt and destroy each other. If there is a god—or gods—this cataclysm is prophetic, for from an island there are no migrations. One is captive. It is a honeyed captivity that provides the false security of unchanging boundaries, and time to pause and appreciate the unrecognized treasures. In Madagascar, the rare lemur with its bat ears, monkey's face and fox's tail is a special genus. An extinct giant of a bird laid eggs six times the size of an ostrich's. Some are still to be found, petrified, in the bush at the southern end of the island. Fossils and petrified shells curved and perfect all these millions of years are harvested from the island earth. It is the most ancient ground I have ever trod and I understand its significance. But the growing fragile population, tiny people with not a bowl full of rice apiece, frightens me. I am overwhelmed with futility; a Cassandra who has nothing to do with the fate of those charming people.

At my workshops the men and women file in quickly to embroider buttonhole stitches in abandon across a limp sampler. I teach them to break all the embroidery rules and to forget the prim borders. They sew ornate leaves and butterflies that I have seen locally. They giggle and work delightfully. I move from one to the next, encouraging and helping. They are quick and agile with a needle. I take chalk and draw on a blackboard, telling the story of perspective and how the small house fits under the shade of the jacaranda, and how the women fit into the house I have drawn. I show how the poplar tree, close to my eyes, towers above the distant mountain, and that a goat is merely a dot as it grazes on the hill. They sit, absorbed by my story like children hearing a new legend full of adventure. I draw a bird in flight, not with two large flapping wings carved of wood, but with motion and size to rest on the branch of the tree beyond. Their amazement and soft smiles encourage me.

I have become on this trip something of a Kipling of art, weaving a story of its origins and secrets in simple absorbing language. When they have understood the story of the distant mountain and the path to their house I move with them to the out-of-doors and urge them to look around them. In Abomey the great baobab in the palace enclosure was an object of surprise for men who had savored its shade all their lives. The central stem fanning like a huge cauliflower utterly surprised them. All their trees to this moment had been fantasy and all leaves came in one shape. In Lesotho, they saw poplars for the first time, and in Botswana at the teachers' training school they learned to draw the roundness of their small cylindrical houses. Even the government officials stayed on to watch me draw the story of their land on a blackboard and, clutching their crayons, moved outdoors to see their town as fellow artists. We laughed together like children under a waterfall, the cool water washing the cobwebs of tradition away and leaving us with fresh discovery.

In Swaziland, the women (only here were the men excluded from my workshops) moved with me into a dusty backyard. I showed them their own green hills asking them to remember that they were soft velvet pillows to rest their eyes on at the end of a long day. One woman carrying her tenth child looped to her waist spoke shyly to tell me she had never drawn a picture or held a pencil in her hand before. Her mountains were bosoms full of fresh milk and I gave her more paper and a sharp pencil and watched her swinging out through the gate onto the hard earth with her small babe on his rumble seat. For this I have come to ten countries and two continents. And I care so much for her, without even knowing her name that even as I write the tears race down my cheeks, curve over my chin. But my tears will not even enrich a centimeter of the parched earth. They will dry before they drop to reach ground, and Africa will go on with the swollen wombs of its women as the greatest and most tragic harvest of all.

It is an irony that those of us who have food and a fresh bowl and a silver spoon sometimes want no children at all. We talk only of the heavy price of education and the test to our patience. And our tragedy is not completed. For if we see the scenery in perspective and know that the trees in our garden seem taller than the mountains, still we do not understand that the perspective of marriage and love is also one of children, of suckling babes and arms as tight as grapevines bearing spring fruit. My tears are for the perspective of living, for where I have failed, and where I have found and given pleasure to others. I have held a pencil in my hand since I can remember, and my mother and father taught me the color of the sky and the shape of the forest before I could read. When I was born, arms held me with tenderness, and as in a slow rhythmic dance the arms changed and the step has quickened. Always there has been great love and a world of many perspectives. Now there are moments of solitude. Without them I could not sort and tuck away each day. Africa offers not only savannahs of the mind and bright jewels of adventure, but also a ribbon of living that unreels as I watch and will continue to unwind without end.

The African adventure is a test of patience. Every change of planes has brought trauma and delay. No matter that we have gone in person to the office of Air Kenya. When we arrive at the airport we find the flight is two hours delayed and we are not even on the manifest! By brandishing official papers and tickets confirmed in their own hand, we join the hapless voyagers who watch the clock. Eleven, twelve, one, and still we sit in the tiny molded chairs like a row of decoy ducks hoping for departure.

This is our fifteenth flight in the odyssey of Africa. The cabin of our wounded bird has gone dark and I become ambivalent. There is a chance we will be here all night like a Nazi victim beneath search lights. There is no confidence that to depart is a better alternative. I am willing to abdicate judgment when I board a plane. I acknowledge it is out of my hands entirely, and once in the air I enjoy the time capsule, the absolute detachment from earth. It is a rich time for writing and thought. Today on the bird flight from the Masai Mara of Kenya to Nairobi I thought only of *Nimbus*, the tapestry I want to create out of cloud and fog and wind, woven together into a suspended mood to move through as easily as we do through the sky today.

Washington, November 1980

And now that I am home, and the pale November weather of dried leaves and frozen stems is about me, I think back to the African adventure as a cathedral with many windows of stained glass, and to my wanderings as that of two pilgrims. Always my hand, whether weary or marveling, clasped within the hand of my loving husband, and the two of us, small figures against a huge landscape vast as the walls of the Cathedral of Toledo. Our passage around each pillar and over the pavement of that continent is as sharp and clear as early morning sunlight on an ornamented window high above us.

The African adventure mimics my life—a great thirsting for fragments of beauty to tuck into my memory and to celebrate living. None of it has been more remarkable than the roll and dissipation of a single wave on the shore of my beloved Mouse Island, but no less wondrous in its suddenness and artless perfection.

My whole life, from the moment of seeding within my mother's womb, has been one of great joy and loving, and with many windows to the world of the finest prisms of oriental beauty. Today I have sat in the narrow pew in church with its mulberry cushions and a wine-colored carpet beneath my feet, and have been filled with the wildest exaltation. For I have shared this joy not only with deep love but shared with God a celebration of living and a thankfulness. The days of my living are as many colors as the yarns in the shelves of my workshop, and all of them have meaning and beauty. The moon that I saw in Africa is no different, neither greater nor less than any other place, but the discovery of silver light above the jacarandas at the edge of Burgers Park in Pretoria or through the lattice of the blinds and balcony looking up to the king's palace at Madagascar has added another room to the mansion in my memory.

This journey has brought me a new sense of peace in the knowledge that my skin is of a color so like the chameleon that I am at home wherever I may go. Will I forget Lanzuo, the slender boy clinging to a pole at the edge of his watery home in Ganvié who answered me when I called softly, *Comme s'appelle?* as I drew him in my color book? Or Thoko Zile, the tapestry maker of African cornrows? Or the endless parade of rumble-seated babies on their mothers' hips. All are part of me forever. I no longer grieve for them. I have no pity as I did when I was young. I see now that we are different planets or shreds of comets in a vast revolving panorama, and the brief glow that we shed upon each other will not change our course or make us sad.

The sharp memories will pale until there are no clear edges. Perhaps the patterns will blend, faded by the light of remembrance, until the mosaic of my days in Africa will be another oriental carpet, soft to my touch, yet woven so tightly that it will sustain my memory as long as I shall live.

Perhaps I can weave some of these memories for the grandchildren with their bright eyes and eager hearts. The grandchildren who have danced in my mind and behind my eyes on this whole trip—for surprisingly they are the ones, not my three tall sons, who are most with me as I travel. It is as though I no longer have a message to impart to those who are my flesh—but instead to the small islands of their making. As we have wandered and laughed and shared, it is the grandones for whom I am storing up the colors of Africa. I have a rainbow that we can travel, with a beginning and an end, and full of the fire of an opal in a warm hand between there and here.

Professional Biography of Nancy Hemenway

1920	Born Nancy Hemenway Whitten, June 19
1926–37	Public Schools, Foxboro, Massachusetts
1937–41	Wheaton College, Norton, Massachusetts
1941	Bachelor's degree in music and art, Wheaton College, Norton, Massachusetts
1941–42	Harvard University, Graduate School of Music; studied composition under Walter Piston
1942	Married Robert Durrie Barton, Washington, D.C.
1942–46	Wartime housing in Washington, D.C., North Carolina, California, and Massachusetts
1945	Robert Bradford Barton born
1946–48	Lived in Montevideo, Uruguay
1947	William Emerson Barton born
1949–52	Lived in Rosario, Argentina
1949	Frederick Durrie Barton born
1953–57	Lived in Madrid, Spain; studied drawing with Pierre Mathieu
1956	University of Madrid, special certificate in Spanish language, art and literature
1957	Exhibit, children's portraits, Casa Americana, Madrid
1957–65	Lived in Bronxville, New York
1957 and 1959	Group exhibit, Uptown Gallery, New York City

1960	Exhibit, Maine Art Gallery, Wiscasset, Maine
1962	Art Student League, New York City; studied with Thomas Fogarty, Robert Brackman, and Joseph Hirsch
1962	Exhibit, "Paintings by Nancy Hemenway," Bronxville Public Library, New York
1962	Group exhibit, Hudson Valley Art Association
1961–64	Columbia University, School of Arts and Sciences; studied Spanish lyric poetry and art with John Heliker
1964	Exhibit, Wheaton College, Norton, Massachusetts
1964–65	Lived in Santo Domingo, Dominican Republic
1965–66	Lived in Washington, D.C.
1966	Columbia University, master of arts degree in Spanish lyric poetry
1966–68	Lived in La Paz, Bolivia
1968	Exhibit, National Museum of Art, La Paz, Bolivia
1968	Created illustrations for *A Short History of Bolivia*, by Robert D. Barton, published by Editorial Los Amigos del Libro, La Paz
1968–72	Lived in Guadalajara, Mexico; founded San Esteban Martir Embroidery School
1969–70	Exhibit, "Creative Stitchery on Hand-Woven Materials from Bolivia by Nancy Hemenway," Pan American Union, Washington, D.C.
1970	Film, *Nancy Hemenway at the Pan American Union*, U.S. Information Agency
1970	Exhibit, Bola Gallery, Mexico City, Mexico
1970	Exhibit, Municipal Gallery, Guadalajara, Mexico
1971	Exhibit, The Art Wagon, Scottsdale, Arizona
1971	Exhibit, Woodmere Gallery of Art, Chestnut Hill, Pennsylvania

1971	Exhibit, Maine Coast Artists, Rockport, Maine
1972	Returned to Washington, D.C.
1972	Exhibit, The Copley Society of Boston, Massachusetts
1972	Exhibit, The Wingspread Gallery, Northeast Harbor, Maine
1974	Catalog, *Ancient Images of Mexico and the Andes,* published by Museum of Fine Arts/Museum of New Mexico, Santa Fe
1974	Exhibit, "Ancient Images of Mexico and the Andes," Oklahoma Science and Art Foundation, Oklahoma City, Oklahoma (exhibit traveled in 1974–75 to Marion Koogler McNay Art Institute, San Antonio, Texas; Museum of Fine Arts, Santa Fe, New Mexico; Montgomery Museum of Fine Arts, Montgomery, Alabama)
1974–75	Project director, "A Celebration of Change," U.S. bicentennial celebration, Boston, Massachusetts
1975	Lecture tour, U.S. Department of State; visited Mozambique, Namibia, South Africa, Zambia, and Zimbabwe
1975	Lecture tour, U.S. Information Agency; visited England, Germany, Netherlands, Spain, Sweden, and Switzerland
1977	Catalog, *Textures of Our Earth: Bayetage Tapestries by Nancy Hemenway, 1972–1977,* published by Nimrod Press, Boston
1977–78	Exhibit, "Textures of Our Earth," Walker Museum of Art, Bowdoin College, Brunswick, Maine; Virginia Museum of Fine Arts, Richmond, Virginia; Seattle Art Museum, Seattle, Washington; The Textile Museum, Washington, D.C.
1979	Exhibit, "Thirteen Tapestries by Nancy Hemenway," Wheaton College, Norton, Massachusetts (with Amy Gray)

1979–80	Exhibitor, "First International Exhibition of Tapestries and Wall Hangings," Pretoria Art Museum; South African National Gallery, Capetown; King George VI Gallery, Elizabeth; Johannesburg Art Gallery, South Africa
1979	Award, Deborah Morton Outstanding Maine Woman Award, Westbrook College, Portland, Maine
1979–80	Fellowship, National Endowment for the Arts, lecture and exhibit under USIA auspices in Cotonou, Benin; Antananarivo, Madagascar; Mbabane, Swaziland; Maseru, Lesotho; and Gaborone, Botswana
1981	Resident artist, Cummington Foundation
1982	Exhibit, "Berenice Abbott, Mildred Burrage, Nancy Hemenway, Dahlov Ipcar, Louise Nevelson," Joan Whitney Payson Gallery, Westbrook College, Portland, Maine
1983	Video, *Salt Shadow, the Making of a Tapestry,* Bonnie B. Durrance Productions, Rockport, Maine
1983	Honorary Doctor of Fine Arts degree, Wheaton College, Norton, Massachusetts
1983	Exhibit, Portland Art Museum, Portland, Maine
1983	Catalog, *Aqua Lapis, Embroidered Wall Sculptures, 1975–1983,* published by Textile Arts Foundation, Washington, D.C.
1983	Exhibit, "Hemenway: Aqua Lapis," Art Institute of Chicago (exhibit traveled in 1984–88 to Edinburgh City Art Centre, Scotland; Farnsworth Art Museum, Rockland, Maine; Los Angeles County Museum of Art, California)
1984	Lived in Boothbay Harbor, Maine
1985	Moved to Birdsong, Southport Island, Maine
1985	Fellow, Djerassi Foundation, Woodside, California

1986	Exhibit, "Aqua Lapis," Farnsworth Museum, Rockland, Maine, and Huntsville Museum, Huntsville, Alabama
1987–89	Exhibit, "Tipi–Waterfall," part of "Frontiers in Fiber: The Americans," U.S. Information Agency exhibit to seven countries in Asia
1988	Catalog, *New England Light,* published by Los Angeles County Museum of Art, California
1988	Exhibit, "New England Light," Los Angeles County Museum of Art, California
1989	Fellow, American Academy, Rome
1991	Exhibit, Carpenter Center, Harvard University, Cambridge, Massachusetts
1994	Exhibit, "New England Light," DePauw University, Greencastle, Indiana
1995	Exhibit, Boothbay Region Art Foundation, Boothbay Harbor, Maine
1995	Exhibit, "Thaw," Maine College of Art, Portland, Maine
1996	Moved to Washington, D.C.
1997	Exhibit, Wheaton College, Norton, Massachusetts
2007	*Abundance: The Poetry of Nancy Hemenway,* published by Hemenway Foundation
2008	Died, in Washington, D.C., February 23

Hemenway Foundation

The publication of *Remembrance and Song* is made possible by the generosity of Robert D. Barton and the Hemenway Foundation.

Founded in 2006, the Foundation exists to promote the artistic works of Nancy Hemenway. Key activities include cataloguing and preserving her tapestries, paintings, watercolors, and writings; creating a repository for their ownership; promoting an understanding of her life and works; and exhibiting her collection. Early efforts have focused on curatorial functions and in the publication of a collection of her poetry in the book entitled *Abundance: The Poetry of Nancy Hemenway*. The publication of her journals, which we are pleased to present here, is an important addition to the understanding of her life.

The Hemenway Foundation is a public benefit corporation that was granted tax-exempt status in 2006.